Irish Lives in America

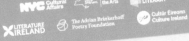

FRIDAY, MARCH 17

IN ASSOCIATION WITH
New York City Council, New York State Assembly,
New York State Senate, Lambda Literary
and Literature Ireland

WITH GENEROUS SUPPORT FROM
The Society of the Friendly Sons of St. Patrick of New York
and the Adrian Brinkerhoff Poetry Foundation

IRISHARTSCENTER.ORG | #IACBOOKDAY

Irish Lives in America

EDITED BY Liz Evers AND Niav Gallagher
FOREWORD BY Ambassador Dan Mulhall

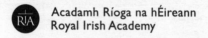

Acadamh Ríoga na hÉireann
Royal Irish Academy

Irish Lives in America

First published 2021
Royal Irish Academy, 19 Dawson Street, Dublin 2
www.ria.ie

The biographies in this book are selected from the Royal Irish Academy's *Dictionary of Irish Biography* (© Royal Irish Academy 2009, 2018; published by Cambridge University Press, reproduced with permission), a comprehensive, scholarly biographical reference work for Ireland, treating the lives of persons from the earliest times to the present day, and encompassing every sphere of human activity. Access to the online version of the *Dictionary* is freely available at www.dib.ie.

ISBN 978-1-911479-80-2 (PB)
ISBN 978-1-911479-94-9 (pdf)
ISBN 978-1-911479-95-6 (epub)

British Library Cataloguing in Publication Data. A CIP catalogue record for this book is available from the British Library.

Copyeditor and project manager: Helena King
Book design: Fidelma Slattery
Index: Eileen O'Neill
Printed in the UK by Clays

Royal Irish Academy is a member of Publishing Ireland, the Irish book publishers' association

5 4 3 2 1

MIX
Paper from
responsible sources
FSC® C018072
www.fsc.org

A NOTE FROM THE PUBLISHER

We want to try to offset the environmental impacts of carbon produced during the production of our books and journals. For the production of our books this year we will plant 45 trees with Easy Treesie.

The Easy Treesie – Crann Project organises children to plant trees. Crann – 'Trees for Ireland' is a membership-based, non-profit, registered charity (CHY13698) uniting people with a love of trees. It was formed in 1986 by Jan Alexander, with the aim of 'Releafing Ireland'. Its mission is to enhance the environment of Ireland through planting, promoting, protecting and increasing awareness about trees and woodlands.

Contents

4. Lives on stage and screen

5. Lives in medicine, science and technology

6. Lives of faith

7. Lives of conscience

8. Lives in art and architecture

9. Lives in print

Foreword

In my time as ambassador I have come to view the Irish American story as an epic tale of travail and transformation, a valiant journey from adversity to achievement. It has been an uplifting experience to encounter communities all over the country, descended from immigrants who arrived generations ago, that retain a deep pride in their Irish heritage. It is fitting that this volume, with its stories of first-generation Irish immigrants who made their mark on America, should appear at a time in which a proud Irish American, President Joe Biden, has ascended to the highest office in the land. He is the twenty-third person of Irish descent to occupy the White House, a building designed by an Irish architect, James Hoban (p. 230).

Of the more than 10,000 lives featured in the *Dictionary of Irish Biography*, over 400 are individuals who died in the USA, most but not all being Irish-born, and a majority having significant careers in America. The fifty biographies collected here are representative of the multitudes of Irish immigrants whose contributions to America were less notable, but no less important. Their descendants, now thirty-five million in number, are to be found in every walk of American life. It strikes me that the extraordinary achievements of Irish Americans could warrant a bumper biographical dictionary of their own!

All told, more than four million Irish people arrived in the USA between 1841 and 1900.[1] The vast bulk of their stories are hidden from view on account of the absence of written evidence documenting their lives. This was brought home to me in the summer of 2019 when I went to Utah for the 150-year anniversary of the completion of the

Transcontinental Railroad. I was asked to propose a toast to the 12,000 Irish immigrants, the 10,000 Chinese and those thousands more of other nationalities who worked on that great project, and was honoured to do so. It struck me at the time that I had little or no information about the lives of those who had played such an indispensable role in connecting America's east and west coasts. The standard books on the railroad pay scant attention to those who laboured to lay those tracks across the continent in extremely difficult conditions.

The best-known illustration of the myriad hidden faces of Irish America is the life of Annie Moore (p. 25). Her place in history stems from the fact that she was the first immigrant to pass through Ellis Island. The remainder of her life's story appears to have been one of toil and tribulation, which ended in an unmarked grave. She has attracted posthumous glory as a symbol of America's extraordinary immigrant odyssey. And, of course, her descendants have had more prosperous and satisfying lives than she was able to live.

While Irish immigrants, notably the Scots Irish, were present in colonial America from the outset, emigration from Ireland stepped up in the first four decades of the nineteenth century, with almost a million people leaving Ireland for North America during that time. It was, however, the great famine and its aftermath that provided the foundation stone for Irish America by bringing millions more across the Atlantic, where they became an integral part of the fabric of modern America. Remarkably, given Ireland's size, in the century between 1820 and 1920 one-sixth of all immigrants from Europe to America came from Ireland.[2]

The lives of the immigrants documented in this collection illustrate the longevity and diversity of the Irish experience in America. The editors are to be applauded for casting light on the lesser-known aspects of the story. I am particularly taken with the examples of Irish people active on the American frontier in the late-eighteenth and early nineteenth century and their interaction with Native Americans. Especially interesting are Mary Jemison (p. 12), who spent most of her life with the Seneca tribe, and John Wallace Crawford (p. 21), who helped create 'the myth of the western hero', which was a mainstay of the cowboy films I watched in my boyhood in the south-east of Ireland.

In my travels around America, I have traced the footsteps of some of those featured here. I have visited the Margaret Haughery (p. 185) memorial in New Orleans, which stands as an impressive testimony to the esteem in which she was held in her adopted city. More imposing still is the tribute paid to Mother Jones (p. 200) by the monument in the Miners' Cemetery at Mount Olive in southern Illinois, built during the great depression. Its scale highlights how revered she was by the miners whose welfare she spent so much of her life seeking to advance. Mother Jones's life continues to be celebrated and, as ambassador, I have participated in a number of events dedicated to her memory and legacy. Epidemics—a nineteenth century reality—ravaged the lives of those two forceful Irish women. The scourge of yellow fever swept away their families, after which Haughery and Jones devoted their lives to the service of others.

Perhaps the outstanding figure in this anthology is Thomas Francis Meagher (p. 45). I say this because, alone among those chronicled in these pages, he was an important figure on both sides of the Atlantic: a romantic revolutionary in Ireland and a significant personality in civil war America. His role in encouraging Irish enlistment in the union army helped cement the position of Irish immigrants in America as the nativist movements that had flourished in the 1840s and 1850s waned.

Meagher is part of a pattern in which the politics of Ireland and America became intertwined in the nineteenth and twentieth century. America, a place of refuge for Irish political exiles, also became an indispensable source of support for Irish movements from the era of Catholic emancipation all the way to the war of independence. There cannot be many nineteenth century Irishmen who are memorialised in four locations on two continents, but Meagher is one. He is remembered by equestrian statues in his home city of Waterford and in Helena, the capital of Montana, as well as on the civil war battlefield at Antietam and at Fort Benton on the Missouri River where his eventful life came to a close. Meagher's role as a civil war general commanding the Irish Brigade also recalls the fact that 57 per cent of all US Medal of Honour recipients have been Irish Americans. And more than half of the Medals of Honour awarded to foreign-born individuals went to the Irish, 257 in all.

Aside from Meagher, the other outstanding patriotic figure represented in these pages is John Boyle O'Reilly (p. 203), a Fenian who was transported to Western Australia, where I once visited the cell he occupied in Fremantle Prison. He daringly escaped to America where he became an important public figure as a poet and owner/editor of the *Pilot*. His activism was not confined to Irish affairs, for he was a dogged opponent of discrimination of all kinds and an advocate in particular for the rights of African Americans, as illustrated in his poem, 'Crispus Attucks':

Oh, we who have toiled for freedom's law,
   have we sought for freedom's soul?
Have we learned at last that human right is
   not a part but the whole?
That nothing is told while the clinging sin
   remains half unconfessed?
That the health of the nation is periled if one
   man be oppressed?[3]

As I wrote this piece with the coronavirus pandemic still raging across America and around the world, I was glad to be reminded of the contribution of Irish immigrants in the field of medicine, represented here by Gertrude Brice Kelly (p. 162), one of New York's first female surgeons who was also a staunch advocate of Irish independence and president of Cumann na mBan in New York, and Limerick-woman Mary O'Connell (Sr Anthony, p. 189), described as America's Florence Nightingale. It is also timely to recall that an Irish immigrant, John Crawford (p. 151) from County Antrim, was one of the first doctors to introduce smallpox vaccination into America.

Of the twentieth-century figures who appear here, two that caught my attention are Kay McNulty (p. 166) and John 'Kerry' O'Donnell (p. 96). McNulty arrived in Philadelphia from Donegal in 1924 and, as a pioneering programmer, helped develop the first electronic digital computer. McNulty was a ground-breaker in a field that has become a mainstay of Ireland's contemporary ties with the USA through the presence in Ireland of so many leading American ICT companies. O'Donnell was a long-time stalwart of the New York GAA. In my years in America, I have come to recognise how important the GAA is to our wider community; not only for Irish-born immigrants, but also for Irish Americans and those whose interest in our sports gives them an affinity with Ireland they would not otherwise have.

The value of Irish American support for Ireland has been much in evidence since my arrival as ambassador in August 2017. The Friends of Ireland caucus, led by its co-chairs, Congressmen Richie Neal and Peter King, both descended from Irish immigrants, was active in support of the Irish government's concerns about the risk posed to the Good Friday Agreement by Britain's departure from the European Union. The visit to Ireland and Britain in April 2019 of a US Congressional delegation, led by Congressman Neal and accompanied by House Speaker Nancy Pelosi, sent a strong signal to the effect that, if the so-called Brexit gave rise to a border on the island of Ireland, this would result in the US Congress blocking a US–UK Free Trade Agreement. This unwavering support for the Good Friday Agreement on the part of Irish American politicians made a real difference and worked greatly to Ireland's advantage at a time when our position might otherwise have been more vulnerable.

This vital Congressional support for Ireland did not come out of thin air. It was built on the backs of the millions of Irish immigrants who crossed the Atlantic during the past 300 years. Their descendants, while proudly and thoroughly American, have continually displayed an affinity with, and an affection for, Ireland. This remains an invaluable asset to our country to this day. This collection throws light on the fascinating history of Irish America, a community that, in different ways, played its part in shaping America—and Ireland.

Daniel Mulhall
Ambassador of Ireland to the United States of America (2017–21)
April 2021

Notes

[1] Kevin Kenny, 'Irish emigration, *c.* 1845–1900', in James Kelly (ed.), *The Cambridge history of Ireland*, vol. iii, *1730–1880* (Cambridge, 2018), 666–67.

[2] David Noel Doyle, 'The Irish in North America, 1776–1845', in W. E. Vaughan (ed.), *A new history of Ireland*, vol. v: *Ireland under the Union, 1801–70* (Oxford, 1989), 683.

[3] Daniel Tobin (ed.), *The book of Irish American poetry: from the eighteenth century to the present* (Notre Dame, Indiana, 2007), 48.

Editors' note

History is shaped by the people who live through it and, although Ireland is a small island, its people have had a disproportionate influence on the history of the world. Nowhere is this more apparent than in the United States, where the impact of Irish immigrants has been profound.

Across nine themed chapters, this selection of fifty entries from the *Dictionary of Irish Biography* attempts to illustrate the breadth of the Irish experience of, and impact upon, American culture, politics and society. We feature individuals across a broad field of endeavour—from political figures to artists and entertainers; soldiers to scientists; slaveholders to abolitionists; from the scouts who opened up the western frontier to the religious who established congregations across the country; from those who spent their lives fighting for the rights of workers to the industry titans who capitalised on the labour of others to become the country's first millionaires.

The biographies were selected with the kind assistance of Professors Margaret Kelleher (University College Dublin) and Maureen O. Murphy (Hofstra University, New York) with clearly defined criteria: the subjects had to be born in Ireland, they had to have contributed significantly (for good or ill) to American history, culture or society and, of course, they had to be interesting. As we curated our selection from the enormously rich corpus of the *Dictionary of*

Irish Biography, our main challenge was whittling down the number to a mere fifty entries. Those that did not make the final cut could fill separate volumes, and some are referred to within these pages. We also wanted to have strong female representation. Eighteen of our selected biographies are of Irish women in America, which, we hope, capture a diverse experience of immigration.

The volume spans over 300 years of American history. The earliest life featured is that of James Logan (1674–1751), public servant and scientist in pre-independence America; the latest is Hollywood actress Maureen O'Hara (1920–2015). O'Hara's biography is one of two new entries written specially for this volume, the other is that of Albert Cashier (1834–1915), a trans man who fought on the union side in the civil war.

Although biography is the history of the individual, we hope that by bringing together these fifty Irish lives in America we have given a sense of the movement of Ireland's people, and their continuous and significant impact on the culture and history of other countries.

Liz Evers and Niav Gallagher
September 2021

1. Lives on the frontier

Introduction

American frontier history and legend has long been dominated by the figure of a lone, grizzled man, leaving behind home and family to brave the undiscovered wilderness. The real frontiers-people were far more diverse—they were European and Native American, of African and Spanish descent, individuals and families. They moved west for land and fortune, the freedom to practice their religion or the opportunity to escape poverty and prejudice in the cities. Less often recorded is the fact that the lands that they moved into were already occupied by Native American populations. The new settlers sometimes coexisted with the indigenous peoples but more often forced them into resistance and, ultimately, retreat and destitution.

The Irish who settled in America were also diverse. The earliest immigrants were mostly Catholic indentured servants fleeing the plantations of Ulster and lives of poverty, or prisoners-of-war sentenced to transportation by Oliver Cromwell's regime. By contrast, Irish immigrants throughout the eighteenth century were mainly Presbyterian planters, those fleeing religious and economic persecution under the penal laws, and by the end of that century more than 2,000 young republican radicals of varying backgrounds who had fled to America following the failed rebellion in 1798. But all of these groups were surpassed by the vast numbers who emigrated from famine-ravaged Ireland during the mid-nineteenth century, with a continuous stream emigrating thereafter into the early twentieth century. While many of these migrants stayed in the cities, numerous others—either by choice or lack thereof—headed west.

Each of these generations of Irish emigrants produced notable characters whose activities helped drive the American project onward, crossing new 'frontiers'. One such is Anne Bonney (*c.*1700–*p.*1721, p. 4), who passed into legend as a fearsome female pirate raiding the coast of Cuba with 'Calico Jack'. To represent the profound struggles of frontier life, we chose Elizabeth Jackson (*c.*1740–81, p. 8), mother of future president Andrew Jackson, who emigrated to an area known as the Waxhaws in the backwoods of the Carolinas, where poor, heavily wooded land, backbreaking labour and political unrest awaited her family. Known as 'Broken Hand', Thomas Fitzpatrick (1799–1854, p. 16), was the first US agent to the tribes of the central plains, while Mary Jemison (1743?–1833, p. 12) chose to live with the Seneca people among the Iroquois nations and supplied a rare account of the tribe's experiences in the colonial and post-colonial periods. John Wallace Crawford (1847–1917, p. 21), born in Black '47, helped create the myth of the western hero, while Annie Moore (1877–1923, p. 25), the first emigrant to pass through Ellis Island, became a symbol of hope and opportunity to all incoming immigrants crossing that particular frontier, though her real life story fell far short of the American dream.

NG

Anne Bonney

*c.*1700–*p.*1721

Disguised as a man
aboard a pirate ship, she
and 'Calico Jack' raided
off the coast of Cuba and
Hispaniola until their
capture in 1720.

Anne Bonney (also Bonny) is thought to have been born in Cork about 1700. While her life story has been somewhat mythologised over time, the lead source about her remains the work of a Captain Charles Johnson (presumed to be the pseudonym of Daniel Defoe), whose *A general history of the robberies and murders of the most notorious pyrates* (1724) also likely mixes fact and fiction to provide a more rounded narrative.

Several historians name Bonney's father as William Cormac, a married man, and her mother as his maidservant, but there is no documentary evidence to support this. According to Johnson, she was disguised as a boy during her early childhood to conceal her identity and later, to avoid local censure, Cormac took mother and daughter to South Carolina where he acquired a substantial plantation. Again, there is no evidence to support this assertion despite land-owning in South Carolina being quite well documented for that period. In the second volume of his work, Johnson provided an appendix to the first volume in which he says he received further information on Bonney from her 'relations'. This new information stated that before May 1719 Anne travelled from the Carolinas to the Bahamas in the company of a woman named Anne Fulworth who acted as her mother. There is quite possibly an element of truth to this tale as a proclamation from governor Woodes Rogers declared 'Ann Fulford, alias Bonny' as being a pirate (5 September 1720). According to Johnson, she married a pirate named James Bonney but, when he accepted the king's pardon in 1718, she joined Captain John Rackham (nicknamed 'Calico Jack' in Johnson's text) and his pirate crew.

Disguised as a man on board ship, Bonney took part in raids off Cuba and Hispaniola and quite possibly bore

Rackham's child during this period. English-born Mary Read (*c.*1695–1721), also joined the crew. On 5 September 1720 the governor of the Bahamas issued a proclamation reporting the theft by Rackham and his associates of an armed twelve-ton sloop from Providence, which was subsequently used for acts of piracy and robbery. The proclamation was published in the *Boston Globe* and, the following month, the vessel was intercepted off the Jamaican coast. The crew, including Bonney and Read, were captured and imprisoned in Spanish Town, Jamaica. Rackham and his male accomplices were tried on 16 November and hanged two days later. On 28 November, at a separate trial in Spanish Town, Bonney and Read were tried for piracy. Although both women pleaded not guilty, the evidence of witnesses was incontrovertible. It was claimed that Bonney and Read were neither kept nor detained by force but that they engaged in piracy of their own free will. Eyewitnesses at the trial stated that the two women, both 'very profligate, cursing and swearing much', were disguised in men's clothing, each armed with a machete and pistol and that, as one of the last defenders of the ship, Bonney was very active on board and willing to do anything.

Although pleas of pregnancy saved both women from the death penalty, Read died in prison and was buried in the Jamaican district of Saint Catherine on 28 April 1721. It is unknown what happened to Bonney or her child. Historians have postulated that her well-connected father secured her release and brought her back to Charlestown where she married, became respectable and lived to the age of eighty-four. Johnson, however, finishes his account merely saying 'What has become of her we cannot tell. Only this we know, she was not executed' (173).

In the twentieth and twenty-first century, Bonney entered popular culture anew. The lead character in the 1951 film *Anne of the Indies* was loosely based on Bonney, while Bonney and Read's exploits were dramatised by playwright Steve Gooch in *The women pirates* (1978). Bonney and Read are also named-checked in the Adam and the Ants song 'Five guns west' (1981). In more recent times, Bonney has been a subject of several books, has appeared in the television series *Black sails* (2014–17), the *Anne Bonnie* (2014) comic book and as a character in the *Assassin's creed* game series.

Frances Clarke and Niav Gallagher

Sources

Captain Charles Johnson, *A general history of the robberies and murders of the most notorious pyrates* (1724); Phillip Gosse, *The history of piracy* (1954); Jennifer Uglow, *The Macmillan dictionary of women's biography* (1989); John C. Appleby, 'Women and piracy in Ireland: from Gráinne O'Malley to Anne Bonny', in Margaret MacCurtain and Mary O'Dowd (eds), *Women in early modern Ireland* (1991), 53–68; *Oxford dictionary of national biography* (2004); David Fictum, 'Anne Bonny and Mary Read: female pirates and maritime women', *Colonies, ships and pirates: concerning history in the Atlantic world 1680–1740* (8 May 2016); Tony Bartleme, 'The true and false stories of Anne Bonny, pirate woman of the Caribbean', *The Post and Courier* (21 November 2018)

Elizabeth Jackson

*c.*1740–81

An ardent patriot,
she travelled through
dangerous wartime
conditions to bring
her son, the future
President Andrew
Jackson, back from a
British prison camp.

Elizabeth Jackson was born in or near the town of Carrickfergus, Co. Antrim. Her father's name was Hutchinson, but this is all we know for certain of her parents. Some sources claim that his name was Francis Cyrus Hobart Hutchinson. In later life, Elizabeth Jackson reportedly talked of her father's voluntary service against an enemy force in Carrickfergus: it seems likely that this was the so-called 'invasion' of the town in 1760 by the French privateer François Thurot. A contemporary source lists a John Hutchinson as one of the valiant defenders of the town, and this was possibly Elizabeth's father.

Her mother may have been a Lisle, but more likely a Leslie, and thus would have been related to a Captain James Leslie, who took emigrants from Carrickfergus to South Carolina in 1755. Passengers on this ship almost certainly included Elizabeth's five older sisters and their husbands (two of whom were Leslies, perhaps their cousins) and their families. They settled in an area that was known as the Waxhaws, in the backwoods of North and South Carolina.

Left in Ireland, Elizabeth Hutchinson married Andrew Jackson, apparently in 1759, in the parish church in Carrickfergus, though the family later identified as Presbyterian. Though they may have suffered from rent increases and other financial impositions, such as Anglican tithes, stories of the family's poverty in Ireland before emigration clearly derive from the American mythology of a poor backwoods boy becoming president. The Jacksons and Hutchinsons were well connected in Ireland, possibly related to Anglican clergy, and fairly well-to-do. (In 1781 a Carrickfergus relative left the young Andrew Jackson a substantial legacy of over £300.) Elizabeth and her sisters were all literate. Andrew and Elizabeth Jackson sold their property in Carrickfergus, possibly including an inn, and emigrated in 1765 with their two infant sons and with Elizabeth's only brother to join her sisters and scores of former Antrim neighbours who had settled in America.

Poverty and misfortune were waiting for them on the poor land in north-west South Carolina. Andrew Jackson, too late to secure a better property, took up 200 heavily wooded acres and struggled alone to clear the land and build a cabin. In February 1767, aged just 29, he died following an accident involving a heavy log. His widow, in the last month of pregnancy, had no other support and had to move in with one of her sisters. Three weeks later, on 15 March 1767, Andrew Jackson junior was born and faced a very uncertain future. Elizabeth Jackson's sister Jane Crawford and her husband James Crawford gave them a home. Elizabeth was involved in all the work in the house and farm, as her sister was an invalid, and she helped raise her nephews as well as her own boys.

When the stirrings of revolution came in the early 1770s, the family were ardent supporters of the patriot cause, all the more so after open warfare broke out in 1775. Elizabeth Jackson is said to have helped nurse wounded rebels after a skirmish in the Waxhaws in 1780. Her oldest son, Hugh, died of heat exhaustion fighting the British at Stono Ferry in coastal South Carolina in 1779, and the two younger sons, still in their early teens, immediately joined the rebel forces. They were taken prisoner in their aunt's house, which was then pillaged by the British. Both young Jacksons were wounded, and both also contracted smallpox in the prison camp at Camden, South Carolina. Elizabeth Jackson negotiated a prisoner exchange to secure the release of her sons, travelling forty miles with two horses to bring the boys back. Andrew was on foot, without coat or shoes, and badly malnourished. The older boy, Robert, died two days after the return to the Waxhaws. Elizabeth nursed Andrew for weeks, but, when he was recovering, she left him to travel 160 miles, through wartime conditions, to Charleston, South Carolina, to try to find her Crawford nephews.

After only a few days visiting and nursing prisoners on the prison ships in Charleston harbour, Elizabeth Jackson contracted fever and died in November 1781. Andrew learned of his mother's death when he received a small bundle of her possessions, perhaps including a small bible she habitually carried. From the age of fourteen, he was on his own. He remembered her principles and precepts throughout his life (though not always living by them), and remained bitterly antagonistic to the British.

Andrew Jackson later tried to find where his mother was buried, so that her remains could be brought to rest in the graveyard of Waxhaw Presbyterian church beside his father and brothers, but her gravesite had been lost. Three later memorials in Charleston and Waxhaw, erected by the Daughters of the American Revolution and others, preserve the memory of Elizabeth Jackson's contribution to American history.

Linde Lunney

Sources

Belfast News Letter, 23 May 1755; 25 August 1944; John Francis Durand, *Genuine and curious memoirs of the famous Captain Thurot* (1760), 32; Robert H. White, 'Elizabeth Hutchinson Jackson, the mother of President Andrew Jackson', *Tennessee Historical Magazine*, series 2, iii, no. 3 (April 1935), 179–84; H. W. Brands, *Andrew Jackson: his life and times* (2005); Sheila Ingle, 'Elizabeth Hutchinson Jackson: the mother of President Andrew Jackson' (7 July 2014), sheilaingle.com; Genealogical sources for Hutchinson/Leslie families, www.wikitree.com/wiki/Space:Hutchinson_Sources

This entry has been abridged for publication. The full version is available at www.dib.ie.

Mary Jemison

1743?–1833

Jemison's life following
her adoption into the
Seneca tribe provides
one of the few authentic
accounts of how
colonial expansion
affected Native
American people.

Mary Jemison, also known as 'Deh-he-wä-mis', was born aboard the ship *William and Mary* as it travelled from Belfast or Larne to colonial Pennsylvania. Her parents Thomas Jemison and Jane (née Erwin) were of Protestant Scotch-Irish heritage. The family settled in Franklin Township, Adams County. On 5 April 1758, aged fifteen, Jemison was captured by a raiding party made up of Shawnee and French forces during a skirmish in the French and Indian War. Her parents, two brothers and a sister all died in the raid. Three subsequent attempts to ransom her back into British Colonial hands failed; Jemison either resisted or avoided them, choosing to live as a Seneca among the Iroquois nations.

She was adopted by two Seneca sisters, who named her 'Deh-he-wä-mis' meaning 'pretty girl or handsome girl, or a pleasant good thing' (Seaver, 59), and married Sheninjee, a Delaware warrior, in 1760. He died within three years of their marriage, which produced a daughter (who died soon after birth) and a son, Tommy, named after Jemison's father. Jemison's second marriage to Hiokatoo (*c*.1763), a husband of her own choosing, lasted over five decades until his death in 1811. They had four daughters and two sons. Knowledge of Jemison's life comes principally from James E. Seaver's, *Narrative of the life of Mrs Mary Jemison* (1824). This account is one of the very few sources depicting the impact of the colonial expansion and ensuing conflagrations on Native Americans, their declining autonomy and the eventual assembly of Seneca peoples into reservations.

Having moved to Genishau, a substantial Seneca town on the Genesee river, New York, Jemison's account of her life captures the great happiness she found in Native American society. Depicting turn-of-the-century Seneca life rich in detail, observing the arrival of alcohol, and futile attempts to convert the Senecas to Christianity, Jemison's account demonstrates the innate happiness and civility manifest in the last vestiges of Native American society, itself highly tolerant of other customs and religions.

Her family was beset by tragedy, however. In July 1811, John, her eldest son by Hiokatoo, murdered her first son Tommy; in July 1812 John also murdered his younger brother, Jesse. In June 1817 John was himself murdered in a drunken altercation.

During the American Revolution the Senecas sided with, and were ultimately abandoned by, their traditional allies the British. The Senecas had to relinquish much of their land and again Jemison's account is an invaluable source of events from the Native American perspective. Jemison was granted 17,927 acres of land along the Genesee River, near Castile, New York, by the Treaty of Big Tree (1797), indicative of her astute negotiating skills. The New York state legislature passed (April 1817) a statute naturalising Mary Jemison, affording her the ability to convey land, thus affirming her title to this land. A grandson, Jacob Jemison, attended Dartmouth College (1816–18).

She lived on her land on the Gardeau Flats until forced to cede it to white settlers in the early 1820s. She then followed other Senecas to the Buffalo Creek Reservation, where she died in 1833. Later reinterred in Letchworth State Park, her remains were moved a second time to an unmarked location in Letchworth Gorge.

At least twenty-eight editions of Seaver's *Life of Mary Jemison: Deh-he-wä-mis* followed its initial publication in 1824. Based on Seaver's interviews with her in November 1823, the book became an instant bestseller.

Seaver presents a captivity narrative—delivered in the first person and ethnographically insightful in reconstructing Iroquois culture—that occasionally betrays the spirited individualism of its subject. Seaver, unable to accept Jemison's confidence, independence and strength, presents her as a passive victim, refusing to acknowledge her deliberate alignment with Native American custom and culture. Jemison's life with the Senecas subverts Anglo-American narrative traditions; she refused to return to colonial society, remaining proudly independent until her death, and she adopted Iroquois matrilineal practice, allowing her to retain her Irish surname through two marriages. Jemison's narrative provides a fascinating account of her life in North America. A bronze sculpture (1910) of her stands in Letchworth State Park, Castile, New York, to mark her grave, while a second monument to her was unveiled near her former home in Adams County, Pennsylvania in 1921.

Turlough O'Riordan

Sources

James E. Seaver, *Life of Mary Jemison: Deh-he-wä-mis* (4th edition, 1856); Susan Walsh, '"With them was my home": Native American autobiography and *A narrative life of Mrs. Mary Jemison*', *American Literature*, vol. 64, no. 1 (March 1992), 49–70; Hilary E. Wyss, 'Captivity and conversion: William Apess, Mary Jemison, and narratives of racial identity', *American Indian Quarterly*, vol. 23, no. 3 and 4 (1999), 63–82; *American national biography* (1999)

Thomas Fitzpatrick ('Broken Hand')

1799–1854

A nineteenth-century
mountain man, he
served as guide to
westward-bound settlers
and was the first US
agent to the tribes of
the central plains.

Thomas Fitzpatrick (known as 'Broken Hand') was born in Co. Cavan, one of three sons and four daughters of Mary Fitzpatrick (née Kiernan) and her husband, whose forename is not known. A Catholic, Thomas received the fundamentals of a sound education before emigrating to America by age seventeen. For some thirty years he played a prominent role in the exploration, exploitation and conquest of the American west, a key participant in many of the historic events of the era. Joining the second fur-trading expedition of William Henry Ashley (1823), when passage up the Missouri river was rendered impossible after armed clashes with Arikara people, Fitzpatrick was designated second-in-command under Jedediah Smith of a party of fifteen men dispatched to blaze a direct overland route to the fur country of the central Rocky mountains. After wintering in the Wind river valley, the party crossed the continental divide at South Pass (March 1824), and descended into the rich beaver country of the Green river and its tributaries, thereby making the effective discovery of the passage that for the next half-century would be the major route through the Rockies to the Pacific ocean. After returning east with a large stock of pelts, Fitzpatrick guided Ashley with a horse train of supplies and trade goods on a winter journey over the new route, arriving at Green river in April 1825. After leading a small trapping band into the Uinta mountains, he reassembled with several other bands and the supply train (July 1825), the first of the sixteen famed annual rendezvous—raucous trade fairs at which trappers sold furs, purchased supplies and revelled after months of solitude in the wilderness.

For the next fifteen years Fitzpatrick led trapping bands, conducted supply caravans to rendezvous and conveyed furs to river posts whence they were boated east to St Louis. Employed by Ashley's firm and its successor until

1830, he was senior partner in the Rocky Mountain Fur Company (1830–34), which contested a fierce trapping and trade war with the mighty American Fur Company of John Jacob Astor. While travelling alone ahead of the 1832 supply train, he endured a harrowing episode under pursuit by members of the Gros Ventre tribe—an experience that reputedly caused the premature greying of his hair—and subsequently led a body of trappers and Native American allies against a party of Gros Ventres in the battle of Pierre's Hole. After the dissolution of the Rocky Mountain company, he was partner in two subsequent firms, before selling out to the American Fur Company (1836), which thereafter employed him annually as a band leader. After suffering the mangling of his left hand by the bursting of his own rifle, probably during a skirmish with Blackfeet in January 1836, he was widely known among Native Americans by the name Broken Hand.

With the fur trade in drastic decline owing to over-hunting and the change in fashion from beaver-skin to silk hats, Fitzpatrick, as a seasoned 'mountain man', served as guide to westward-bound settlers, exploration parties and military expeditions. He guided the first two Pacific-bound emigrant wagon trains (1841 and 1842) along the old trappers' route, now known as the Oregon trail, to Fort Hall on the Snake river; the 1841 train joined forces with the first Catholic missionary party to cross the Rockies under the Belgian-born Jesuit priest Pierre-Jean De Smet, whom Fitzpatrick accompanied to the Flathead country of northern Idaho. He guided John C. Fremont's fourteen-month expedition of 1843–4 through the Oregon country and California, which achieved a daring winter crossing of the Sierra Nevada; functioning as expedition quartermaster, he frequently commanded the main section and baggage train when Fremont led smaller parties on exploring forays. As war with Mexico loomed after America's annexation of Texas, he guided two of the three western military reconnaissance missions of 1845: the Kearny expedition of five companies of dragoons across the central plains into the Rockies, and the Abert expedition through the internationally disputed territory of the Texas panhandle and western Oklahoma. When war was declared, he guided Kearny's army of the west, which invaded Mexican territory and occupied Santa Fe (August 1846).

Appointed 'Indian agent' for the region of the Upper Platte and Arkansas (1846–54), he was thus the first US agent to the tribes of the central plains: Cheyenne, Arapaho and several bands of Lakota Sioux. He married (November 1849) Margaret Poisal, daughter of a French-Canadian trapper and an Arapaho woman; they had one son and one daughter. Near Fort Laramie in September 1851 Fitzpatrick convened the largest Native American council ever held in the west, attended by some 10,000 plains and mountain tribespeople, and successfully negotiated a treaty whereby tribal chiefs pledged peace among themselves and with Euro-Americans, and guaranteed safe passage of westward-bound emigrant traffic through defined tribal territories, in return for government annuities of $50,000 in goods. He subsequently obtained ratifications from the signatory tribes of US senate amendments reducing the term of annuities from fifty years to fifteen. At Fort Atkinson in July 1853 he concluded a similar treaty with the Comanche, Kiowa and plains Apache. Summoned to Washington to discuss the latter treaty, he fell ill with pneumonia and died 7 February 1854. He was buried in the congressional cemetery.

Of medium height, spare but muscular in frame, remarkably coolheaded and adaptable, Fitzpatrick is ranked alongside Kit Carson and James Bridger as the three greatest of the mountain men, though he did not achieve their fame due to a comparative dearth of publicity surrounding his exploits. A devotee of Jacksonian democracy and manifest destiny, he regarded Native Americans as inferiors and advised retribution for acts of violence but opposed policies of extirpation as tantamount to extermination. He insisted on just and honest relations and counselled the gradual 'civilisation' of the semi-nomadic hunting plains peoples by patient training in tillage and trade. Though he was remembered favourably by such leaders as Black Kettle of the Cheyenne and Little Raven of the Arapaho—who called him the 'one fair agent' his people ever had—their judgements were perhaps influenced by the depths of fraud and betrayal their tribes subsequently encountered.

Lawrence William White

Sources

Dictionary of American biography (1928–58); LeRoy R. Hafen and Ann W. Hafen, 'Thomas Fitzpatrick', in LeRoy Hafen (ed.), *The mountain men and the fur trade of the far west*, vii (1969); LeRoy R. Hafen, *Broken Hand: the life of Thomas Fitzpatrick: mountain man, guide, and Indian agent* (1973); Charles Phillips and Alan Axelrod (eds), *Encyclopedia of the American west* (1996)

This entry has been abridged for publication. The full version is available at www.dib.ie.

John Wallace Crawford

1847–1917

This frontier scout, writer and entertainer from Donegal helped create the myth of the Wild West hero.

John Wallace Crawford was born 4 March 1847 in Carndonagh, Co. Donegal, the son of John Austin Crawford, a Glasgow tailor, and Susie Wallace. His father moved to Minersville, Pennsylvania, to work in the coalmines in 1854; his mother followed in 1858 and the children two years later, in 1860. When his father enlisted in the union army in 1861, Crawford and his brothers went to work in the coalmines to help support the family. During the next two years Crawford twice tried to enlist in the army but was denied for being too young. He was eventually accepted in 1863, when he joined Company F of the 48th Pennsylvania volunteer infantry. After being wounded on 12 May 1864 at Spottsylvania, Pennsylvania, he was hospitalised in west Philadelphia, where he was taught to read and write by a member of the Sisters of Charity. On 2 April 1865 he was wounded a second time, and later that year was honourably discharged from the army and returned to be with his dying parents. He supposedly made a deathbed promise to his mother to abstain from alcohol.

In 1869 he married Anna Marie Stokes of Numidia, Pennsylvania, and they had five children together. By the early 1870s Crawford was serving as an army scout in campaigns against the Sioux and the Apache, and for most of the 1870s he lived on the American frontier while his wife and family remained in Pennsylvania. In August 1875 he was appointed first captain of the Black Hills Rangers militia, organised to protect miners from native raids. He was also an (unsuccessful) gold prospector at the time and correspondent for Omaha and Cheyenne newspapers. He helped found several frontier towns, including Deadwood, Custer City and Spearfish in South Dakota, and Crook in Wyoming. In the autumn of 1876, he left the Black Hills to co-star with fellow scout William F. 'Buffalo Bill' Cody in his 'Wild West' melodramas. Crawford was wounded in the groin during a performance in Virginia City, Nevada, in the summer of 1877, and while recuperating wrote his first play, 'Fonda, or, The trapper's dream', which became a great success. He ended his partnership with Buffalo Bill, toured California with the play, and was approached to take it to Australia, but could not finance the trip. Known as 'Captain Jack' and the 'Poet Scout', in 1879 he published his first collection of poetry, *The poet scout*, and by the early 1880s he was a well-known composer of verse.

In 1880 Crawford was a scout in New Mexico for the army in the war against the Apache, and in 1881 his family joined him at Fort Craig, New Mexico, where he was a post trader and later a special agent of the Indian Bureau. He established a ranch on the Rio Grande in 1886, though he also had a home in Brooklyn, New York. In 1889 he was appointed a special agent in the justice department to investigate illegal liquor traffic on native reservations in the western states and territories. Four years later he embarked on a career as a public lecturer, recounting the 'Wild West' he knew from his experiences in an attempt to counteract the sensationalist version depicted in dime novels. He gained a nationwide reputation from his performances, though he abandoned them between 1898 and 1900 to prospect for gold in the Klondike.

In 1903 he again left his family and returned to Brooklyn, where he continued his literary work—which helped create the myth of the western hero—though he never received the recognition he felt he deserved. One of the first cowboy balladeers, he published more than a hundred short stories. His other major works are *Camp fire sparks* (1893), *Lariattes* (1904) and *The broncho book* (1908). He died on 28 February 1917 at his Brooklyn home.

Adam Pole

Sources

D. J. O'Donoghue, *The poets of Ireland: a biographical and bibliographical dictionary of Irish writers of English verse* (1912); *Dictionary of American biography* (1928–58); Stanley J. Kunitz and Howard Haycraft (eds), *American authors, 1600–1900* (1964); Brenda Hanrahan, *Donegal authors: a bibliography* (1982); William F. Cody, *The life of Buffalo Bill* (1994); *American national biography* (1999); Robert A. Carter, *Buffalo Bill Cody* (2000); Darlis A. Miller, *Captain Jack Crawford: buckskin poet, scout and showman* (2012)

Annie Moore

1874–1924

As the first immigrant
to land on Ellis Island
she became a symbol
not only of Irish
immigrants, but of
all who landed there.
Her real experience,
however, fell far short
of the American dream.

Annie Moore was born on 24 April 1874 in Cork, the second child and only daughter of Matthew Moore and Julia Moore (née Cronin). Annie's parents emigrated to New York in 1888, and she and her younger brothers, Anthony and Philip, followed three years later. The trio left Cork on 20 December 1891, travelling steerage aboard the *Nevada*. They arrived in New York on 1 January 1892 just in time for the opening of the new federal immigration depot at Ellis Island. Annie Moore was first in line to disembark the ship. She was greeted by federal, state and city dignitaries. Colonel Weber, the superintendent of immigration, presented her with a ten-dollar gold piece. Annie and her brothers were reunited with their parents who were living at 32 Monroe Street in the city's fourth ward, a neighbourhood of tenements. Matthew Moore, who had worked as a longshoreman, died in 1907.

For many years, the biographical details of Moore's life were erroneously reported. In 2006, genealogist Megan Smolenyak and Brian G. Andersson, the commissioner of records and information for New York City (2002–10), announced that the Annie Moore who moved with her parents first to Indiana and then to Waco, Texas, was not the Ellis Island Annie Moore as had long been supposed. The Texas Annie Moore had in fact been born in Illinois and married a Patrick O'Connell who died during the Spanish 'flu epidemic. She was struck by a train and killed in 1924. The Ellis Island Annie Moore had in fact stayed in her Lower East Side neighbourhood in New York. In 1895 she married Joseph Augustus Schayer (1876–1960), the son of German immigrants who worked at the Fulton Street Fish Market, at St James's Catholic church, James Street. She gave birth to eleven children and buried six of them. The death certificates of the infants show death by poverty or neglect. Of the five who survived infancy, three had children of their own.

Moore died of heart failure on 6 December 1924 at 99 Cherry Street. She was fifty. A photograph taken late in life shows a stout woman frowning in front of a doorway. A story told about her is that she was too overweight to bring down the stairs, so her body had to be passed out the window. Annie Moore Schayer, five of her children and James Doherty, a neighbour's infant, were buried in an unmarked grave in Calvary cemetery in Queens, New York. After Smolenyak and Andersson produced the evidence describing Moore's life, plans were made by Irish American organisations to mark her grave with an Irish limestone headstone carved in Co. Clare. The grave was marked and dedicated on 11 October 2008.

The centenary of Ellis Island turned Annie Moore into a cultural icon. The Irish American Cultural Institute promoted the idea of making her the symbol not only of Irish immigrants but of all those who arrived at Ellis Island. Irish artist Jeanne Rynhart (1946–2020) created two pieces to commemorate the centenary: one of Annie Moore and her brothers departing Ireland, which was installed outside the Cobh Heritage Centre; the second was installed at Ellis Island pier depicting Annie alone, carrying her bag and holding her hat. Both were unveiled in 1993 by President Mary Robinson.

The merchandising of Annie Moore followed. The Irish American Cultural Institute introduced a commemorative ornament series with a brass replica of the New York Rynhart statue. Belleek Pottery produced a commemorative plate called 'The first sight of Miss Liberty', which sold out immediately. An Annie Moore doll came with the poem 'Grandma Annie' that explained the significance of the heirloom gold coin she received on her arrival in America. She was also commemorated in song, the Irish Tenors' March 2001 Ellis Island concert featured the Annie Moore ballad 'Isle of hope, isle of tears', while the refrain in Tim Sparling and Allen Werneken's 'Immigration island', includes the line, 'You're the first through this island in a new land, Annie Moore'.

Eithne Loughrey wrote three young adult novels that invent the life that Annie led in America: *First in line for America* (1999), *Annie Moore: New York City girl* (2000) and *Annie Moore: the golden dollar girl* (2001). Eve Bunting's *Dreaming of America* (2000) is another account of Annie's arrival in New York for the young reader.

These fictional accounts bear little resemblance to the grinding poverty and lost children of the real-life Annie Moore, however. Of the hardship she experienced, Megan Smolenyak wrote:

> …as is so often the case with immigrants, her sacrifices led to greater opportunities for her descendants who have since flourished. At least one remained in the Lower East Side until this century, but most fanned out to New Jersey, Maryland, Wisconsin, Arizona, and elsewhere. They took on a variety of professions, worked their way up the economic ladder, and married others with diverse backgrounds so that Annie's Irish genes have now blended with Hispanic, Jewish, Scandinavian, and more (10 January 2017).

The Annie Moore Award was established by the Irish American Cultural Institute in 1995 to honour individuals who have contributed significantly to the Irish American community.

Maureen O. Murphy

Sources

National Archives of Ireland microfilm M237-581, 8; *New York Herald*, 2 January 1892; *New York Mirror*, 2 January 1892; *Causeway*, v, no. 1 (1998), 5; Edward O'Donnell, 'Annie Moore arrives', *Irish Echo* (27 December 2000–2 January 2001), 14; Susan Kelly and Stephen Morton, 'Calling up Annie Moore', *Public Culture*, xvi (2004), 119–30; Ray O'Hanlon, 'Cardinal clears the way for Annie headstone', *Irish Echo*, 23–29 January 2008; Megan Smolenyak, '125th anniversary of Annie Moore and Ellis Island', 10 January 2017, www.megansmolenyak. com/125th-anniversary-of-annie-moore-and-ellis-island/; Annie Moore revisited, https://anniemoore.net/home.html

2. Lives of politics

Introduction

From the beginning of the seventeenth century France, Spain and England jostled for domination of the New World, establishing colonies throughout the Americas and displacing, enslaving or murdering indigenous people. By the closing decades of the eighteenth century America had established itself as an independent country and was poised to become an economic and military powerhouse in the nineteenth century.

Irish immigrants played a significant role in the politics and administration of the new country. They were governors and military leaders, signatories to the declaration of independence, framers of the constitution and even presidents—twenty-three of America's forty-six presidents can claim Irish ancestry. Some, such as William Johnson (1715–74, p. 34) of Meath, walked a fine line between colonial administration and respect for indigenous tribes. He was given the name Warraghiyagey ('Chief Big Business' or 'Doer of great things') by the Mohawks.

In the war for America's independence, eleven of the fifty-six delegates to the first Continental Congress (1774) were born in Ireland, and nine of the signatories to the declaration of independence were of Irish birth or ancestry. The Irish were also part of America's two great defining conflicts—the war of independence and the civil war—and served as soldiers and sailors, financiers and politicians. In the civil war that raged from 1861 to 1865 the first two recorded combat deaths were Irishmen, and, in total, more than 150,000 Irish signed up to fight on the union side, including Thomas Meagher (1823–67,

p. 45) who commanded the Irish Brigade at the battles of Malvern Hill, Antietam and Fredericksburg. A lowly private, Albert Cashier (1834–1915, p. 56) left Ireland poor and illiterate and joined the union army at Illinois. When the war was over, he worked in a variety of jobs in a small town, wearing his uniform proudly in the annual veterans' parade. What makes Albert's story extraordinary is that he was born Jennie Hodgers and, at the end of his life, was forced to wear a dress and answer to that name. His army comrades ensured that, at least in death, Albert's life as a veteran was honoured.

Although significantly fewer fought on the confederate side, there were at least six confederate generals of Irish birth, and units such as the Charleston Irish Volunteers were formed. Regrettably, many Irish supported the institution of slavery from the start. In 1787 Pierce Butler (1744–1822, p. 39), a soldier and slaveholder from Carlow had the unfortunate distinction of being the man who insisted that the 'fugitive slave clause' be inserted into the US constitution.

Our final choice in this selection of political lives is John 'Old Smoke' Morrissey (1831–78, p. 52), a famed and formidable New York prize-fighter, Tammany Hall operative and gang leader who fought street battles against 'Bill the butcher', and became a senator representing New York state from 1875 until his death in 1878.

NG

Sir
William
Johnson

1715–74

Called 'Chief Big
Business' by the
Mohawk tribe, Johnson
was superintendent of
Indian affairs in colonial
America and the founder
of Johnstown, New York.

William Johnson was born at Smithtown, Co. Meath, one of seven children (three sons and four daughters) of Christopher Johnson, tenant farmer, and Anne Johnson (née Warren). Both the Johnson and Warren families conformed to the Church of Ireland, probably during the early eighteenth century.

In early 1738 Johnson arrived in America to oversee the Mohawk valley estate of his uncle, Vice-admiral Sir Peter Warren, at Warrensburg, New York, near the mouth of the Schoharie river and covering twenty-two square miles. By 1740 he had built his own home, Mount Johnson, across the river from Warrensburg. To run the household he chose a German indentured servant, Catherine Weisenberg, who became the mother of three of his children: a son, Sir John Johnson (who became a loyalist leader in the American revolution, later settling in Canada), and two daughters, Ann ('Nancy') and Mary. For the farm he recruited twelve families from Meath. Throughout his career Johnson chose to settle Irish immigrants on his estates, as well as Palatine Germans, to serve as a buffer against the often antagonistic Albany Dutch, who had long held a virtual monopoly on trade with the Iroquois and also carried on an illegal trade with the French and native peoples in Canada.

During this period, Johnson began trading with the Six Nations (Iroquois confederacy), as well as supplying the settlers in the Mohawk valley. His close relationship with the Six Nations, particularly the Mohawks, led him into the political and military arenas, influencing his ideas of how the colonies should manage trade and westward expansion. By 1745–8, when he participated in the war of the Austrian succession (called 'King George's war' in North America), he had already gained the confidence of Tiyanoga, a Mohawk sachem (administrative chief), known to the Dutch as 'King Hendrick', who had travelled to England in 1709–10 and again in 1740. Johnson's friendship with the Mohawks was so great that he was adopted into the tribe and renamed Warraghiyagey ('Chief Big Business' or 'Doer of great things'). Johnson learned the Mohawk language, and he also adopted their clothing and customs when among them.

In 1746 the New York assembly voted to provide Johnson with funds to supply Fort Oswego on Lake Ontario and he was named 'colonel of the...Six Nations and commissary for Indian affairs' by the royal governor of New York, George Clinton (son of the Irishman Charles Clinton). Returning to the Mohawk valley following the end of the war, in 1748 Johnson began building Fort Johnson, a stone house still in existence. Johnson participated in the Albany congress (1754) which helped formulate British policy toward native peoples. In April 1755 the crown confirmed Johnson as superintendent of Indian affairs with full powers to treat with the Six Nations and their allies, and he was also commissioned major-general by the northern colonial governments.

Increasing French encroachments on the north-western frontier eventually led to the Seven Years' War (officially 1756–63, though it began and ended earlier in North America, where it is called 'the French and Indian war'). Although Johnson's expedition to capture the French fort at Crown Point failed, he soundly defeated the French under Baron Dieskau at Lake George (September 1755) and later established Forts Edward and William Henry. In November 1755 the king made him a baronet (only the second in the American colonies). He participated in the siege of Niagara (1759), which fell to him on 25 July, and in 1760 he served with General Jeffery Amherst in the capture of Montreal. That year the Mohawks bestowed the title of sachem on him. In 1761 he journeyed to Detroit, part of a diplomatic mission to pacify the Native Americans of that region. In 1762 he founded Johnstown, New York, where he established his principal residence.

After Catherine Weisenberg's death (1759), Mary ('Molly') Brant, daughter of the sachem Nichuls Brant (Aroghyiadecker) and sister of Joseph Brant, the Mohawk leader during the American revolution, came to manage the household, first at Fort Johnson and later at the Georgian-style Johnson Hall, built in 1763, and also still in existence. Between 1759 and 1773 she bore William nine children, of whom eight survived, two sons and six daughters. One son, Peter Johnson, was killed aged seventeen fighting on the British side during the American revolution, and Molly (known also as Degonwadonti) herself led Mohawk warriors. After that war, Molly and her family settled in Kingston, Ontario, where she died in 1796, aged about sixty. Sir William Johnson had died on 11 July 1774, aged fifty-nine, probably from cirrhosis of the liver, undoubtedly a result of years of hard drinking and entertaining Native Americans and Europeans at Fort Johnson and Johnson Hall, which were renowned centres of hospitality in the Mohawk valley.

Portraits of Johnson may be found in the Public Archives of Canada, Albany Institute of History and Art, New York Historical Society and Derby Museum and Art Gallery (the last, by Benjamin West, shows him rescuing a French officer from a tomahawk-wielding Iroquois). His papers were edited by the New York State Division of Archives, Albany (13 vols, 1921–62).

James E. Doan

Sources

Arthur Pound with Richard E. Day, *Johnson of the Mohawks: a biography of Sir William Johnson, Irish immigrant, Mohawk war chief, American soldier, empire builder* (1930, reprint 1971); James T. Flexner, *Lord of the Mohawks: a biography of Sir William Johnson* (1959, revised edition 1979); Milton W. Hamilton, *Sir William Johnson: colonial American, 1715–1763* (1976); Paul Redmond Drew, 'Sir William Johnson—Indian superintendent', *Early America Review*, i, no. 2 (Fall 1996) [electronic journal]; Fintan O'Toole, *White savage: William Johnson and the invention of America* (2005)

Pierce Butler

1744–1822

British colonial officer who married into South Carolina's wealthy slave-owning elite, switched allegiances in the war of independence and soon thereafter entered politics. He was responsible for the 'fugitive slave clause' in the US constitution.

Pierce Butler was born in Ballintemple House, Co. Carlow, on 11 July 1744, the third son of Sir Richard Butler, 5th baronet of Cloughgrenan and member of the Irish parliament, and his wife Henrietta (née Percy), daughter of the mayor of Dublin, Anthony Percy, whose family laid claim to the dukedom of Northumberland, albeit unsuccessfully. Although he enjoyed a privileged upbringing, as the third son of an Anglo-Irish aristocrat Butler was unlikely to inherit his father's lands or titles; thus when he was eleven years old his father purchased a commission for him in the 22nd Regiment of Foot (known later as the Cheshire Regiment) and he entered active service.

By the age of fourteen Butler was a full lieutenant and in command of troops at the Siege of Louisbourg in French Canada in 1758, where he was wounded. The following year he again fought against the French at the battle of the Plains of Abraham. In 1762, when word came that the regiment was being dispatched to Louisiana, Butler took the opportunity to transfer to the 29th Regiment of Foot (known later as the Worcestershire and Sherwood Foresters), then stationed in Ireland. He remained in Ireland until 1765 when the regiment was sent to garrison Nova Scotia, and a year later he was promoted to major, a title he continued to use even after resigning his commission.

Having established his military career, Butler allegedly attempted to elope with a fifteen-year-old South Carolina heiress in 1768—a marriage that was forestalled by the girl's stepfather. On 10 January 1771 he made an advantageous match when he married Mary Middleton, daughter of Thomas Middleton, a South Carolina planter and slave importer. On 10 November the same year she inherited Middleton's estates and, through her, Butler now owned vast estates in Toogoodoo, Bull's Island and Hilton Head. The couple went on to have eight children, of whom five survived—one boy and four girls. He also gained significant social and political links to South Carolina's elite through the marriage: Mary Middleton's uncle was Henry Middleton, who presided over the continental congress for several days in 1774, and her cousin was Arthur Middleton, one of the signatories of the American declaration of independence.

Having ended French territorial claims in North America, permanent garrisons were required to maintain British gains. The cost of financing these troops fell upon American colonists and, as unrest spread, the 29th along with the 14th Regiment of Foot were sent to maintain the king's peace in Boston. On 5 March 1770 a detachment from Butler's regiment opened fire on a crowd at the Boston customs house killing five people, in what became the opening shots of the American Revolution. Butler remained in the regiment for a further three years but when they received orders to return to Britain in 1773, he resigned his commission and used the money to increase his landholding significantly. Between 1772 and 1786 he bought almost 10,000 acres in Georgia and South Carolina and he also began to accumulate small coastal ships in order to move his produce more easily.

When war broke out between America and Britain in 1775 Butler joined with several former British officers, such as Charles Lee and Richard Montgomery, in siding with his adopted country. Initially his involvement was administrative rather than military. In 1776 he accepted the post of justice of the peace for Beaufort district, and in 1778 he was elected to the house of representatives for Prince William district (a position he held until 1789).

From 1779 onwards, however, his participation was more significant. Early in the year John Rutledge, governor of South Carolina, appointed him adjutant-general, a position that carried the rank of brigadier-general, and tasked him with organising the state's militia. In retaliation for this betrayal of his oath to king and country, his principal residence at the Eutaw plantation was burned by the British in May 1779 and his name was placed on a proscribed list of rebel officers of both South Carolina and Georgia.

In May 1780 the British captured Charleston and with it most of the state's government and military. Butler, out recruiting for the militia, evaded capture and joined General Gates's army in North Carolina, where he was placed in command of 150 militia guarding British prisoners of war in Salisbury. Although the war was effectively over by October 1781 when the British, under Lord Cornwallis, surrendered at Yorkstown, preliminary peace terms were not signed until November 1782. On 14 December that year Butler brought his family back to Charleston from their exile in Philadelphia. He had suffered significant losses, both financial and physical, during the war: his residence had been burned down, slaves confiscated, ships sunk and crops destroyed. After the Treaty of Paris was signed on 3 September 1783 Butler returned to Europe, ostensibly to see his family in Ireland and enrol his son Thomas in an exclusive school in London, but also to raise loans and open new markets for his produce. He returned to America in late 1785 and does not appear to have left his adopted country again.

For the latter half of his life Butler was deeply involved in American politics. Already a representative in the South Carolina legislature, in March 1787 he was elected one of four delegates to represent the state at the Philadelphia convention, originally intended to redraft the articles of confederation but which ultimately resulted in a new constitution.

Accompanied by the other South Carolina delegates Charles Pinckney, Charles Cotesworth Pinckney and John Rutledge, Butler spoke approximately seventy times at the convention. He also proposed Article IV, section 2, clause 3, known as 'the fugitive slave clause', which stated a 'person held to service or labour in one state...escaping into another, shall...be delivered [back to that] party to whom such service or labour may be due.' It was adopted into the constitution almost verbatim. It is unsurprising that Butler's greatest concern for the new constitution was that it would protect wealth and property, given that he owned a large number of slaves until his death, and that his heirs did likewise. On 17 September 1787 Butler was one of forty men who signed the constitution of the United States of America, and when the South Carolina House of Representatives met on 22 January 1789 he was elected as one of the first United States senators.

Butler served three terms in the senate: 1789–92; 1792–6, when he resigned and returned to his state, and again from 1802 to 1806, when he completed the term of a colleague who died in office. His name was also suggested as a vice-presidential running mate for Thomas Jefferson in 1796 but that does not appear to have been a serious proposal. In 1816 he was appointed as one of five government directors of the Bank of the United States and, upon completion of his three-year term, President James Monroe expressed 'high respect and sincere friendship' for him (*Butler papers*, 1 January 1819).

After he retired from politics in 1806 Butler spent a lot of time in Philadelphia where he continued with his business interests, becoming one of the wealthiest men in

America. He died at home on 15 February 1822 and was buried in the family vault at the episcopal Christ Church, Philadelphia. Many of the accounts of Butler's life portray him as a contradictory man, one who supported a broad franchise but also defended slavery, a man who was born into aristocracy and wealth but who was fierce in his opposition to monarchy, and a soldier who fought against the French and the British and then spent a lifetime decrying war. He was not contradictory in his central belief, however, in a strong central government that protected the rights of the private citizen. Even so, he found the constitution that he helped to draft flawed, declaring at the end of his life: 'our system is little better than [a] matter of experiment…[and] much must depend on the morals and manners of the people at large' (*Soldier-statesmen of the constitution*, 76–78).

Niav Gallagher

Sources

Dictionary of American biography (1928–58); S. Sidney Ulmer, 'The role of Pierce Butler in the constitutional convention', *Review of Politics*, 22 (1960), 361–74; Linda Grant DePauw, *et al.* (eds), *Documentary history of the first federal congress of the United States of America* (1972), 824–30; Francis Coughlan, 'Pierce Butler, 1744–1822, first senator from South Carolina', *South Carolina Historical Magazine*, 78 (April 1977), 104–19; Lewright B. Sikes, *The public life of Pierce Butler, South Carolina statesman* (1979); James H. Hutson, 'Pierce Butler's records of the federal constitutional convention', *Quarterly Journal of the Library of Congress*, 37 (1980), 64–73; Robert K. Wright Jr and Morris J. MacGregor (eds), *Soldier-statesmen of the constitution, Washington, D.C.* (1987), 76–8; Malcolm Bell Jr, *Major Butler's legacy: five generations of a slaveholding family* (1987); *American national biography* (1999); Terry W. Lipscomb (ed.), *The letters of Pierce Butler, 1790–1794: nation building and enterprise in the new American republic* (2007); *The Irish Times*, 12 February 2019; *Biographical directory of the United States Congress*, https://bioguideretro.congress.gov/

Thomas Francis Meagher

1823–67

A born adventurer, Meagher went from a Young Ireland revolutionary to a transported convict, a civil war general to a Wild West territorial governor.

Thomas Francis Meagher was born 3 August 1823 in Waterford city, the eldest child of Thomas Meagher and his wife Alicia Quan. Both parents came from well-to-do Catholic merchant families. His father was a shipowner, specialising in the Newfoundland trade, who went on to become mayor of Waterford (1842–4) and an O'Connellite MP for the city (1847–57). Young Tom had a comfortable, even privileged, upbringing. He was sent to Clongowes Wood college, Co. Kildare (1833–9), and then to the sister Jesuit college at Stonyhurst, Lancashire (1839–43).

Returning to Waterford in 1843, he supported Daniel O'Connell's movement for repeal of the act of union. In January 1844 he moved to Dublin and registered as a law student at King's Inns (nominated by O'Connell). He became actively involved in the affairs of the Repeal Association, and within a year had abandoned his law studies. This was a period of growing division between O'Connell's old guard and the Young Ireland group. Influenced strongly by Thomas Davis, Meagher was firmly in the Young Ireland camp, though consistently among its more moderate majority. In the critical meeting of the Repeal Association on 28 July 1846, at which Young Ireland seceded, he gave a stirring speech in defence of the ultimate right of recourse to arms, which earned him the sobriquet 'Meagher of the Sword'. When the seceders established the Irish Confederation in January 1847, he was appointed to its national council and was prominent among its leaders. In February 1848 he stood as a Confederation candidate in a by-election in Waterford, where his father was one of two MPs for the city. The vacancy was created by the resignation of the other MP (O'Connell's son, Daniel), who had accepted a government appointment. His bid for the seat was unsuccessful.

On 15 March 1848 Meagher, whose passionate oratory made him a great favourite with the Confederate clubs, addressed a mass meeting in Dublin that adopted a congratulatory address to the new French revolutionary government, and was one of three delegates chosen to carry the address to Paris. He and William Smith O'Brien were prosecuted for seditious speeches made at this meeting, but were acquitted (16 April). While still on bail, Meagher went to Paris and on 3 April presented the address to the French government, returning with the green, white and orange tricolour. Over the next few months Meagher addressed Confederate clubs in Dublin and the south-east, encouraging them to arm, and was appointed to the Confederation's war directorate. On 12 July he was arrested in his father's house in Waterford and was removed to Dublin. Again he was released on bail and when the government suspended habeas corpus on 22 July, Meagher pressed for action, travelling to the south-east with the other leaders to organise an insurrection. Attempting to raise support in the surrounding area, Meagher was not present at Ballingarry, Co. Tipperary, on 29 July 1848, the principal engagement in the abortive rising. In his later account of these events, he blamed the failure of the rising on the timidity of his fellow leaders and the opposition of the Catholic clergy.

After the collapse of the rising he went on the run and was arrested on 13 August near Cashel and charged with high treason. Together with Smith O'Brien, T. B. McManus, and Patrick O'Donohoe he was tried in Clonmel and on 23 October 1848 sentenced to death. After appeals, the sentences were commuted to transportation for life, and on 29 July 1849 Meagher began the three-month voyage to Tasmania aboard the *Swift*. He signed a ticket of leave and upon arrival took lodgings in the village of Ross. Though forbidden to associate with his fellow convicts, he regularly met O'Donohoe, John Mitchel and Kevin Izod O'Doherty. He married Catherine Bennett, the daughter of an Irish settler family, on 22 February 1851. Meanwhile, plans for the escape of the Young Ireland convicts were being developed by Irish exiles in New York, and on 3 January 1852 Meagher slipped aboard the *Elizabeth Thompson* off the east coast of Tasmania. Four months later he arrived to a hero's welcome in New York, and was immediately taken into the heart of the Irish-American establishment.

For the next ten years Meagher was a newspaper publisher, lawyer, public speaker and social celebrity. He was admitted to the New York bar in 1855, founded and published the *Irish News* for a number of years, and made two expeditions to Central America, exploring commercial possibilities. His wife, who had remained in Tasmania, gave birth in March 1852 to a son, who died four months later. In March 1853 Catherine moved to Waterford and subsequently travelled to New York. Returning to Waterford, she had a second son and died, aged twenty-three, on 15 May 1854. Two years later Meagher married Elizabeth Townsend, daughter of a wealthy New York railroad and steel family. He had no children with his second wife. His son was brought up in Waterford, subsequently emigrated to the US, and died in Manila in 1909.

The years before the civil war brought mixed fortunes to Meagher. His principal activity (and source of income) was lecturing, generally on Irish revolutionary matters. His success as a newspaperman and lawyer was modest. When in New York he lived at his American wife's family home. As a celebrated revolutionary, he was able to command a position as a leading figure among Irish Americans, and to build a network of political connections with American politics. As his American base expanded, however, his commitment to Irish revolution decreased. James Stephens sought his support for the plans of the newly established Irish Republican Brotherhood (IRB) and their sister organisation in America, the Fenians, in 1858, and came away disappointed.

When the American civil war began in April 1861, Meagher was an American citizen, and one of the acknowledged leaders of Irish America. As a staunch Democrat, he supported the party's position of non-interference with slavery, and was initially ambivalent about the war, but soon swung enthusiastically to the union cause. He lent his name and energies to the recruitment drive, and was commissioned as a captain with the 69th Regiment in time to play a full part in the first battle of Bull Run in July 1861. The union forces were routed, and the 69th, having lost 150 men, returned to New York to regroup. By November three regiments were sent back to the war front in northern Virginia as the Irish Brigade, with Meagher as their commanding officer. He was commissioned as brigadier-general on 3 February 1862. For some eighteen months he commanded the brigade on continuous active service. It was engaged in all the major battles of the period, suffering heavy losses at Malvern Hill (1 July), Antietam (17 September) and Fredericksburg (13 December 1862). At this stage the brigade, originally 3,000 strong, was reduced to fewer than 500 men, and Meagher wrote to the secretary of war requesting that it be withdrawn from active service to regroup and recruit. When this request was not accepted he tendered his resignation, which was accepted by the president on 14 May 1863. The following year, after much badgering of the war department, he returned to the service and was given command of a rearguard garrison brigade in Tennessee. After a mismanaged transfer of his troops to join Sherman's Carolinas campaign, he was relieved of duty (24 February 1865) on the initiative and orders of the commander-in-chief, General Ulysses S. Grant. Meagher emerged from the war with a mixed reputation: brave, eloquent, convivial, inspiring; skill or effectiveness as a commander are not mentioned by contemporaries.

After the war Meagher's stock was low. He had lost favour with many Irish Americans for his continued support for the war and his backing of the Republican candidates Lincoln and Johnson in the 1864 election. There was little prospect of success in his former business pursuits. He persistently sought an official appointment from the Johnson administration and, when disappointed, travelled to Minnesota to seek opportunities in the west. While there he was notified of his appointment as secretary for the territory of Montana, not yet a state. This was still a wild frontier, and on arrival Meagher became acting governor. He threw himself fully into his new duties, which included the preparation of legislation for the territory, the maintenance of law and order, and the containment of hostilities with the Sioux. His tenure was controversial, and relatively brief. Even his death was controversial. On 1 July 1867, while on an official tour of duty connected with the Sioux campaign, he fell overboard from a steamer moored on the Missouri River at Fort Benton. It may have been an accident, but his friends and supporters had sufficient belief that he was murdered by his political enemies that they put up a reward for the discovery of his killers. The mystery remains.

Meagher was forty-three when he died. In each of his multiple careers as a Young Ireland revolutionary, a transported convict, a New York celebrity, a civil war general and a territorial governor in the Wild West, he made a mark. His most notable monuments are fine equestrian statues in front of the state house in Helena, Montana, and on the Mall in Waterford.

E. P. Cunningham

Sources

D. P. Conyngham, *The Irish Brigade and its campaigns* (1869, reprinted 1994); Arthur Griffith (ed.), *Meagher of the Sword: speeches on Ireland 1846–1848* (1916); John Mitchel, *Jail journal* (1913); Robert G. Athearn, *Thomas Francis Meagher: an Irish revolutionary in America* (1949); *Decies: Waterford Archaeological and Historical Society*, no. 59 (2003); John M. Hearne and Rory T. Corish (eds), *Thomas Francis Meagher. The making of an Irish American* (2005)

John Morrissey

(1831–78)

Nicknamed 'Old Smoke', this prize fighter fought street battles against 'Bill the butcher' before entering politics as the Democratic representative for New York's fifth district.

John Morrissey was born 12 February 1831 at Templemore, Co. Tipperary, the only son among eight children of Timothy Morrissey, factory worker, and Julia (or Mary) Morrissey. In 1834 the family emigrated to Canada and then the United States, settling at Troy, New York. From the age of ten Morrissey worked, first in a mill, and then as an iron worker due to his size and strength. Morrissey became involved in various street gangs, developing a reputation as a pugilist of great strength and resolve. As leader of the Downtowns he defeated six members of the rival Uptown gang in a single afternoon in 1848. He took work on a Hudson River steamer and married Sarah Smith, daughter of the ship's captain. They had one child, who died before reaching adulthood.

In a New York saloon Morrissey challenged Charley 'Dutch' Duane to a prize fight and, when he was not to be found, with typical bravado Morrissey extended the challenge to everyone present. This impressed the owner, Isaiah Rynders, the Tammany Hall politician, and he employed Morrissey to help the Democratic party: this involved Morrissey in intimidating voters at election time. A fistfight with gang rival Tom McCann earned Morrissey the nickname 'Old Smoke'. Mid-fight he was forced on to a bed of coals, but despite having his flesh burned refused to concede defeat; he fought his way back and beat McCann into unconsciousness. Stowing away to California to challenge other fighters, he began a gambling house to raise money, and embarked on a privateering expedition to the Queen Charlotte Islands in a quixotic attempt to make his fortune.

In his first professional prize fight (21 August 1852) he defeated George Thompson in dubious circumstances, and began calling himself the 'champion of America'. It was only on 12 October 1853, however, that he officially earned this title, when he won the heavyweight championship of America in a bout at Boston Corners, New York, against Yankee Sullivan. The fight lasted thirty-seven rounds, and Morrissey had the worst of most of them, but he was awarded the contest after a free-for-all in the ring.

Increasingly involved in New York politics, he and his supporters fought street battles against the rival gang of William Poole, known as 'Bill the butcher', a Know Nothing politician later fictionalised in the film *The gangs of New York* (2002). On 26 July 1854 the two men fought on the docks, but Morrissey was beaten badly and forced to surrender. This marked the beginning of a bitter feud between the two parties, with heavy casualties on both sides, which climaxed on 8 March 1855 when Poole was murdered. Morrissey was indicted as a conspirator in the crime, but was soon released because of his political connections. On 20 October 1858 he fought John C. Heenan (1835–73) in another heavyweight championship bout. Heenan broke his hand early in the fight and was always at a disadvantage; after taking much punishment Morrissey finally made his dominance count. There was a rematch on 4 April 1859, which Morrissey again won, and after this he retired from the ring. Investing his prize money, he ran two saloons and a gambling house in New York. With the huge profits from his gambling empire he invested in real estate in Saratoga, opening a racetrack there in 1863, which has endured to become America's oldest major sports venue.

A political career beckoned as a reward for his consistent support for the Democratic party. He was elected to the house of representatives in 1866 representing New York's fifth district, was re-elected the following year, and served until 3 March 1871. He supported President Andrew Johnson against demands for his impeachment and was sceptical about the Radicals' plans for reconstruction in the south. In his final years he served as a US senator for New York State (1875–8). He died at the Adelphi Hotel, Saratoga Springs, on 1 May 1878, and was buried at Saint Peter's cemetery, Troy. On the day of his funeral, flags at New York's City Hall were lowered to half-mast, while the *National Police Gazette* declared 'few men of our day have arisen from beginnings so discouraging to a place so high in the general esteem of the community...' (4 May 1878). His name is included in the list of 'pioneer' inductees in the Boxing Hall of Fame in Canastota, New York, and each year the John Morrissey Stakes are held at Saratoga racecourse in honour of its founder.

Patrick M. Geoghegan

Sources

William E. Harding, *John Morrissey: his life, battles and wrangles* (1881); St. George L. Sioussat, 'Notes of Colonel W. G. Moore, private secretary to President Johnson, 1866–1868', *American Historical Review*, xix (1913), 98–132; Herbert Asbury, *Gangs of New York* (1927); Albert V. House, 'The speakership contest of 1875', *Journal of American History*, lii (1965), 252–74; Elliott J. Gorn, *The manly art: bare-knuckle fighting in America* (1986); Elliott J. Gorn, '"Good-bye boys, I die a true American": homicide, nativism, and working-class culture in antebellum New York City', *Journal of American History*, lxxiv (1987), 388–410; James C. Nicholson, *The notorious John Morrissey: how a bare-knuckle brawler became a congressman and founded Saratoga Race Course* (2016)

Albert Cashier

1834–1915

Born female into an
impoverished family in
Louth, he stowed away
to America to find a
better life and shortly
thereafter enlisted in
the union army, serving
with distinction in the
civil war.

Albert Cashier was born Jennie Irene Hodgers on 25 December 1843 in Clogherhead, Co. Louth. Very little is known about Cashier's early life—he gave conflicting accounts of it throughout his life and he was suffering from dementia when he spoke about it in 1913—but it would seem that his parents were named Patrick and Sallie Hodgers. Cashier was born two years before the start of the Irish famine into what must have been very poor circumstances: he remained illiterate throughout his life and, although born female, he dressed as a male from an early age and was sent out to work by his stepfather in order to support the family. It is believed that his mother died while he was young, and in 1859 he left Ireland for America, travelling as a stowaway first to Liverpool and then to New York. From there Cashier travelled to Belvidere, Illinois, where he worked in a shoe factory, and then as a labourer, farmhand and shepherd for a farmer named Avery.

At the beginning of August 1862 Albert D. J. Cashier, aged nineteen, responded to Abraham Lincoln's call for soldiers and enlisted in the 95th Illinois infantry, G Company, signing his enlistment papers with an X. He was described as having a light complexion, blue eyes and auburn hair and, at just five foot three, was the shortest soldier in the company. Cashier was one of more than 400 documented cases of soldiers who were born female but enlisted as men to fight in the civil war. Some were discovered during the war through injury or capture and some chose to return to living as female after the war but there were others, like Cashier, who lived as men until the end of their lives. The motivations of these women were as varied as those of the men going to fight the war— they joined out of desire for adventure, for steady wages, motivated by patriotism or perhaps following a loved one into battle. They also stood very little chance of discovery unless they were injured: the initial physical examination consisted of checking they had teeth to rip open powder cartridges, and four functioning limbs for marching and firing weapons. Heavy, ill-fitting uniforms concealed body shape and, because many youths joined up, a lack of facial hair was not seen as suspicious. Cashier had the added advantage of small-pox scars, which gave him a more masculine look.

From August to November 1862 G Company trained at Camp Fuller. From there they went to Cairo, Illinois, and then on, via river steamer, to Columbus, Kentucky. As part of the army of Tennessee, at one time under the command of General Ulysses S. Grant, the 95th took part in more than forty battles, including the siege of Vicksburg, the battle of Guntown where the regiment suffered heavy losses, and the battle of Nashville in December 1864, the last major battle of the western theatre. In total, Cashier's regiment travelled almost 9,000 miles by foot, rail and boat and lost 289 soldiers to death and disease. Cashier was a brave and able soldier—he was a skilled marksman and allegedly fearless in his encounters with the enemy. One comrade recounted that during the siege of Vicksburg, Cashier was captured during reconnaissance but escaped by wrestling a gun away from his captor and running all the way back to union lines. Sergeant C. W. Ives recalled in his diary that Cashier, despite being cut off from the rest of his company, taunted confederate soldiers yelling, 'Hey you darn rebels, why don't you get up where we can see you?' (*Chicago Tribune*, 29 August 2019), while on another occasion he reportedly rescued his company's flag and hung it from the highest branch of a tree.

The 95th were camped near New Orleans when General Robert Lee surrendered to General Grant at the battle of Appomattox courthouse on 9 April 1865, effectively bringing an end to the civil war, although sporadic fighting continued for some weeks. On 15 August the 95th marched into Belvidere as returning heroes, and two days later Cashier was mustered out, having served a full three-year enlistment. Initially he settled in Belvidere. An army comrade, Amos Morton, invited Cashier to join him and his wife in Iowa, but Cashier chose to stay, opening a plant-nursery with another comrade, Samuel Pepper. For reasons unknown, the venture came to an end and in 1869 Cashier moved to the small town of Saunemin, south-west of Chicago in the county of Livingston, Illinois. He initially took work as a farmhand, living with his employer Joshua Chesbro and his family in exchange for work, but he also worked for the town and was variously employed as church janitor, cemetery worker and street lamplighter over the next forty years. In 1885 Chesbro built a small house for him and the 1900 census lists Cashier as 'head of house, white, male…age 57, born in Ireland with both parents also born in Ireland, worked as a janitor, cannot read or write, owned house.' He was immensely proud of his military service, and each year at the annual Memorial Day parade he marched in his civil war uniform, buying ice-cream and treats for the children afterwards despite their teasing, calling him a 'bugle boy'.

Living as a man, Cashier was able to vote in elections, hold a bank account and eventually claim a military pension, all things that would have been denied to Jennie Hodgers, and he maintained his independence until 1911 when an accident forced him into sheltered accommodation. In that year he was underneath the car of state senator Ira Lish carrying out repairs when the senator accidently drove over him. Despite Cashier's protests, Lish called for the doctor and in the course of the examination his birth gender was uncovered. It was clear that Cashier's injuries were severe and he could no longer look after himself, and on 5 May 1911 Lish arranged for him to be admitted to the Soldiers' and Sailors' Home in Quincy, Illinois. Cashier lived there happily for two years. He was in receipt of a veteran's pension, which W. J. Singleton, a banker in Quincy, had helped him apply for, and he was visited by old army comrades, including the captain of G Company. As his mental condition deteriorated, however, his secret leaked into the press. On 6 May 1913 the *Syracuse Herald* ran an article headlined 'Civil War Veteran is a Woman', while in December the *Irish Independent* told 'the romantic story of a woman named Hodgens...who enlisted in the American army...' (13 December 1913).

By March 1914 Cashier's dementia was so advanced that he was moved to the Western Hospital for the Insane at Watertown, Illinois, now the East Moline State Hospital. His committal papers described him as having no memory and being 'noisy at times, [a] poor sleeper and feeble' (Clausius, 386). Such a move necessitated a court hearing and, when word of his birth gender reached the national press, the US government launched an investigation into whether Cashier had obtained his pension by fraud. Several comrades from the 95th came forward to testify on his behalf, including Corporal Robert D. Hannah who confirmed that he had served with Albert D. J. Cashier, and Cashier's pension was secured. His final months in the asylum, however, were very unhappy. In contrast to the veterans' home where Cashier lived as he always had, the state hospital took away his union uniform and forced him to wear a dress, despite protests from former comrades and friends. Frail and confused, he attempted to fashion the dress into trousers but the unaccustomed clothing caused him to trip, breaking his hip. He was bedridden for his final months and died on 10 October 1915.

Albert Cashier was given an official Grand Army of the Republic funeral on 12 October and was buried in Saunemin with full military honours—he was dressed in his union uniform, his casket was draped with the American flag and his tombstone recorded his military service: 'Albert D. J. Cashier, Co. G, 95 Ill. Inf.' His estate, valued at $282, remains on the county books to this day, his executor, a Mr Singleton, having failed to find a convincing heir. Cashier was a veteran of the civil war whose military service was a source of enormous pride throughout his life. Although he was born Jennie Hodgers, he died Albert Cashier, a soldier, and his name is listed on the internal wall of the Illinois memorial at Vicksburg Military Park.

Niav Gallagher

Sources

Syracuse Herald, 6 May 1913; *Irish Independent,* 13 December 1913; *Washington Post,* 29 March 1914; *Moberly Weekly Monitor,* 23 February 1915; Gerhard P. Clausius, 'The little soldier of the 95th: Albert D. J. Cashier', *Journal of the Illinois State Historical Society* (1908–1984), vol. 51, no. 4 (winter 1958), 380–7; DeAnna Blanton, 'Women soldiers of the civil war', *Prologue Magazine* (spring 1993), vol. 25, no. 1; Elizabeth D. Leonard, *All the daring of the soldier* (2001); DeAnna Blanton and Lauren M. Cook, *They fought like demons: women soldiers in the American civil war* (2002); Lon Dawson, *Also known as Albert D. J. Cashier: the Jennie Hodgers story, or how one young Irish girl joined the union army* (2005); Damian Shiels, *The Irish in the American civil war* (2013); *Guardian,* 22 August 2017; Jill McDonough, 'The soldier: Albert D. J. Cashier (1843–1918)', in Mark Bailey (ed.), *Nine Irish lives: the thinkers, fighters and artists who helped build America* (2018), 73–98; *The Irish Times,* 10 April 2018; American Battlefield Trust; *Chicago Tribune,* 29 August 2019

3. Lives in business

Introduction

In January 1925 President Calvin Coolidge declared 'The chief business of the American people is business'. From the outset American settlers had several advantages in terms of going into business: no aristocracy or powerful guilds controlling access to practice of entreprise; colonial governments were less intrusive than the monarchies and empires of Europe; and although challenging, settling the new land provided opportunities for innovation and employment.

Irish emigrants played a prominent role in the founding of iconic American businesses from the start. Oliver Pollock (c.1737–1823), enormously wealthy in his own right, is credited with creating the '$' symbol, while Thomas Fitzsimons (1741–1811) was one of the founders of the Bank of North America, the country's first bank. William James (1771–1832), grandfather of writer Henry and psychologist William, amassed one of the largest fortunes in America and helped to create the American 'rags to riches' success myth, while Irishman James Gamble (1803–91) was one half of the partnership that founded the enormously successful Procter & Gamble Company.

From the middle of the nineteenth century, the combination of railroads, telegraph lines, factories and finance created a wealthy class of businessmen and professionals who, in turn, created white- and blue-collar jobs. Alexander Brown (1764–1834, p. 74), for example, set up a linen business in Baltimore, which he used to finance America's earliest railroad, a vital link in transatlantic trade. Alexander Turney Stewart (1803–76, p. 80) opened the world's largest purpose-built retail store in New York in 1862. It covered a full city block, had eight floors and nineteen departments, and reimagined retail for the next hundred years. His innovations included buying in bulk, a one-price policy and departmentalisation.

The Irish made a significant contribution to American publishing too. Mathew Carey (1760–1839, p. 66) founded one of the longest running and most successful publishing houses in America and published the first general atlas of the country, while Peter Fenlon Collier (1849–1909, p. 84) brought books within popular reach when he established a system of small monthly payments for works of great literature, and launched the magazine *Collier's Weekly*. Although men dominated the business world, women made their mark too. Belinda Mulrooney (1803–91, p. 88) was for a time the richest woman in the Klondike. At the peak of her wealth she lived in a turreted stone mansion known as Carbonneau Castle and owned a large tract of farmland in Yakima, Washington. Her unladylike behaviour, however, precluded her from being accepted into polite society and a series of lawsuits and unsuitable investments ate away her riches. She ended her career cleaning steel welders in a shipyard.

In the twentieth century, John 'Kerry' O'Donnell (1899–1994, p. 96) became synonymous with Gaelic games and Irish identity, making his fortune running the New York GAA for decades.

NG

Mathew Carey

1760–1839

Having fled Ireland
to escape prosecution
for libel, this audacious
printer and politico
founded one of America's
longest running and
most successful
publishing houses.

Mathew Carey was born on 28 January 1760 in Dublin, one of five sons to Christopher Carey, a baker who prospered provisioning the British navy, and Mary Carey (née Sheridan). Small and lame from infancy (having been dropped by his nurse), Mathew was a withdrawn child and so became a voracious reader. In 1775 he secured a position for himself as a printer's apprentice to Thomas McDonnell, co-publisher of the pro-American *Hibernian Journal*. In 1777 it published his first essay against duelling, and he quickly emerged as an outspoken radical. His first pamphlet, *The urgent necessity of an immediate repeal of the whole penal code* (1779), argued for Catholic emancipation; its radical tone angered Catholic leaders, who offered a reward to have the author identified. To avoid the possibility of prosecution, Mathew's father sent him to France, where his pro-American reputation gained him an introduction to Benjamin Franklin, who employed him at his press in Passy. He also gained vital experience under the great printer Didot *le jeune*, and met the Marquis de Lafayette. Back in Dublin by late 1780, he successfully edited the pro-Volunteer *Freeman's Journal* for three years before establishing his own *Volunteer's Journal* in October 1783, with the financial support of his father. Adopting a strongly popular line on the issues of parliamentary reform and protective duties, Carey persistently criticised Ireland's connection with Britain. His *Journal* grew to attain the second-largest circulation in Ireland, but its outspokenness was halted when on 5 April 1784 he published a woodcut depicting the hanging of John Foster, the chancellor of the exchequer. Arraigned before the house of commons along with his brother Thomas, he was jailed for a time in Newgate. On his release, with a libel case still pending against him, he fled for America on 7 September

1784. According to legend, he was smuggled on board ship dressed as a woman.

Carey reportedly arrived in Philadelphia in November with just £25, having lost much of his money en route to card sharps. He had letters of introduction from Franklin, however, and was fortunate to be reintroduced to Lafayette, who sent him a note of encouragement and $400 with which to start a newspaper, and also commended him to George Washington. Forty years later Carey persuaded Lafayette to accept a return of the $400. His initial efforts to acquire printing equipment were frustrated by the conservative Republican publisher Eleazer Oswald, who feared this skilled Irish rival with his extensive European contacts and experience of journalism. Carey, siding with the Constitutionals, persevered and spent most of his capital setting up the *Pennsylvania Evening Herald*, which appeared on 25 January 1785, just three months after his arrival in Philadelphia. Its anti-English and pro-Irish tone limited its appeal, but when Carey introduced innovative reporting of state assembly debates in the summer, based on his own notetaking, circulation soared. In 1786 he became embroiled in a public quarrel with Oswald when he published a bitter satire against him entitled *The Plagi-Scurriliad*. Oswald, a former army officer, claimed Carey used his infirmity to protect himself from personal insults, and challenged him to a duel. Carey took eighteen months to recover from the wound he sustained in the fight, and wryly noted the paradoxical situation of having begun his career condemning duelling.

In September 1786 he co-launched *Columbian Magazine*, a monthly journal that also included two fine engravings with each issue. In December, however, he withdrew from the partnership and established a rival publication, the *American Museum*, the first publication to promote American literature. Although it secured his national reputation, it ceased publication in late 1792 due to continuing distribution problems. This prompted Carey, over time, to pioneer a distribution network that ensured the success of his later bookselling and publishing. During the constitution ratification debates of 1787–8, he adopted a non-partisan stance by printing arguments for and against and, as his reputation grew, he earned the backing of the Federalist party and recommendations from George Washington. Carey's precarious financial situation was also bolstered when he began a partnership with Mason Locke Weems, a legendary salesman and popular author, publishing his *Life and memorable actions of George Washington*, a bestseller of the nineteenth century.

Carey married Bridget Flahavan on 24 February 1791, and later acknowledged his gratitude to her for the role she played in running the business he had struggled to establish. Six of their nine children lived to maturity and his son, Henry, became chief economic adviser to Abraham Lincoln. Having maintained lucrative links in London, Edinburgh and Dublin, Carey imported works of all kinds in vast quantities, and his Philadelphia Company of Printers and Booksellers became one of the largest in the country. Patrick Byrne was one of his many Irish trading partners, and he successfully distributed Byrne's Dublin imprints, also helping him settle when he eventually emigrated to America in 1800. Carey's private acts of charity were innumerable, and he was repeatedly honoured by his fellow citizens. When yellow fever struck Philadelphia in August 1793, Carey was appointed on the relief committee. His *Short account of the malignant fever* (1793), first a pamphlet then a book, was an influential account, widely read in Europe and republished in five editions. Publishing further works on the disease, he became extensively involved in medical publishing. Constantly seeking new markets, he also published literature and technical 'how to' books as well as works on science, agriculture, humour, travel, material of interest to women, scholarly texts, grammars, dictionaries and important early accounts of the frontier.

Carey dominated the American atlas market for several years, and two of his publications were among the most ambitious titles yet to appear in America without a prior subscription sale. These were William Guthrie's *A new system of modern geography* (1794), featuring an atlas of about fifty large maps and charts, and Oliver Goldsmith's *A history of the earth and animated nature* (1795) with fifty-five plates. Their maps established the basis for several further updated atlases, most notably his *American atlas* (1795), the first general atlas of the US. Carey was also the first prominent Catholic bookseller in America: in 1790 he published the Douai translation of the Vulgate, in effect the first Catholic bible in America, and was instrumental in launching America's first Sunday school society in 1795.

In 1790 he founded Philadelphia's Hibernian Society for the relief of Irish immigrants and, as secretary, he urged them to integrate and become civic-minded Americans. He also involved himself in national politics, moving away from the Federalists and joining the Society of Constitutional Republicans (or 'Quids') who lobbied for Irish support for Jefferson in 1796. When the terms of Jay's Treaty between Britain and America were leaked during the ratification debates in 1795, Carey published Alexander Dallas's *Features of Mr Jay's treaty*, one of the first and most lucid attacks on it, as well as *The American remembrancer* (1795–6). In 1796 he published a direct attack on the Federalists in *Address to the house of representatives*, not even sparing Washington, and he clashed with the exiled United Irishman James Reynolds on the issue. His correspondence with Patrick Byrne kept him informed of Irish politics and the activities of the United Irishmen. When the Philadelphia Society of United Irishmen first met in June 1797, he attended but supposedly declined joining, though in 1798 his name appeared (with that of his brother James, also exiled and involved in printing) on a published list of members. Although he vehemently denied having taken the test, 'his private correspondence tells a very different story' (Wilson, 44). Despite his success in business, Carey experienced financial pressures that were compounded by the accusation of membership of the United Irishmen and general attacks upon his politics by William Cobbett, using the pseudonym 'Peter Porcupine'. This public quarrel and the possibility of prosecution under the aliens and sedition acts threatened Carey's reputation and his credit, but he countered successfully with *A plumb pudding for…Peter Porcupine* and *Porcupiniad, a Hudibrastic poem* (both 1799).

Carey held two positions of public office: a short term on the city council, and a term as a director of the Bank of Pennsylvania, the latter finally ensuring his financial stability. Forming the Philadelphia Society for the Promotion of National Industry (1819), he wrote a series of *Addresses* for them, appropriately printed on the first American machine-made paper, arguing for domestic manufacture through protective tariffs and championing the nationalist school of economics. Over time he wrote at least 450 pamphlets, which ranged from promoting improvements to the transportation system, canals and railways, prison discipline, colonisation, female labour and the oppression of women, infrastructure and a host of other topics. He involved himself in international issues, forming in 1827 a Greek Committee to aid that country's independence struggle and publishing *African colonization* (1829) and *Appeal in behalf of the expatriated Poles* (1834).

In 1814 he published *The olive branch: or, faults on both sides, Federal and Democratic*, a plea for national unity in the face of the rift between Federalists and Republicans. The expanded volume from this work became the most widely read political book in America since Thomas Paine's *Common sense*, going through ten editions by 1819. When civil war threatened during the nullification crisis, Carey again assumed this role, penning *The new olive branch: a solemn warning on the banks of the Rubicon, to the citizens of South Carolina* (1830). He remained committed to Ireland and Catholic emancipation, and one of his proudest achievements was publishing his *Vindiciae Hibernicae* (1819), a reaction to William Godwin's novel *Mandeville* (1817), which exploited the 1641 massacres in Ireland. Advised by William James MacNeven on sources, and having conducted thorough scholarly research, Carey examined and refuted falsehoods claimed by historians regarding the numbers of Protestants massacred, and the extent of plotting and violent outrages committed by Catholics. It was highly influential and contributed significantly to the emerging Catholic historiographical movement: Thomas Davis quoted from it and Daniel O'Connell's *Memoir on Ireland, native and Saxon* (1844) was significantly influenced by it. James Madison praised him for demonstrating how the Irish nation had been so 'traduced by the pen of history' (Wilson, 166). His first

Autobiographical sketches appeared in 1829 and were serialised (1833–4) in the *New England Magazine*.

In 1821 Carey turned the management of his business (M. Carey & Sons) over to his son Henry and son-in-law Isaac Lea, so he could devote all his energies to social issues. The new firm, H. C. Carey & I. Lea, was financially sound and expanded to become even more of a dominating force in American publishing than Carey himself had been. After passing through the hands of various relations and business partners, with attendant name changes, the firm became Lea & Febiger in 1907, and traded under that name until its sale in 1990. Carey accumulated a sizeable fortune but through habit lived frugally till the end, attributing his achievements as an immigrant to 'care and indefatigable industry' (Durey, 175). He died on 16 September 1839, and his funeral procession was one of the largest the city of Philadelphia had ever seen.

Johanna Archbold and Sylvie Kleinman

Sources

Carey papers, Historical Society of Pennsylvania; Library Company of Philadelphia; Earl L. Bradsher, *Mathew Carey, editor, author and publisher: a study in American literary development* (1912); Mathew Carey, *Autobiography* (1942); Edward C. Carter II, 'The political activities of Mathew Carey, nationalist, 1760–1814' (Ph.D. thesis, Bryn Mawr College, 1962); William Clarkin, *Mathew Carey: a bibliography of his publications, 1785–1824* (1984); James N. Green, *Mathew Carey: publisher and patriot* (1985); Michael Durey, *Transatlantic radicals and the early American republic* (1997); David A. Wilson, *United Irishmen, United States: immigrant radicals in the early republic* (1998); *American national biography* (1999); *Oxford dictionary of national biography* (2004); Maurice J. Bric, *Ireland, Philadelphia and the re-invention of America 1760–1800* (2008); 'Special issue: Ireland, America and Mathew Carey', *Early American Studies*, vol. 11, no. 3 (Fall, 2013)

Alexander Brown

1764–1834

Merchant, banker
and founder of one
of America's earliest
railroads, Brown was
one of the country's
first millionaires.

Alexander Brown was born 17 November 1764 in Ballymena, Co. Antrim, one of four surviving children of William Brown and Margaret Brown (née Davison). As a young man Brown achieved some success as a linen dealer and auctioneer in Belfast. In 1783 he married Grace Davison, possibly his cousin, from Drumnasole, Co. Antrim, and they had four sons who survived infancy. These boys were sent to school with Reverend J. Bradley in Catterick, Yorkshire.

While there is no evidence that Brown was involved in the rebellion of 1798, he did go into hiding in its aftermath and, perhaps as a consequence of the resulting political and economic conditions in Ireland, he emigrated to America. Several years earlier Brown's brother-in-law, Dr George Brown, and his younger brother, Stewart, who had sold linen goods supplied by Alexander, had emigrated to Baltimore, Maryland. Thus it was to Baltimore, a growing port town of just over 26,500 people on the upper Chesapeake Bay, that Brown, his wife and son William (the younger sons remained in school in Yorkshire) sailed in 1800. By 20 December Brown had established an 'Irish linen warehouse' and was able to publish in the *Federal Gazette* and *Baltimore Daily Advertiser* that he had for sale linen goods, three dozen mahogany chairs and four clocks. This was the beginning of a thriving business for Alexander Brown & Company, importing general merchandise and Irish linens to Baltimore, the latter supplied by his cousin William Gihon and friends in Ulster, and exporting tobacco and cotton to Liverpool from the American south. In 1803 he brought his three younger sons to Baltimore, and by 1805 took William into partnership with him as Alexander Brown & Son; five years later George was included in the partnership to form

Alexander Brown & Sons, which would extend into merchant banking, the first such bank in the United States. (The company is still trading and is currently partnered with Raymond James, a wealth management firm.)

Brown realised that Liverpool was the key to the transatlantic trade in which he was engaged, and in 1809 he sent William, who it was thought would also benefit from a less humid climate, to Liverpool to carry out shipping and merchandising arrangements for his father's interests. William founded a company in his own name in 1810, later changed to William & James Brown & Company, with his brother, and still later to Brown, Shipley & Company, with Joseph Shipley, an American who joined the firm in 1826 and who was instrumental in saving it during the panic of 1837 by negotiating a £1,950,000 loan from the Bank of England.

Alexander Brown's initial business was based on trade in goods; he even acquired his own fleet of merchant ships. In the aftermath of the war of 1812, however, he realised that there was less risk and more money to be earned handling the finances of the transatlantic trade. As Brown began to provide financial services for other merchants, buying sterling bills from cotton and tobacco exporters in the American south and selling them to importers of British merchandise in Baltimore, the Liverpool operation became a vital link in the process of handling currency exchange and of providing credit for international commerce, that is, accepting (guaranteeing) bills of exchange, issuing letters of credit, and furnishing information on the financial reliability of firms engaged in the transatlantic trade. In 1863 offices were opened at Founder's Court in the City of London and in 1888 the Liverpool operations were closed. Brown, Shipley continues in several British cities as part of Quintet Private Bank of Luxembourg.

Brown appointed agents in the key southern cities of Petersburg, Charleston, Savannah, Huntsville, Mobile and New Orleans—the so-called 'cotton triangle'—to facilitate the export of cotton. Baltimore had flourished during the years of the Napoleonic wars; however, better port facilities and better access to inland markets made Philadelphia and New York increasingly thriving business centres for both imports and exports during the 1820s and 1830s. To take advantage of this evolving situation, the third son, John, was sent to Philadelphia in 1818 to found John A. Brown & Company (later Brown & Bowen); the youngest son, James, who had worked with William in Liverpool, went to New York in 1825 to found Brown Brothers & Company. James also opened a branch of Brown Brothers in Boston in 1844 and reorganised Brown & Bowen, of Philadelphia, into Brown Brothers in 1859. This bank, the oldest and one of the largest private banks in the United States, still exists as Brown Brothers Harriman (the merger with the Harriman banks taking place in 1931), with offices in several cities in the United States and overseas. These family banks created a financial network with a reputation for prudence and integrity that dominated credit, currency exchange and shipping arrangements for British-American trade during the nineteenth century, financing a major portion of United States international commerce, overtaking Baring Brothers & Company as the leading Anglo-American merchant bankers and carrying on into the twenty-first century.

Alexander Brown and his son George were founders of the Baltimore & Ohio Railroad in 1827, one of the earliest railroads in the United States, which was intended to keep Baltimore competitive with New York after the completion of the Erie Canal. Alexander Brown was also a shareholder in the Second Bank of the United States, and when that bank closed in 1836 the Browns were able to take a leading role in foreign exchange in the United States. Alexander Brown died on 4 April 1834 in Baltimore, one of the first millionaires in America.

George Brown (1787–1859) married (1818) Isabella McLanahan of Baltimore. He retired from the bank in 1839 to pursue private financial affairs and to support such philanthropic activities in Baltimore as the Peabody Institute. He died on 26 August 1859.

William Brown (1784–1864) married (1809) Sara Gihon of Ballymena, was active in public life in Liverpool in addition to his work with Brown, Shipley. He was elected alderman in 1831, stood for parliament in 1844 as an Anti-Corn Law League candidate, and was elected MP in 1846, advocating free trade and decimal currency. In 1856 he raised and equipped the first brigade of the Lancaster Volunteer Artillery, in which he served as lieutenant-colonel. In 1860 he opened the Free Public Library and Derby Museum in Liverpool, toward which he had contributed £60,000, and for which he was rewarded with a baronetcy in 1863. William Brown died on 21 May 1864.

John Alexander Brown (1788–1872) married (1813) Isabella Patrick of Ballymena and, after she died, Grace Brown, the daughter of Dr George Brown of Baltimore. He retired in 1837 and devoted himself to Presbyterian church activities in Philadelphia. He died on 31 December 1872.

James Brown (1791–1877) married (1817) Louisa Kirkland Benedict and, after she died, he married (1832)

Eliza Maria Coe. He remained active in the affairs of Brown Brothers & Company until his death on 1 November 1877, during which time the New York bank emerged as the headquarters of several firms. James Brown was a trustee of the New York Life Insurance Company and the Bank for Savings; he took a particular interest in Union Theological Seminary, of which he was a director, and he was involved in numerous charities.

Francis M. Carroll

Sources

Alexander Brown & Sons papers, Library of Congress; Brown Brothers & Company papers, New York Historical Society; photocopies of Brown, Shipley & Company papers, Liverpool Public Library; *Dictionary of national biography* (1885–1901); John Crosby Brown, *A hundred years of merchant banking* (1909); Brown Brothers and Company, *Experiences of a century, 1818–1918* (1919); Frank R. Kent, *The story of Alex. Brown & Sons* (1925, new edition 1950); *Dictionary of American biography* (1928–58); Aytoun Ellis, *Heir of adventure: the story of Brown, Shipley & Co., merchant bankers, 1810–1960* (1960); John A. Kouwenhoven, *Partners in banking: an historical portrait of a great private bank, Brown Brothers Harriman & Co., 1818–1968* (1983); Edwin J. Perkins, *Financing Anglo-American trade: the house of Brown, 1800–1880* (1975); *American national biography* (1999)

Alexander Turney Stewart

1803–76

Merchant, entrepreneur
and community planner,
Stewart opened the
world's largest purpose-
built retail store in
New York city.

Alexander Turney Stewart was born 12 October 1803 in Lisburn, Co. Antrim, son of Alexander Stewart and Margaret Stewart (née Turney). Born into a family with Scottish and Huguenot ancestry, Stewart's father died shortly before his birth. When he was a year old his mother remarried and moved to America, leaving the infant in the care of his maternal grandfather John Turney. He was educated at Belfast Academical Institute and, although his formal education ended at second level, it provided him with basic knowledge and a lifelong interest in the classics. In 1818 Stewart emigrated to New York where he found employment as a tutor. He returned to Ireland in 1823, apparently to collect an inheritance from his grandfather's estate, and while there he may have received goods and credit that enabled him to begin his career as a merchant. He returned to New York later in the year and opened his first small store on Broadway. Shortly afterwards he married Cornelia Mitchell Clinch, the daughter of a wealthy ship chandler.

Stewart gained prominence as a dry-goods merchant by introducing a policy of one retail price for all customers, with occasional general sales and mark-downs. He was an innovator in advertising, in providing credit and for his policy of accepting returned goods for exchange or cash. His retail store catered to wealthy New York women, while his wholesale department sent products throughout the country. In 1846 he opened the first retail emporium built for that purpose. Faced in marble, it became known as his 'Marble Palace'. In 1862 he added a new store on Broadway that was then the largest retail store in the world. As part of his mercantile empire, Stewart operated offices and warehouses in Ireland, England, Scotland, France, Germany and Switzerland. In addition, he became owner of the Grand Union Hotel, the Metropolitan Hotel, the Globe Theatre and Niblo's Garden, all well-known New York landmarks of the time.

After assuring his business success and accumulating great wealth, Stewart took a more active role in public affairs. During the civil war, he supported the union cause, actively working with the Union Defense Committee. When General Ulysses S. Grant was elected president in 1868, Stewart was offered the position of secretary of the treasury but he was unable to take up the post because of a provision in the treasury act (1789) that prohibited merchants or importers from heading the department.

Stewart had a reputation for being a strict and parsimonious employer, but he was generous in times of public need. He raised funds for the Irish suffering during the famine period and later he came to the aid of Irish mill workers severely affected by the northern embargo on cotton and blockade of southern ports. In May 1863 he chartered a ship, filled it with food, and sent it to the impoverished weavers in his native region of Lisburn. He offered free passage on its return trip to those who wished to emigrate to America. He also sent a shipload of flour to the French to alleviate hardship following the Franco–German war, and gave aid to the people of Chicago in 1871 after the disastrous fire.

In 1869 Stewart embarked on perhaps his most ambitious venture. He purchased 7,000 acres of the Hempstead Plains, then the Town Commons, to create a model suburban community. In addition to attractive houses and wide streets, Stewart's Garden City was to be provided with a railroad connection to New York city, a waterworks, a hotel and a nearby brick manufacturing plant to produce the needed building material.

Stewart died on 10 April 1876, before his plans for Garden City could be completed, and his wife commissioned construction of a cathedral to serve as a mausoleum for her husband and herself. In a final bizarre event, however, Stewart's coffin was stolen from the family vault before the crypt was ready and a ransom was paid for its return. The Stewarts had no surviving children, and their mercantile empire did not survive long after its founder's death. The mansion built on Fifth Avenue was demolished in 1901 and most of their personal papers were destroyed. Today a bronze bust of Stewart by Granville W. Carter and a thoroughfare through Garden City named Stewart Avenue are the main reminders of the young Irish immigrant who became one of the richest men in America.

Mildred Murphy DeRiggi

Sources

New York Times, 11–15 April 1876; *Dictionary of American biography* (1936), ix, 3–5; Stephen N. Elias, *Alexander T. Stewart: the forgotten merchant prince* (1992); Vincent F. Seyfried, *The founding of Garden City, 1869–1893* (1969); M. H. Smith, *History of Garden City* (revised edition, 1980)

Peter Fenelon Collier

1849–1909

Publisher and businessman, he founded *Collier's* magazine and published classic works of literature at low prices, making them available to the American masses.

Peter Fenelon Collier was born 12 December 1849 in Myshall, Co. Carlow, son of Robert C. Collier and Catherine Collier (née Fenelon). After an education in local schools, he emigrated to America at seventeen and entered Saint Mary's seminary in Cincinnati, Ohio. He did not join the priesthood, however, and after a variety of jobs, including a period as a carpenter in Dayton, Ohio, he found employment in the early 1870s as a salesman for a firm of publishers of Catholic books in New York.

When his employers dismissed his novel suggestion of selling books on an instalment plan, he began publishing and selling Catholic books from a basement store, on an independent basis, and built up a strong trade, founding P. F. Collier & Son Ltd in 1875. The marked success of the use of an instalment plan led him to use it as the means to expand his business, and in 1877 he began to publish the classic works of literature at low prices. Beginning with Shakespeare and Dickens, he pioneered bringing literature within popular reach through the system of small monthly payments. Over the following three decades Collier & Son printed almost 60 million books at its extensive works in New York, which had a staff of 700 and could produce 20,000 volumes a day, using the most modern printing technology. These books were distributed by numerous company branches across the country, employing sales-men, deliverers and collectors. A strong believer in the educational value of books, Collier refused to publish any-thing he regarded as inferior or morally suspect, such as the works of Tolstoy, while an edition of the works of Balzac, whom he particularly admired, was published without *Contes drolatiques*, a series of Rabelaisian stories. In 1909 he introduced the Harvard classics, an inexpensive set of classics bound in maroon cloth with gold lettering, which proved particularly popular with middle-class households. He always refused to publish more expensive editions for a limited public and took great pride that his inexpensively priced books enjoyed a mass readership, allowing him to become rich in what he regarded, with some pride, as a morally just manner.

In 1888 he launched a magazine, *Once a Week*, which he subsequently replaced (1896) with *Collier's Weekly: An Illustrated Journal*. This upmarket journal, initially edited by his son Robert, campaigned against corruption and for higher standards in politics and business, becoming widely respected as an independent observer of national affairs. Its wholesome nature, and that of its proprietor, was emphasised by its refusal of advertisements for alcohol or for patent medicines, and the exclusion of articles making extravagant claims on putative investment returns. The establishment of the journal was costly, but it is claimed that Collier wished it to be a force for good rather than a commercial success.

A passionate horseman, he was the master of the Meadowbrook Hunt Club on Long Island, winning numerous prizes, including the prestigious champion cup at Philadelphia on his renowned horse Punch. For many years he played on the Rockaway polo team. He imported horses from Ireland and his visits to Ireland invariably coincided with the hunting season. In 1905 and 1906 he stayed at Athlumney House, Co. Meath, where he entertained local children, and in 1907 he stayed at Killeen Castle, the seat of the earl of Fingall, riding with the Meath hunt, and becoming its master before his death. While in Ireland he made several notable friends, including T. P. O'Connor, and was a benefactor to Irish libraries and literary associations. He regretted being unable to start a major publishing company in Ireland to give work in his native country.

Devoutly Catholic, his outlook was coloured by the poverty of his childhood and a near-fatal bout of typhoid fever in the 1870s, and he is credited with numerous charitable deeds. A boundless, almost frenzied, energy characterised all aspects of his life, and his gregarious nature helped ensure that he pursued his leisure as vigorously as his work. He died 24 April 1909 astride one of his horses at the New York Riding Club. After a service at Saint Patrick's Cathedral, New York, he was buried on a hill overlooking his farm at Wickatunk, New Jersey.

He married (1873) Catherine Dunn of Carlow; they had one son, Robert.

Paul Rouse

Sources

The Times (London), 26 April 1909; Robert Collier, *In memoriam Peter Fenelon Collier* (1910); *Dictionary of American biography* (1928–58); Henry Boylan, *A dictionary of Irish biography* (3rd edition, 1998); *American national biography* (1999)

Belinda Mulrooney

1872–1967

A serial entrepreneur, Mulrooney was early to the Klondike where she quickly amassed a fortune selling supplies and providing accommodation to gold prospectors. She was worth $1 million at her peak and proclaimed the richest woman in the Klondike.

Belinda Mulrooney (Carbonneau) was born 16 May 1872 (though her official birth certificate stated 10 June) at her maternal grandparents' twenty-one acre farm near Carns, Co. Sligo, the first child of one son and four daughters of John Mulrooney from Carra, Co. Mayo, and his wife Maria (née Connor). Soon afterwards her father left for America, to be followed within a few years by her mother. Raised in Carns by her grandparents, Belinda had a happy childhood, mostly spent roughhousing with her uncles, who were only slightly older. Her primary school education, however, was cut short when she quarrelled with the teacher.

Wanting help in raising their younger children, her parents sent for her in 1885 to join them in Archbald, Pennsylvania, where her father was a coal miner. Once there, she hated living in a cramped house in that soot-covered town. Although a bright student, she quit school because she was teased for her accent and kept getting into fights. She reacted against her mother's fervent Catholicism by not going to Mass and resented being steered towards conventionally feminine roles, preferring instead to earn money by picking berries and hauling coal. For some years she aimed to save enough to return to Ireland. Aged seventeen, she escaped Archbald by visiting her aunt in Philadelphia and staying there, finding employment as a nurse-maid in a wealthy household.

Around the end of 1891, she moved to Chicago and bought a site amidst the construction work underway for the 1893 World's Fair. The rent she earned from storing a Ferris wheel went towards erecting a new building on her property, which she sold profitably in order to take over, and thrive further off, a busy sandwich counter nearby. In 1894 she moved to San Francisco where she lost all her money when a building she had rented and redeveloped burned down. From spring 1895 she spent eighteen months as a stewardess aboard a steamship serving the Alaska route, during which she developed a side-line selling clothes, goods and whiskey in Alaskan ports, prompting the company to open a store for her in Juneau in July 1896. She had quit by September and departed Juneau briefly, returning that winter just as rumours arrived of gold discoveries in Canadian territory along the Klondike River.

Getting there from Alaska's south-eastern panhandle entailed first hiking over the Coast Mountains and then boating down an often-hazardous network of waterways, all while carrying her wares and winter supplies. Abandoning her first attempt, she was better equipped and accompanied upon setting out on 1 April 1897. She climbed the 3,400ft high Chilkoot Pass over twenty times, hauling her gear piecemeal on backpacks and sleds between two camps. That June she completed the 600-mile journey by reaching Dawson, the Klondike's nascent boomtown, well ahead of the gathering host of fortune seekers. By packing niceties as well as necessities, she made a killing from selling her supply of hot-water bottles, cotton cloth and silk women's undergarments. These gains were used to buy food and rafts from newcomers for the purposes of running a canteen and building log cabins for sale in what was still a tent settlement. As most transactions were in gold dust, she inflated her already considerable profits by manipulating her weighing scales.

In July she travelled the eleven miles to the gold fields at the aptly named Bonanza Creek, where she built a roadhouse called the Grand Forks Hotel. Completed in mid-August, it was a sixteen by thirty-two foot, two-storey, log structure with large paned windows, comprising a bar and dining room on the ground floor and a row of bunk beds on the upper floor. She shamed drunken customers into behaving by being pleasant, good-humoured and prim (by Klondike standards). The money-spinning Grand Forks served as a trading depot, a lumberyard, a gold-dust deposit, a brokerage for swapping claims and a collection centre for Canadian government royalties. Even the daily sweepings could yield $100 in stray gold dust.

To accommodate the fresh wave of 'stampeders', she built an elegant three-storey hotel in Dawson called the Fairview, which opened in July 1898 after she personally supervised the hauling of furnishings over the mountains. (When her carrier, Joe Brooks, dumped these valuables on the trail upon receiving a better offer, she hired toughs who violently seized Brooks's packhorses, using them to deliver her cargo). A key player in Dawson's frenzied development, she founded the area's telegraph company and a venture selling much needed boiled and purified water. She also generously supported the charity work undertaken by local churches, despite being dismissive of religion.

Being privy to the latest mining gossip, she accumulated interests in claims from 1897, sometimes by purchase, sometimes by getting a share in return for providing financing or equipment. In 1899 she sold the Grand Forks and leased the Fairview to concentrate on mining the hill-sides above Bonanza and Eldorado Creeks. She relished supervising the miners, her ferocity best instanced by a dispute with another operator's foreman that she resolved by clubbing him to the ground. An observer described her as 'Irish—distinctly so—short, dark, angular, masculine, could swear like a trooper' (Armstrong, 49). Involving generous production bonuses for workers and the use of tram cars to move the dirt, her relatively sophisticated operations flourished. She was worth over $1 million at her peak and hailed as the richest woman in the Klondike.

In October 1899 she embarked on a tour of America and Europe, taking in visits to her family in Archbald and her grandmother in Sligo. Becoming close to her immediate family, she endowed her parents with money and property, and made sure her younger siblings, and later her nieces and nephews, were well educated. By then she was in a relationship with Charles Carbonneau, a Québécois of humble origins posing as a French count. Busily forming Klondike mining ventures for ensnaring distant investors, he was an obvious swindler, yet she admired his dash and sophistication, and was lonely after several years of shrewdly avoiding being overfamiliar with her fellow Klondikers. Neither was she above sharp practice, having promoted a dubious mining investment vehicle of her own in 1897 and acted as a front for government officials barred from owning claims. Mulrooney and Carbonneau married in the Catholic church near Dawson on 1 October 1900 and spent the subsequent winters travelling Europe at great expense, enabling Charles to canvass banks and investors there.

In 1902 the Carbonneaus accomplished the largest Klondike-related stock floatation yet through their new company, the Gold Run (Klondike) Mining Company, which bought $1.175 million worth of claims at Gold Run Creek, sixty-six miles from Dawson. By summer 1903 Belinda was managing hundreds of employees there, but this venture foundered amid a lack of investors and complaints of broken promises from partners and bankers. During spring 1904 she realised that Charles had only married her for her wealth, the remainder of which he had committed to what proved a failed shipping venture. She returned to the Klondike without him that summer, bidding to salvage something, only to be ousted by the banks from the Gold Run company. Fleeing an impending conviction for fraud in France, Charles stole $17,000 worth of valuables belonging to Belinda and briefly abducted her younger sister Agnes. Belinda never met him after 1904 and obtained a divorce in 1906, passing herself off as a widow long before he died in prison in 1919.

Embroiled in assorted lawsuits and pursued by creditors, she left the Klondike in September 1904 for the new gold mining settlement in Fairbanks, Alaska. Backed financially by her family, who now repaid her earlier generosity, she engaged in prospecting before establishing a bank in 1906 at Dome City, a creek settlement eighteen miles from Fairbanks, in partnership with a miner, Jesse Noble. The Dome City Bank advanced loans but thrived mainly off buying gold dust for onward shipment to the US mint. Recognising that her legal difficulties owed much to her dislike of paperwork, she delegated administrative matters to her sister Margaret, a business school graduate. Animosities arising from the collapse of Noble's marriage to her sister Nell led him to sue Belinda for fraud in October 1907. The case was dropped when Noble bought out Belinda while agreeing to retain her at the bank.

In late November 1908 she resettled in Yakima, Washington, where she bought farmland worth $125,000 and built a turreted stone mansion known as Carbonneau Castle, living there in some style with her parents and several of her siblings. More suited to operating within chaotic gold-rush surrounds, she failed to develop a financially viable orchard on her estate. Likewise, her bid for social respectability was undone by her unladylike proclivities for smoking, gambling, drinking whisky (albeit in moderation) and sitting with her feet on the table. She was also embroiled in a discreditable legal battle with two former business partners who claimed she had established the Dome City Bank with misappropriated funds. Threatening her with financial ruin, the case lasted until 1917 before she triumphed. Furthermore, on 27 January 1911 Noble's new partner at the Dome City Bank, August Ruser, sued her sister Margaret for embezzlement just as another of her sisters, Nell, was pursuing Noble for failing to honour the terms of their divorce settlement. Within days Belinda lured Ruser to a hotel room in Seattle where two men held him down while she horsewhipped him. She pleaded guilty to this and was fined $150; Ruser dropped the case against Margaret.

As the money ran out in the 1920s, she leased Carbonneau Castle and then gradually sold off her Yakima property, moving to a smaller house in Seattle in 1925. There she maintained both herself and family members with the rent from another property and by working as a seamstress. During the second world war she cleaned steel welders in a Seattle shipyard, enjoying it so much that she joined a commercial shipyard following the war. In 1957 she entered a local nursing home, remaining sharp and lively into advanced old age. Latterly she was transferred to a nursing home in Redmond, Washington, eventually dying in the Swedish Hospital, Redmond, on 3 September 1967. Having re-joined the Catholic church late in life, she was buried in Holyrood Catholic cemetery in King County, Washington. In 1927–8 she reminisced about her life to 1900 in a series of unpublished interviews. The notes are in the Bancroft Library of the University of California, Berkeley. She was played by Abbie Cornish in the American television series *Klondike* (2014).

Terry Clavin

Sources

General Registry Office (birth certificate); Mary E. Hitchcock, *Two women in the Klondike* (1899), 215; *Yakima Herald*, 1 February 1911; Nevill A. D. Armstrong, *Yukon yesterdays: thirty years of adventure in the Klondike* (1936); Pierre Berton, *Klondike: the life and death of the last great gold rush* (1960); David Wharton, *The Alaska gold rush* (1972); Melanie J. Mayer and Robert N. De Armond, *Staking her claim: the life of Belinda Mulrooney, Klondike and Alaska entrepreneur* (2000); Myles Dungan, *How the Irish won the West* (2006); 'Belinda Mulrooney—the richest woman in the Klondike', Smithsonian National Postal Museum (https://postalmuseum.si.edu/ accessed February 2021)

John 'Kerry' O'Donnell

1899–1994

Dictatorially ruling
New York GAA,
he capitalised on
Gaelic sports' surging
popularity in the 1940s
and placed himself at
the epicentre of Irish
émigré culture.

John O'Donnell was born on 15 November 1899 in Gleann na nGealt, Castlegregory, near Camp, Co. Kerry, the eldest child of Michael O'Donnell, a local farmer, and his wife Johanna (née O'Connor). At age nineteen he emigrated to Canada and was a lumberjack operating north of Montreal before moving to New York city and then in 1922 to Detroit, where he worked in a Dodge car factory, played baseball and attended night school. A New York bricklayer from 1926, he bore a name common among Irishmen in the city, so acquaintances distinguished him as John 'Kerry' O'Donnell. He grew obsessed with Gaelic football during a 1928 visit to Ireland and played for Camp in the West Kerry League alongside his brother Tim (1907–2003), who won three all-Ireland titles with Kerry. Back in New York, John lined out for the Kerry Gaelic football club there until 1942.

He entered the bar trade once prohibition ended and opened his first tavern-restaurant in 1935, accumulating a further four such establishments over the next decade. In 1934 he married Helen O'Callaghan, a New York city native whose parents were from Brosna, Co. Kerry. They settled in the Bronx at Riversdale, and had three sons and five daughters.

From 1929 he engaged in the administration of the New York Gaelic Athletic Association (GAA) and, despite being dogged by rumours concerning his business affairs, served as either its secretary or treasurer for much of the 1930s, while organising social events, tours to New York by visiting Irish GAA teams, and the tour to Ireland in 1937 by New York's Kerry club. In 1944 he leased the Bronx venue used for Gaelic games in order to prevent its takeover by a soccer organisation. The cost of doing so and of upgrading the grandiosely renamed Croke Park obliged him to sell all but one of his taverns. He struggled initially, as GAA activity in New York had lapsed during the wartime ban on immigration and the absence of young men on military service.

He failed in his attempt to have the replayed 1946 all-Ireland football final held in New York, but, with the assistance of Canon Michael Hamilton, managed to get the 1947 final replayed in the city.

From the late 1940s surging Irish immigration produced a GAA boom in New York, which soon boasted sixty-five clubs. O'Donnell's stadium, which became known as Gaelic Park, hosted four matches every Sunday watched by some 4,000 spectators. Gaelic Park also staged the touring Irish sides' secondary exhibition matches and their headline encounters against New York selections, from 1959. Operating the main social outlet for the Irish in New York, O'Donnell thrived off the large bar, drawing accusations of exploiting vulnerable immigrants. Yet he was a generous benefactor, who charged cheap admissions, found employment for struggling new arrivals, and closed early on Sunday nights to prevent customers from getting into trouble at work.

Dictatorially ruling New York GAA until well into the 1970s, O'Donnell was elected its president on seven occasions (1940, 1955, 1958–60, 1972–3) and served repeatedly as vice-president, treasurer and secretary, and as manager of the New York Gaelic football team. (He was also the president and patron of the Kerry club.) The always-fraught relationship between the New York board and Dublin headquarters was especially bad when the compulsively quarrelsome O'Donnell was in his gleefully disreputable pomp. Upholding New York's unaffiliated status, he disdained his antagonists as incompetent and scorned their principled amateurism; his restless, outsized personality and financial permissiveness clashed irreconcilably with the Irish GAA's cumbersome power structures and obsessive dogmatism.

GAA purists took umbrage at the sale of alcohol during matches in Gaelic Park, the sponsorship deals O'Donnell struck on behalf of New York GAA with breweries, and his poaching of players from Ireland through financial inducements and soft jobs. Furthermore, he by-passed the central council and disrupted the GAA calendar by enticing county teams and clubs to New York for unofficial exhibitions. Although he barred uncooperative journalists from Gaelic Park, the Irish media lapped up his withering criticisms of the central council.

Commencing in 1950, the regular GAA tours—both to New York by Irish teams and to Ireland by New York teams—proceeded amid constant wrangling rooted in O'Donnell's bravura brinksmanship. Differences arose over finances, format, dates, choice of referee, New York's selection of players deemed ineligible by central council, and the New York team's physicality. Reminiscent of how Gaelic games were played in Ireland during O'Donnell's youth, the roughhousing owed something to his fiery dressing-room orations and was consistent with the robust fare normally on offer at Gaelic Park, which American reporters dubbed the 'Bronx bloodpit' and where visiting teams and referees were menaced by New York supporters and officials.

From 1962 O'Donnell invited leading GAA players in Ireland to participate in the Cushing Games, a series of exhibition matches held in Boston and New York in support of the Catholic missions in South America (initiated by Cardinal Richard Cushing of Boston). Continuing annually until 1973, the Cushing Games earned O'Donnell a knighthood of Saint Gregory from the Catholic church in 1969 and inspired the GAA all-star tours. Similarly, he arranged 'compromise rules' encounters between New York and Australian rules football teams, which were later adopted by the GAA in Ireland, and took New York on world tours in the 1960s and 1970s. His calculated generosity meant he had supporters as well as detractors across Ireland, especially in Kerry. Made assistant trainer of the Kerry footballers for their 1969 all-Ireland triumph, he was sacked a year later for arguing with the county chairman over the Kerry team's world tour.

Despite his efforts as national treasurer of the American Irish Immigration Committee, changes to the US immigration laws in 1965 curtailed Irish immigration, and Gaelic Park attendances fell from the late 1960s. (Many Irish also left the Bronx during this period.) Paying Irish-based players to travel over for weekend club matches alleviated this decline, as did the regular staging of rock festivals in Gaelic Park during the 1970s.

As his financial position weakened in the late 1960s, the previously astute O'Donnell imprudently escalated tensions with the GAA central council before relations sank to a new low in 1970 when, following a ferocious encounter between the Cork and New York hurlers at Gaelic Park, the referee was assaulted and suffered a broken jaw. After the New York board refused to accept the central council's ensuing suspension of one of its players for life, official tours to New York were banned until 1973. A younger generation of New York GAA officials reacted by advocating a more constructive attitude towards the central council in opposition to O'Donnell.

He repelled this challenge, partly by stoking the New York GAA's traditional republicanism through his characteristically fervent and outspoken support for the

Provisional IRA. Frequently embarrassing the central council on this divisive issue, he was heavily involved from 1970 in the Irish Northern Aid Committee (NORAID), an organisation established ostensibly to provide relief for distress in Northern Ireland, but widely assumed to be funding arms purchases for the Provisional IRA. NORAID operated hand-in-glove with the New York GAA, its collectors a ubiquitous feature of Gaelic Park. When O'Donnell arranged a tour to New York by a 'six-counties' football team in 1971, the central council refused permission (though it proceeded nonetheless), because there was no assurance that the money raised would go solely to the distressed.

The New York GAA finally slipped from O'Donnell's grasp in the late 1970s, but as manager of Gaelic Park he continued to provoke the central council. Soon after the dismal failure of his bid for the presidency of the GAA in 1981, his animosity towards the Roscommon-born New York GAA official Terry Connaughton led him to pilfer the Sam Maguire Cup, then on show in New York, and spread rumours that the culprit was a Roscommon supporter disgruntled by his county's recent all-Ireland final loss. The trophy eventually reappeared, daubed with pro-Roscommon and pro-IRA graffiti.

Renewed Irish immigration during 1985–90 produced bumper crowds at Gaelic Park, but exposed a more expectant generation to the deplorable state of what had become a glorified drinking den. O'Donnell's longstanding failure to develop Gaelic Park embarrassed the New York GAA, which also challenged him regarding his unsupervised collection of the gate receipts. Disputes over admission prices led to the ground being closed to the GAA for a month during 1986 and to the cancellation of the New York club final replay in 1987.

While he did not officially retire, he did delegate the daily running of Gaelic Park to his children. Determined efforts were made from within the Irish community to oust him when his lease came up for renewal in 1990, but despite a damning consultants' report on his tenancy and the rival bidders' readiness to invest more in the stadium, the Metropolitan Transportation Authority made the controversial and politically motivated decision to award O'Donnell a twenty-year lease. This entailed a much higher rent and was conditional on $1.5 million worth of renovations, for which he needed the New York GAA's help. After months of tense negotiations, a projected deal unravelled in April 1991.

O'Donnell retained the bar, but the pitch was leased to Manhattan College. Partly to deprive him of custom, the New York GAA unsuccessfully sought an alternative venue before coming to terms with Manhattan College in 1994 following three calamitous years of staging matches in an open field. Just as this agreement was reached, O'Donnell died in Montefiore Hospital in the Bronx on 21 April 1994 after a short illness and was buried in Gate of Heaven cemetery, Hawthorne, New York. In confronting the GAA with its uncomfortably violent past while portending its commercially tainted future, O'Donnell epitomised the diaspora's unsettling influence on the insular pieties of post-independence Ireland.

Terry Clavin

Sources

General Registry Office (birth certificate); *Advocate*, 1 April, 7 October 1944; *Western People*, 31 December 1966; 14 December 1968; 28 June 1969; 29 January, 11 March, 8 April, 9 September 1972; Pádraig Puirséal, *The GAA in its time* (1982); John Joseph Concannon and Frances Eugene Cull (eds), *The Irish American who's who* (1984); Donal O'Donovan, *Dreamers of dreams: portraits of the Irish in America* (1984); David Guiney, *Good days and old friends* (1985); Seán Óg Ó Ceallacháin, *Seán Óg: his own story* (1988); *Cork Examiner*, 13 December 1988; *Irish Echo*, 11 November 1989; 16 January, 17, 24 April, 15 May 1991; 27 April 1994; *New York Times*, 12 October 1990; 11 February 1991; *Longford Leader*, 3 May 1991; John Scally, *The Earley years* (1992); Michael O'Hehir, *My life and times* (1996); Mick Dunne, *The star spangled final* (1997); Seamus J. King, *The clash of the ash in foreign fields: hurling abroad* (1998); Seán Óg Ó Ceallacháin, *Tall tales and banter* (1998); Pat Spillane with Eddie McGoldrick, *Shooting from the hip: the Pat Spillane story* (1998); Keith Duggan, *The lifelong season: at the heart of Gaelic games* (2004); Brian Hanley, 'The politics of Noraid', *Irish Political Studies*, xix, no. 1 (summer 2004), 1–17; Paul Darby, *Gaelic games, nationalism and the Irish diaspora in the United States* (2009); Weeshie Fogarty, *My beautiful obsession: chasing the Kerry dream* (2012); Paul Fitzpatrick, *The fairytale in New York: the story of Cavan's finest hour* (2013); Eugene McGee, *The GAA in my time* (2014); *Irish Independent, Irish Press, The Irish Times, Kerryman, Sunday Independent, passim*

The entry and related sources have been abridged for publication. The full version is available at www.dib.ie.

4. Lives on stage and screen

Introduction

Many of America's first music 'superstars' were Irish. John McCormack (1884–1945, p. 108) was the biggest popular music idol of his day, filling venues beyond capacity around the country, and indeed around the world. McCormack's predecessors include Patrick Sarsfield Gilmore (1829–92), the bandmaster who wrote 'When Johnny comes marching home' (as Louis Lambert) and held legendary monster concerts: his first in New Orleans had a chorus of 5,000 and an orchestra of 500, including cannon. Before Sarsfield there was Thomas Moore (1779–1852), who married his poetic lyrics to classic Irish airs in his collected *Irish melodies* to deliver a runaway success in American 'parlour music'.

Some of America's first matinee idols too were Irish. On stage, there were dashing Shakespearian actors such as John McCullough (1832–85) and James O'Neill (1845–1920, father of playwright Eugene); while in the cinema, Irish emigrants such as Sara Allgood (1883–1950), Barry Fitzgerald (1888–1961), Maureen O'Sullivan (1911–98) and Maureen O'Hara (1920–2015, p. 135) were all highly bankable stars. Behind the camera, early Hollywood was home to great Irish talents in directors Herbert Brenon (1880–1958), thought to have worked on up to 300 silent films, and William Desmond Taylor (1872–1922), who is celebrated annually in his native Carlow at Taylorfest. Perhaps the most influential was Rex Ingram (1893–1950, p. 117), an early Hollywood film director described by David Lean as his 'idol' and by Michael Powell as 'the greatest stylist of our time'.

Irish playwrights, producers and actors also made an outsized contribution to the development of American theatre. From impresario John Brougham (1810–80) who staged a huge variety of wildly popular entertainments from serious theatre to burlesque, to playwright Dion Boucicault (1820–90), whose highest career moments were on the American stage, including with productions of 'The colleen bawn' and 'The shaughraun'; he also introduced the matinee performance, and innovated new forms of trapdoor and fireproof scenery in American theatres.

In our selection we feature two women who helped develop twentieth-century American theatre: Mary Manning (1906–99, p. 122), who founded the avant-garde Cambridge Poets' Theatre in Boston, and introduced America to Dylan Thomas and works by Beckett and Joyce; and Geraldine Fitzgerald (1913–2005, p. 126) who, despite a successful film career, disdained Hollywood commercialism and returned to the stage. She distinguished herself in the plays of Eugene O'Neill among others, and dedicated herself to making theatre accessible to a broader audience.

LE

John
McCormack

1884–1945

From the choir of
Dublin's Pro-Cathedral
to the massive New York
Hippodrome, this tenor
was one of the first music
superstars in America.

John Francis McCormack was born 14 June 1884 in Athlone, Co. Westmeath, the fourth of five children to survive in a family of eleven of Andrew McCormack and his wife Hannah (née Watson), both Scottish mill workers who had migrated to Ireland. The tenor's paternal grandfather had emigrated to Scotland from Co. Sligo. McCormack won a scholarship from the Marist Brothers in Athlone (1896) to attend the Diocesan College of the Immaculate Conception, or Summerhill College, in Sligo (later Sligo College) where he excelled in mathematics and languages, maintaining himself there with further scholarships. Shortly after leaving school (1902) he joined the Palestrina Choir of the Pro-Cathedral, Dublin, under its famed choirmaster, Dr Vincent O'Brien. In 1903 he won the gold medal in the tenor section of the Feis Ceoil. The myth persists that James Joyce competed in the same year, whereas in fact he entered the following year and won the bronze medal. Joyce remained a lifelong admirer of McCormack, who was a model for Shaun the Post in *Finnegans wake*.

After an aborted visit to the St Louis exposition in 1904, where the young tenor objected to being asked to do a stage-Irish turn, he went to Milan for lessons from Maestro Sabatini, with whom he was to spend less than a year. He made his operatic debut in the title role of Mascagni's 'L'amico Fritz' at the Teatro Chiabrero, Savona (13 January 1906). After some engagements in minor Italian opera houses McCormack found himself unemployed. He headed back to London, where he had made recordings two years earlier, and made an impression with appearances at the Boosey ballad concerts, then much in vogue. His main break came in 1907, when he made his debut at the Royal Opera House, Covent Garden, in the role of Turridu in Mascagni's 'Cavalleria rusticana'. At twenty-three he was the youngest tenor ever to sing a major in that house. In a short time he was partnering the most celebrated sopranos of the day, Luisa Tetrazzini and Nellie Melba included; and such was his own success that he remained with Covent Garden for eight consecutive seasons, until 1914. With the exception of singing the role of Cassio to Giovanni Zenatello's Otello, he sang only major roles, fourteen in all; Don Ottavio ('Don Giovanni'), Rudolpho (Puccini's 'La Bohême'), Cavarodossi ('Tosca') and Edgardo ('Lucia di Lammermoor') among them.

In 1909 McCormack sang at Oscar Hammerstein's Manhattan Opera House in New York, partnering again the coloratura soprano Luisa Tetrazzini, with whom he was to continue to share many triumphs on both sides of the Atlantic. The same year, through his friendship with the baritone Mario Sammarco, he sang at the San Carlo Opera House, Naples. Despite favourable reviews, his own estimation of his success was only moderate, and he did not sing in Italy again.

In 1910 he appeared at the Metropolitan Opera House, New York, making his debut there with Melba in 'La traviata'. In 1911 he appeared in the world premiere of 'Natoma' by Victor Herbert, first in Philadelphia and then at the Metropolitan, singing the role of Lieutenant Paul Merrill opposite Mary Garden in the title role as the Native American. The critics, however, were unimpressed. The same year he toured Australia as Melba's leading tenor, and returned to Australia as a recitalist in 1913.

An indifferent actor, McCormack was nevertheless greatly admired on the opera stage for his polished vocalism. On one occasion in Boston the conductor Felix Weingartner put down his baton and led the applause during a performance of 'Don Giovanni' after McCormack had sung 'Il mio tesoro', for which he was justly famous. It was by his recording of this aria (1916) that he said his reputation should be judged. There are other records in the same category. He was perhaps the finest singer of Handel and Mozart of his time. 'O sleep, why dost thou leave me?' (1920) from Handel's 'Semele' and 'Come my beloved' ('Care selve', 1924) from Handel's 'Atalanta' are models of their kind. In these vintage McCormack recordings the voice floats on the tip of the breath, as it were, the economy of means, and the arching, lucid phrases, delivered with exquisitely judged portamenti.

Despite having a voice of only moderate size, at the Metropolitan he was cast in Verdi and Puccini operas. At Covent Garden, Monte Carlo and the Manhattan Opera House, and with the Chicago–Philadelphia Opera Company (formed after the Manhattan had closed), he had the opportunity to sing in early nineteenth-century operas by Rossini, Donizetti and Bellini, for which his mellifluous voice was ideally suited.

In 1912, under the management of Charles L. Wagner, a noted impresario of the day, McCormack made a concert tour in the United States. This proved to be a turning point. The tenor realised that the recital was his true *métier*. By himself, as himself, on the concert platform he could hold an audience in his hand as few other singers could. Audiences responded to the charm of his singing, which sounded entirely natural and unforced, no matter how large the auditorium. McCormack had something much more than good diction: he had a feel for words, an ability to converse on a musical line, to point up a story in song, in a manner that was entirely his own. His gift for intimate communication in recital became legendary.

To the Irish in America McCormack was an icon of the age who brought solace to those experiencing poverty and the tragedy of emigration. His singing of such songs as 'I hear you calling me', 'Macushla' and 'Mother Machree' represented a consolation, direct and heartfelt, of the sadness and heartbreak of those times. He brought humour too in his renditions of 'The garden where the praties grow' or 'Off to Philadelphia', in which his vocalisation is whimsical and never forced.

By the middle war years, McCormack could fill virtually any concert hall in any part of the United States to over-capacity. Standing room and seats on stage became the norm. At one point he was making concert tours of eighty and ninety dates per season. In New York he would move between Carnegie Hall, the Metropolitan Opera and the massive Hippodrome (where he would give eight or ten recitals during the season), always to brimming audiences. His repertoire was extensive. In the 1915–16 season in New York, he did not repeat one song or aria in twelve programmes (excluding encores). In Boston he could sing four times in the space of a week.

As a recitalist, his concert repertoire was divided into groups made up of seventeenth- and eighteenth-century arias; the work of modern English and American composers; often Rachmaninoff, one of his favourite composers and a personal friend; and German lieder, in all of which he excelled. The Irish ballads—for which the Irish émigrés would be waiting in 'impatient silence' would then round off the evening, but, despite perceptions to the contrary, he never gave concerts exclusively of ballads.

As a consequence of his success as a recitalist, McCormack's opera appearances became less frequent. His last season was at the Monte Carlo Opera (1923), when he created the role of Gritzko in Moussorgsky's 'La foire de Sorotchintzi'. He was not yet forty when he retired from opera.

He made a notable tour of middle Europe in 1923, taking in Berlin and Prague, where he was much admired for his lieder and for the range of his repertoire. He had a particular affinity with the songs of Hugo Wolf, recording 'Ganymed' (1931) for the Hugo Wolf Society subscription series. In 1924 he took part in the Beethoven Festival at the Théâtre des Champs-Élysées in Paris under the direction of Walter Damrosch, when he sang, as he had in Berlin, the aria from Beethoven's oratorio 'Christus am Ölberge'. In 1930 he recorded the recitative in both German and English, and the aria in English. At this point in his career he had just sufficient voice left to encompass the aria, and its combination of technical ease and religious fervour make it one of the great recordings of its kind. No matter where he sang, his engagement with his audience was noted. He triumphed as far afield as South Africa, Hawaii and Japan.

Writing some time after hearing him at the Queen's Hall, London, in 1924, the Irish pianist Charles Lynch summed up the experience in this way:

> When McCormack's voice entered I realized that I was listening to the most perfect voice I had yet heard...The voice literally floated through the hall, with the words, seemingly floating on top of it. This had the effect of making the words seem separate from and, at the same time emotionally one with, the vocal line. Consequently the simultaneous perfection of both vocal and verbal articulation was truly memorable. (*Capuchin Annual 1946–47*)

Having applied for citizenship early in 1914, McCormack became a naturalised American citizen in

June 1919. This made him *persona non grata* for a time in Britain and in Australia, where a concert tour in 1920 had to be abandoned. Among many honours he received, he was made Doctor of Literature at Holy Cross College, Massachusetts, as early as 1917; became a freeman of the city of Dublin in 1923; and was awarded a Doctorate of Music by the National University of Ireland (1927). In 1928, for his unstinting services to charity, he was made a hereditary count of the papal court, later serving as a papal chamberlain. At the pontifical high mass in Phoenix Park, Dublin, which closed the eucharistic congress of 1932, and with a million of the faithful present, McCormack, on the steps of the high altar, sang César Franck's 'Panis angelicus'.

With the advent of radio in the 1920s he reached new audiences. He made his debut with the soprano Lucrezia Bori and went on to appear with the likes of Bing Crosby, becoming a popular radio celebrity in the 1920s and 1930s.

He took the lead in the film *Song o' my heart* (1930), the first sound feature film shot in Ireland, which also featured the nineteen-year-old Maureen O'Sullivan in her first film role. He later appeared, awkwardly overweight and in indifferent vocal form, as himself in *Wings of the morning* (1937; the first Technicolor feature film made in Britain or Ireland).

His recording career matched his popularity as a recitalist. He first recorded in 1904, right at the beginning of the industry, and continued until well into the second world war, a remarkable span that reveals his development as an artist and his expanding repertoire. The youthful timbre of his voice, which did not last long, was best heard between 1910 and 1920. Off stage he enjoyed good living, and his lifestyle and excessive weight appear to have taken a toll on his voice. But his art never ceased to develop. As his vocal range shortened he made more of language in song; the immediacy and freshness of his communication remained right until the end. Along with the Italian tenor Enrico Caruso and the Romanian-American soprano Alma Gluck, John McCormack was the mainstay of the RCA Victor recording catalogue for many years.

His last concert appearance in the United States was on 16 March 1937 at Buffalo, New York, after which he made a farewell tour of Britain and Ireland, culminating in a tearful farewell at the Royal Albert Hall in London (27 November 1938). He came out of retirement during the second world war to sing on behalf of the Red Cross and continued to make recordings until 1942, when the onset of emphysema made further singing impossible. He lived for some months at the Shelbourne Hotel, Dublin, before finally retiring to his last home, 'Glena' in Booterstown, Co. Dublin, where he died on 16 September 1945, aged sixty-one. He was buried, as he wished, in his papal uniform in Deansgrange cemetery, Co. Dublin.

A bronze statue of McCormack by sculptor Elizabeth O'Kane (2008) stands in the Iveagh Gardens at the rear of the National Concert Hall, Dublin, and shows him in characteristic pose: 'his head thrown back, his eyes closed, in his hands the little black book he always carried, open but never glanced at, as he wove a spell over his completely hushed listeners', as the American critic Max de Schauensee recalled. de Schauensee was not alone in remarking on the illusion that no matter how large the auditorium, he had the sensation that the tenor was singing to him alone. After the tenor appeared in concert in Tokyo, the reviewer for the *Japan Times* commented:

> Once he got settled by the piano he'd not shift his position at all, hardly; and you'd find yourself

listening to that quiet soothing voice, that just came with no apparent effort, and seemed to be talking confidentially to each individual in the theatre (5 May 1926).

He married (1906) in the Pro-Cathedral, Dublin, Lily Foley of Dublin, a singer who had also performed in St Louis in 1904; she and their two children survived him. His correspondence with Charles L. Wagner is in the Heinman Collection case, Library of Congress, Washington, DC.

Gordon T. Ledbetter

Sources

Florence French, 'First authentic story of John McCormack's life and career', *Musical Leader* (June 1917); Pierre V. R. Key, *John McCormack: his own life story* (1918); Charles. L. Wagner, *Seeing stars* (1940); L. A. G. Strong, *John McCormack* (1941); *Capuchin Annual 1946–47*; Lily McCormack, *I hear you calling me* (1950); Gerald Moore, *Am I too loud?* (1962); R. Foxall, *John McCormack* (1963); J. Scarry, 'Finnegans wake: a portrait of John McCormack', *Irish University Review*, iii, no. 2 (autumn 1973); P. Dolan, 'John McCormack, mastersinger: a short account of his American career', *The Sword of Light* (spring 1974); Henry Pleasants, *The great singers from the dawn of opera to the present* day (1977); Gordon T. Ledbetter, *The great Irish tenor* (1977); Paul W. Worth and Jim Cartwright, *John McCormack: a comprehensive discography* (1986); John Ward, 'McCormack on Brighton pier', *Record Collector*, xxxvii (1992); Gearóid O'Brien, *John McCormack and Athlone* (1992); Kevin Rockett, *The Irish filmography* (1996); *American national biography* (1999); *The letters of John McCormack to J. C. Doyle*, edited and with introduction by G. T. Ledbetter (2006); *The people's tenor*, DVD documentary directed and produced by Martin Dwan (2006); Pádraic O'Hara, *The greatest Irish tenor: John McCormack a life in letters* (2008); Paul Worth with Doreen McFarlane (ed.), 'John McCormack Discography' (2018), available at https://archive.org/details/MCCORMACKJOHNtenorARCHIVEDISCOGRAPHY (accessed September 2020); Paul Worth with Doreen McFarlane (ed.), *John McCormack, a singer's life: memoirs and career of the beloved tenor* (2019)

This entry has been abridged for publication. The full version is available at www.dib.ie.

Rex Ingram

1893–1950

An innovative and prolific early-Hollywood director, his film credits include the influential cinematic masterpiece *The four horsemen of the apocalypse.*

Reginald Ingram Montgomery Hitchcock was born 18 January 1893 at 58 Grosvenor Square, Rathmines, Dublin, the elder of two sons of Francis Ryan Montgomery Hitchcock, clergyman and Donnellan lecturer at Trinity College Dublin (1912), and his wife, Kathleen Hitchcock (née Ingram). Educated first at Nenagh, Co. Tipperary, Reginald (known as 'Rex') moved to Kinnitty, King's Co. (Offaly), when his father was made rector. In 1905 he was sent to Saint Columba's College, Dublin, where he excelled in boxing and rugby but often fell foul of the school authorities. The death of his mother in October 1908, and his subsequent failure to gain admittance to Trinity College, had a decisive influence on his life and he resolved to leave Ireland. He arrived in New York on 3 July 1911, shortly before his father's remarriage, and never visited Ireland again.

In 1912 he entered Yale University School of Art, where he studied sculpture under Lee Lawrie. At that time New York was the centre of the nascent film industry. Ingram was introduced to Charles Edison, son of the inventor and part of the famous Edison Studios based in the Bronx, and he abandoned his studies for film (despite never finishing his degree, Yale conferred on him a Bachelor of Fine Arts degree in 1921, the first academic recognition of film as one of the fine arts). Employed first as an artist, he drew titles and painted sets, but he was also employed as a script writer and performer on screen. Moving to the Vittagraph Company in 1914, he continued to act in films, where his dashing good looks photographed well, but his acting limitations were exposed. In 1915 he was hired by the Fox Company and changed his name to Rex Ingram in honour of his mother. Moving to Universal in 1916, he directed his first silent film, *The great problem*, and three more films followed that year. When the film industry relocated to Hollywood, so did Ingram, and he directed four films in 1917 before being dismissed by the studio. For the Paralta–W. W. Hodkinson Corporation he directed six more films between 1918 and 1920.

Ingram was briefly in the Royal Canadian Signal Corps in late 1918, and apparently suffered an injury (not combat-related) that tormented him for the rest of his life. Having established a reputation for being brilliant but impossible to work with, he was hired by the Metro Picture Corporation (afterwards MGM) in 1920, where he was under the supervision of June Mathis, screenwriter and the first female executive for Metro/MGM. During the filming of *Shore acres* in 1920 he again fell out with his cameraman and was given the young cinematographer John Seitz to work with, which marked the start of a great collaborative partnership. With *The four horsemen of the apocalypse* (1921), based on the novel by Vicente Blasco Ibáñez, Ingram created a cinematic masterpiece of enduring quality. Shooting began in July 1920 and lasted six months—unheard of since D. W. Griffith's epics. Together with June Mathis, who wrote the screenplay for the film, he insisted on engaging an unknown actor, Rudolf Valentino, to play the lead, and made him an international icon in the process; Alice Terry played the heroine. Colonel Francis Clere Hitchcock (1896–1962), the director's brother, advised on military matters, and the filming involved 12,000 people. The eleven reels of the finished film display Ingram's mastery of the camera, his stunning narrative ability, and his visual audacity. A perfectionist, he always insisted that his cast say their lines in the language of the country in which a scene was set, even though the films were silent. *The four horsemen* was an international success, though on its opening in Dublin in January 1923 it was savaged by the press. It was followed by *The conquering power* (1921), which had the same leading actors and was greeted with more critical acclaim. Relations between Ingram and Valentino soured, however, and they never worked together again. More popular success followed in 1922 with *The prisoner of Zenda*, again starring Alice Terry. Determined to prove that he could make any good-looking actor a star, he took one of his players, Ramon Samaniegos and, changing his surname to Novarro, set out to make him as big a success as Valentino.

Disillusioned with the Hollywood studio system, and never afraid of voicing his criticisms, Ingram moved to France in 1923, determined to make his own films. He established himself in Nice, where he modernised the Studios de la Victorine de Saint-Augustin and directed *Scaramouche* (1923), *Mare nostrum* (1925), and *The garden of Allah* (1927; it is believed that he converted to Islam at this time). After some initial antagonism, he gained the friendship of the director Erich von Stroheim, and in 1925 was entrusted with the cutting of his classic film *Greed*; the film was afterwards further cut, despite both men's protests. In 1926 he was awarded the Légion d'honneur française. In 1927 his MGM contract was not renewed, and he purchased the Nice studio for $5 million, though he later lost control (being erratic and unreliable when it came to business). In 1928 he established the Ingram Hamilton Syndicated Ltd production company in London. He is said to have met the young British director Alfred Hitchcock in 1929 and advised him to change his name if he wanted to get anywhere. *The three passions* (1929) was his last silent film, and with the advent of sound he lost interest in directing. His only attempt at the new form was *Baroud* (1931), in which he played the lead himself, but it lacked the assurance of his earlier work and he decided to retire. In 1934 he moved to

Egypt, before returning to Hollywood in 1936. He published two novels, *The legion advances* (1934) and *Mars in the house of death* (1940), both melodramas.

Ingram married twice: his first marriage (15 March 1917) to Doris Pawn ended in divorce; on 5 November 1921 he married his leading actress, Alice Frances Taaffe (Terry), whose father came from Co. Kildare. Ingram died in July 1950 in California, and was cremated; he had one adopted son, Abd-el-Kadar.

Arrogant, and with a reputation as a hedonist, Ingram was a controversial figure, but one of the true giants of cinema. A genuinely innovative director, he helped to define and develop the cinematic medium, leaving an enduring legacy for future directors; David Lean called him 'my idol', while Michael Powell insisted that he was 'the greatest stylist of our time' (O'Leary, x). Erich von Stroheim, who considered Ingram the world's greatest director, said of him 'He was a very proud man and wouldn't have done the things I did. He never stooped, he never gave any publicity and was a little huffy—he was very Irish' (O'Leary, 57). Perhaps the most fitting epitaph was given by James Joyce in *Finnegans wake*: 'Rex Ingram, pageant master.' For his contribution to the motion picture industry, he has a star on the Hollywood walk of fame.

Patrick M. Geoghegan

Sources

René Prédal, *Rex Ingram, 1893–1950* (1970); Liam O'Leary, *Rex Ingram: master of the silent cinema* (1980); Ian Graham, 'Rex Ingram: a seminal influence, unfairly obscured', *American Cinematographer*, iv (1993), 74–80; Laurie Collier Hillstrom (ed.), *International directory of film and filmakers*, ii: *Directors* (1997); Henry Boylan, *A dictionary of Irish biography* (3rd edition, 1998); Ruth Barton, *Rex Ingram: visionary director of the silent screen* (2014)

Mary Manning

1905–99

This Dublin-born
playwright and novelist
founded the avant-
garde Cambridge Poets'
Theatre, and introduced
America to Dylan
Thomas and works by
Beckett and Joyce.

Mary Manning was born 30 June 1905 in Dublin, the eldest of three children, to Fitzmaurice Manning, a civil servant in the colonial service, and his wife Susan (née Bennett), sister of the suffragist and peace activist Louie Bennett. Manning's father was a distant figure to his children: his work kept him abroad for two-year periods at a time, and he was killed in 1918 whilst serving in West Africa during the first world war, leaving the family in straitened circumstances. Her mother ran a celebrated teashop, 'The sod of turf' in Dublin city, which was much frequented by writers and poets. When her mother inherited money, the family moved to Wellington Place and Mary was educated at Morehampton House school and Alexandra College.

On leaving school, Manning studied acting at the Abbey School under the auspices of Sara Allgood and Ria Mooney. She had small parts with the Irish Players in England, and with the Abbey, before joining the Gate Theatre as publicity manager; she founded and edited *Motley*, the theatre's short-lived but influential magazine that published the works of Austin Clarke, Frank O'Connor, Francis Stuart and Mainie Jellett, among others. Micheál MacLiammóir, who appeared in her first play, 'Youth's the season…?' (1931), wrote that 'her brain, nimble and observant as it was, could not yet keep pace with a tongue so caustic that even her native city was a little in awe of her' (*All for Hecuba*, 146), but he also noted her impulsive sympathy. The play was well-received and subsequent critics have termed it one of the most accomplished first plays ever seen in Dublin. Unique in dealing with Dublin high life, it had a note of sardonic disillusionment and was given the modernist touch by the presence of an eerily silent character, Egosmith, included at the suggestion of Manning's lifelong friend Samuel Beckett. She wrote two further plays for the Gate, 'Storm over Wicklow' (1933), which was also well-received, and 'Happy family' (1934), which was less so. Neither was subsequently published.

In 1935 Manning emigrated to America, where she married Harvard law professor and civil rights activist Mark de Wolfe Howe. The couple settled in Cambridge, Massachusetts, and had three daughters: the poets Susan and Fanny Howe, and the sculptor Helen Howe Braider. She wrote her first novel *Mount Venus* (1938) and continued to engage with theatre in Cambridge. She initially ran the Radcliffe drama programme, where she directed a young Jack Lemmon as Christy in a student production of 'The playboy of the western world', and in 1950 she founded a small theatre company known as the Poets' Theatre, which became a site of pioneering experimental verse drama, setting young American writers such as John Ashbury, Richard Eberhard, Alison Lurie and Frank O'Hara on their paths to long and illustrious careers. In 1952 the Poets' Theatre brought Dylan Thomas over for his first American reading, and in 1956 actress Siobhán McKenna and playwright Brendan Behan were brought over to speak. One of Manning's career highlights was her staging of *Finnegans wake* (1955). During this period she wrote her second novel, *Lovely people* (1953), about the Boston upper middle classes.

Manning returned to Dublin following her husband's death in 1968 where she was the drama critic for *Hibernia*, *The Irish Times* and other publications. Her perceptive, caustic reviews were occasionally threatened with libel actions. She also returned to playwriting, producing a widely praised adaptation of Frank O'Connor's novel *The saint and Mary Kate* (1968), and wrote a series of short stories entitled *The last chronicles of Ballyfungus* (1978) that took a satiric look at modern Ireland. In 1980 she returned to America and married Boston lawyer Fanaeuil Adams. She remained gregarious and well-loved—just two weeks before her death she hosted one of her famous parties in the reception room of her retirement home. She died on 27 June 1999.

Bridget Hourican

Sources

Micheál Mac Liammóir, *All for Hecuba* (1946); Robert Hogan, *After the Irish renaissance* (1967); Peter Luke, *Enter certain players* (1978); Deirdre Bair, *Samuel Beckett* (1978); *The Irish Times*, 8 July 1999; Donna Casella, 'Mary Manning', in Jane Gaines *et al.* (eds), *Women film pioneers project* (2013); Paige Reynolds, 'The avant-garde doyenne: Mary Manning, the Poets' Theatre and the staging of "Finnegans Wake"', *The Canadian Journal of Irish Studies*, vol. 39, no. 2 (2016), 108–133

Geraldine Fitzgerald

1913–2005

This versatile actress
abandoned Hollywood
for the stage and
worked to make theatre
accessible to all sectors
of American society.

Geraldine Mary Wilma Fitzgerald was born 24 November 1913 at 85 Lower Leeson Street, Dublin, one of two daughters and two sons of Edward Martin Fitzgerald (1886–1965), a lawyer, who was Roman Catholic, and his wife Edith Marie (née Richards) (c.1890–1963), a Protestant. The family later lived in Greystones, Co. Wicklow.

Educated at convent schools, Fitzgerald studied for three years at the Dublin Metropolitan School of Art before turning to acting, and was coached by her maternal aunt, the actress Shelah Richards. She appeared in eight plays in the 1933/4 season at Dublin's Gate Theatre; she was praised for 'a quality of poise which is not usually found in combination with her youth and charm' (Hobson, 50). Her most substantial Gate role was that of Isabella Linton in a stage adaptation of 'Wuthering Heights', starring Micheál MacLiammóir as Heathcliff; she also played the high-spirited Ilse in 'Children in uniform', the controversial lesbian-themed drama by Christa Winsloe. Moving to London in 1934, she began acting in films, and was well-reviewed in *Turn of the tide* (1935), about two feuding Yorkshire fishing families, and as the heroine, Maggie Tulliver, in *The mill on the Floss* (1937).

Fitzgerald married (1936) Edward William Lindsay-Hogg (1910–99), who latterly succeeded as 4th baronet (1987), a gentleman horse-racing enthusiast and dilettante playwright; the marriage was dissolved in 1946. Hoping to further her husband's song-writing ambitions, Fitzgerald moved with him to New York in 1938, and soon appeared on Broadway in the ingénue role of Ellie Dunn in the Mercury Theatre production of 'Heartbreak House' by George Bernard Shaw, directed by and starring another Gate Theatre alumnus, Orson Welles. (Fitzgerald and Welles are thought to have embarked on an affair that resulted in Welles fathering Fitzgerald's son Michael

Lindsay-Hogg (b. 1940), 5th baronet, a theatre, film and television director. Lindsay-Hogg has remained ambiguous on the issue.)

Signed to a seven-year contract by Warner Brothers Pictures, Fitzgerald insisted on a clause (conceded reluctantly by the studio) that allowed her perform in theatre for six months every year. Her first two Hollywood films, released in the same month (April 1939), were both box-office smashes. In the Warner melodrama *Dark victory* she gave a 'sentient and touching portrayal' (*New York Times*, 21 April 1939) as the responsible, devoted friend of a vibrant but wilful socialite (played by Bette Davis, who remained a lifelong personal friend) doomed by a malignant brain tumour. On loan to the Goldwyn studio, she reprised her role as Isabella Linton in *Wuthering Heights* (directed by William Wyler) opposite Laurence Olivier in his breakthrough cinematic role as Heathcliff, resulting in an Oscar nomination for best supporting actress.

Despite these promising debuts, Fitzgerald's Hollywood career rapidly foundered. Over the next seven years, she made twelve more films with co-stars including Alan Ladd, John Garfield, Peter Lorre, Sidney Greenstreet, Barbara Stanwyck and Loretta Young. She either refused or was denied by studio executives (sources differ) the lead femme fatale role of Brigid O'Shaughnessy in *The Maltese falcon*, and refused the part of Melanie Hamilton (played by Olivia de Havilland) in *Gone with the wind*.

She disdained Hollywood commercialism, aspired only to make worthy films with solid scripts, and defied the rigid strictures of the studio system by her undaunted commitment to live theatre (acting regularly in stage plays in the Los Angeles area), and spirited refusals of what she deemed inferior roles. The Warner Bros studio retaliated by confining her to B pictures and second female leads, and regularly suspended her for insubordination, or loaned her to rival studios. She supported Davis again in *Watch on the Rhine* (1943; screenplay by Dashiell Hammett from the play by Lillian Hellman), as the dissatisfied wife of an aristocratic Nazi agent. After appearing in *Wilson* (1944) as Edith, the eponymous American president's resolute second wife, she was featured glamorously in a *Life* magazine cover story (7 August 1944). In the weirdly compelling thriller *The strange affair of Uncle Harry* (1945), she played the neurotically (perhaps incestuously) possessive sister of the title character (played by George Sanders).

Directed by Max Reinhardt (in his last professional undertaking), Fitzgerald returned triumphantly to the Broadway stage in 'Sons and soldiers' (1943), opposite Gregory Peck. Fitzgerald married (1946) Stuart Scheftel (1910/11–1994), a wealthy New York businessman, heir to the Macy's department store fortune, patron of the arts, civic leader and occasional political aspirant; their one daughter, Susan, became a clinical psychologist. On leaving Hollywood, Fitzgerald resided permanently in New York, on Manhattan's Upper East Side. She made two films in Britain, both with dark Victorian settings: *So evil my love* (1948), with Ray Milland, and *The late Edwina Black* (1952), with Roland Culver. In the early 1950s she concentrated on television work, appearing in many anthology drama series.

Resuming her stage career in the mid-1950s, Fitzgerald appeared widely in classical and contemporary drama, performing many of the leading female roles of the twentieth-century repertoire. She played Jennifer Dubedat in Shaw's 'The doctor's dilemma' (1955); was directed by and acted opposite Orson Welles, as Goneril in his controversial Broadway production of 'King Lear' (1956); and was directed by John Houseman, as Gertrude in 'Hamlet' (1958), in the American Shakespeare Festival Theatre, Stratford, Connecticut. Her interpretations of Eugene O'Neill were especially distinguished. She played Essie Miller in 'Ah, wilderness!' at Ford's Theatre, Washington, DC (1969), and at the Long Wharf Theatre, New Haven, Connecticut (1974); the latter production, directed by Arvin Brown, transferred to Broadway's Circle in the Square Theatre (1975), and was filmed for television by the Public Broadcasting Service (PBS) (1976). Her most critically acclaimed role was in another O'Neill play, as Mary Tyrone in 'Long day's journey into night' (1971), directed by Brown in an off-Broadway production. She reprised the role with the Philadelphia Drama Guild (1975) (where she also played Amanda Wingfield in 'The glass menagerie' by Tennessee Williams). She was Nora Melody in O'Neill's 'A touch of the poet' (1977).

Her long association with Arvin Brown and the Long Wharf included the part of Juno Boyle in 'Juno and the paycock' (1973) by Sean O'Casey; she also starred, opposite Milo O'Shea, in Brown's revival of a long-neglected musical version of the play, staged initially at the Williamstown Theatre Festival (1974), and (under the title 'Daarlin' Juno') at the Long Wharf (1976). She performed twice, in separate roles, in Thornton Wilder's 'Our town', as Mrs Webb with American Shakespeare Theatre (1975), and as the Stage Manager in Williamstown (1976). She played Felicity, a dying hospice resident, in 'The shadow box' (1977), the Pulitzer Prize and Tony Award winning drama by Michael Cristofer, which opened at the Long Wharf, then transferred to Broadway's Morosco Theatre. While concentrating on stage direction (both straight plays and musicals) in the 1980s, she acted in 'I can't remember anything', the opening play in Arthur Miller's diptych 'Danger: memory!' (1987).

Believing that theatre and other arts should be purged of elitism and accessible to all sectors of society, Fitzgerald was actively involved with public arts programmes, and served on the arts councils of New York city and state. Amid the social and political convulsions of the period, in 1969 she co-founded Everyman, a community theatre company that produced plays in deprived areas of the city, often with amateur casts recruited locally; she wrote, acted and directed for the company, and helped initiate the inaugural Everyman Community Street Theater Festival at the Lincoln Center (1971). For her work with Everyman, Fitzgerald was awarded the Handel Medallion by the city of New York, the municipality's highest cultural award, the first actress so honoured (1973).

On the basis of two off-Broadway productions, Fitzgerald won the 1981 Outer Critics Circle's Lucille Lortel award for outstanding new director: for 'Mass appeal' (1980), a dramatic comedy about the conflicts between a complacent parish and a firebrand seminarian; and for an Everyman production of 'Long day's journey into night', with an all-black cast (1981). She returned to Dublin to direct the European premiere of 'Mass appeal' (summer 1981), then directed the play on a successful Broadway run (1981–2). One of the first women to direct on Broadway, she received both Tony and Drama Desk nominations for best director. (In 1982, another play with a Catholic theme, 'Agnes of God', began a lengthy Broadway run, directed by Michael Lindsay-Hogg, the first occasion ever that a mother and son were directing separate Broadway plays at the same time.) She wrote the lyrics and directed an off-Broadway production of 'Sharon' (1993), a musical based on the play 'Sharon's grave' by John B. Keane.

Fitzgerald's versatility was evident in the varied character roles that she played in film and television. She was a goading, socially ambitious small-town attorney's wife in *Ten North Frederick* (1958), opposite Gary Cooper; a widowed social worker who seeks to befriend a lonely concentration-camp survivor (Rod Steiger) in *The pawnbroker* (1964); a crazed revivalist preacher in *Rachel, Rachel* (1968), supporting the Golden Globe-winning Joanne Woodward in Paul Newman's directorial debut; and the fetching but memory-impaired old flame rediscovered by a displaced pensioner (the Oscar-winning Art Carney) during his cross-country travels in *Harry and Tonto* (1974). She received a best actress nomination from the Australian Film Institute for *The mango tree* (1977), and played the hare-brained, sherry-tippling, billionaire grandmother of the title character (Dudley Moore) in the hit comedy *Arthur* (1981), with Liza Minnelli, and in the ill-received sequel, *Arthur II: on the rocks* (1988), her last feature film.

Her television work included a worthy adaptation of *The moon and sixpence* (1959), from the novel by Somerset Maugham, playing the abandoned bourgeois wife of a Gauguin-like stockbroker-turned-artist (Laurence Olivier). She made guest appearances in such television series as *Naked city*, *The nurses*, *The defenders*, *Lou Grant*, *Trapper John, M. D.*, *Cagney and Lacey*, and *St Elsewhere*. For her performance in 'Rodeo Red and the runaway' (1978) in the after-school series *NBC special treat*, she won a 1979 Daytime Emmy award for outstanding individual achievement by a performer in children's programming. She played the redoubtable matriarch Rose Kennedy, opposite E. G. Marshall as Joseph Kennedy, and supporting Martin Sheen in the title role, in the award-winning television mini-series *Kennedy* (1983). She twice guested, in separate roles, in *The golden girls*, her first appearance (1988) receiving a Primetime Emmy nomination for outstanding guest performer in a comedy series.

After taking singing lessons in her mid-fifties, Fitzgerald began singing in nightclubs and Everyman stage productions, and played the part of Jenny in 'The threepenny opera' (1972). For many years she toured in a full-length, one-woman cabaret show, 'Streetsongs', incorporating songs and connecting narration; during a lengthy off-Broadway run in 1979 the show was televised on PBS. Her repertory songs, notable for novel interpretations, included Irish popular ballads, music hall and Tin Pan Alley standards, Percy French, Noel Coward, Vera Lynn, Edith Piaf and the Beatles. A live recording of a 1981 performance at the Great Lakes Theatre Festival, Cleveland, Ohio, was released as *Geraldine Fitzgerald in Streetsongs* (1983).

A consistently compelling performer of great authenticity and distinctive presence, Fitzgerald was witty, forthright, idealistic and intelligent. Incapacitated by Alzheimer's disease from the mid-1990s, she died at her home on 17 July 2005, and was buried in Woodlawn cemetery in the Bronx, New York. Relatives in the theatrical profession include the Irish stage director Caroline Fitzgerald (niece), Irish actress Susan Fitzgerald and British actress Tara Fitzgerald (grand-niece). She is honoured by a pavement star in the Hollywood Walk of Fame.

Lawrence William White

Sources

General Registry Office (birth certificate); Gate Theatre programmes, 1933–4 (National Library of Ireland, Ir 3919 D2); Bulmer Hobson (ed.), *The Gate Theatre Dublin* (1934), 50, 138; *New York Times*, 21 April 1939; 11 August 1976; 11 December 1983; 9 February, 8 March 1987; 21 January 1994; 19 July 2005; Micheál MacLiammóir, *All for Hecuba: an Irish theatrical autobiography* (1961 edition); *Irish Law Times and Solicitors' Journal*, xcix, no. 5117 (6 March 1965), 89; John Houseman, *Run-through: a memoir* (1973); *The Irish Times*, 18 July 1981; 23 July 2005; John Houseman, *Unfinished business: a memoir* (1986); Christopher Fitz-Simon, *The boys* (1996); Simon Callow, *Orson Welles*, i: *The road to Xanadu* (1997); Simon Callow, *Orson Welles*, ii: *Hello Americans* (2006); Kenneth Ferguson (ed.), *King's Inns barristers 1868–2004* (2005); *Independent* (London), 19 July 2005; *Guardian*, 20 July 2005; *San Francisco Chronicle*, 20 July 2005; *Washington Post*, 20 July 2005; *Daily Telegraph*, 27 July 2005; Don B. Wilmeth (ed.), *Cambridge guide to American theatre* (2007 edition); Chris Welles Feder, *In my father's shadow: a daughter remembers Orson Welles* (2010); *Observer*, 31 January 2010; 'Taking it out of doors', Playbill Arts (8 July 2010), www.playbillarts.com/features/article/8417.html (accessed 29 April 2021); Michael Lindsay-Hogg, *Luck and circumstance: a coming of age in Hollywood, New York, and points beyond* (2011); Internet Movie Database, www.imdb.com (accessed 29 April 2021); Internet Broadway Database, www.ibdb.com (accessed 29 April 2021); Lortel Archives: The Internet Off-Broadway Database, www.lortel.org (accessed 29 April 2021); Film Reference, www.filmreference.com (accessed 29 April 2021); Irish Theatre Institute: Irish Playography, www.irishplayography.com (accessed 29 April 2021); Primetime Emmy® Award Database, www.emmys.com (accessed 29 April 2021); 'About us: show archive', Long Wharf Theatre, www.longwharf.org (accessed 29 April 2021); 'Background and history', Great Lakes Theater Festival, www.greatlakestheater.org (accessed 29 April 2021); 'Production archives', Williamstown Theatre Festival, www.wtfestival.org (accessed 29 April 2021); Noir of the Week, www.noiroftheweek.com (accessed 29 April 2021); Find a Grave, www.findagrave.com (accessed 29 April 2021)

This entry has been abridged for publication. The full version is available at www.dib.ie.

Maureen O'Hara

1920–2015

Iconic movie star known for her roles in big-budget swashbucklers and John Ford pictures, she was one of the first people to be recognised as Irish, and not 'English', in her American citizenship paperwork.

Maureen O'Hara was born Maureen FitzSimons on 17 August 1920 at the family home at 32 Upper Beechwood Avenue in Ranelagh, Dublin. Her father, Charles Stewart Parnell FitzSimons, managed a high-end clothing company and was part-owner of Dublin's Shamrock Rovers soccer team. Her mother, Marguerita (Rita) FitzSimons (née Lilburn), was a clothes designer, actress and singer. O'Hara, the second of six children (four girls and two boys), reminisced in her 2004 memoir 'Tis herself about the happy and creative house she grew up in: all of her siblings were drawn to the arts and enjoyed varying degrees of success in music, dance, theatre and film.

O'Hara attended the girls' primary school on John Street West off Thomas Street, Dublin, and secondary school with the Sisters of Charity in Milltown, Dublin. She gave her first performance at a school concert at the age of six and was 'bitten by the acting bug that night...I wanted to become the greatest actress of all time!' ('Tis herself, 13). Shortly thereafter she was enrolled in the Ena Mary Burke School of Elocution and Drama, as well as taking singing and dance lessons. At ten she joined the Rathmines Theatre Company. O'Hara entered and won various amateur acting competitions and feiseanna, and earned her first professional fees with roles in radio dramas for 2RN (later Raidió Teilifís Éireann (RTÉ)).

In 1934, aged fourteen, O'Hara joined the Abbey Theatre company, initially doing background jobs such as set building and cleaning. After a year at the Abbey, she started getting walk-on parts in bigger productions, slowly progressing to parts with one or two lines. Just before she performed her first substantial role at the Abbey aged seventeen, she was 'discovered' by visiting American entertainer Harry Richman. He recommended O'Hara for a screen test in London. While at Elstree Studios a few days later, she was invited to deliver one line in Richman's comedy, *Kicking the moon around* (1938), marking her film debut.

The screen test, however, did not go well: 'They dressed me in a gold lamé gown…and transformed me with heavy makeup into a Mata Hari look-alike…I looked like a ten-dollar hooker' (*'Tis herself*, 20). Thankfully for O'Hara a meeting with actor Charles Laughton at his Mayflower Pictures production company was more fruitful, and she was offered a seven-year contract. Her first film was *My Irish Molly* (1938), a low-budget musical and the only film in which she appeared under her real name. Her next role was in *Jamaica Inn* (1939), based on the best-selling novel by Daphne du Maurier, co-starring Laughton and directed by Alfred Hitchcock. Her performance was confident and well-reviewed. When it came to publicising the film, Laughton told her that her surname was too long for marquees and would have to be shortened: thus Maureen O'Hara was born.

While filming in England, O'Hara met production team member George Brown, and was persuaded to date him by a mutual friend. By her account Brown was dogged in his romantic pursuit, and in her naivety she consented, aged eighteen, to a hasty marriage on 13 June 1939, just prior to leaving for Hollywood to shoot her next film with Laughton, *The Hunchback of Notre Dame* (1939). Brown was meant to join her later in Hollywood but was prevented by the outbreak of the war. The marriage was annulled in 1941. O'Hara's mother had accompanied her to Hollywood in June 1939 and the two became effectively trapped there when travel to and from Europe was barred. It would be some time before either woman could return to Ireland: Rita FitzSimons via a circuitous route in 1941, O'Hara in 1946.

On the set of *The Hunchback of Notre Dame* O'Hara became friendly with dialogue director William Price, a charming Mississippian who became her frequent companion at social events. She again blundered into a marriage in December 1941 in which her feelings were not engaged: 'Like a half-witted idiot, I jumped from the frying pan into the fire and became Mrs William Houston Price' (*'Tis herself*, 73). This second marriage would be a tumultuous one, Price was reportedly an alcoholic and lavish spender of her film-star income, buying a succession of ostentatious houses at desirable Los Angeles addresses. The marriage lasted ten years and they had one child, Bronwyn (1944–2016). Over the years many of O'Hara's family members, including her parents, joined her in California.

Despite the success of *Hunchback*, Laughton broke the news to O'Hara that his production company was in financial trouble and that he had sold her contract to RKO Pictures. In her memoir, O'Hara expresses the opinion that had she not been bound by the RKO contract and able to return to Europe earlier, she would have become a more serious, character-actor: 'But the studios had different plans for me. Hollywood would never allow my talent to triumph over my face' (47).

After three mediocre films with RKO, she was offered a role in director John Ford's Welsh coal-mining epic *How green was my valley* (1941) for 20th Century Fox. It was the first of five films she would make with Ford and it won five Oscars in 1942, including best picture, beating *Citizen Kane*. A significant portion of O'Hara's 2004 memoir is devoted to recalling her intense and often troubled friendship with John Ford, the son of emigrants from Spiddal,

Co. Galway. O'Hara became a regular visitor to his home and spent many weekends with the Ford family aboard their yacht, the *Araner*. In 1942 Ford offered O'Hara the lead in a film that would take another ten years to be made: *The quiet man* (1952). The two worked together over the next several years to develop the draft script while Ford tried in vain to secure financial backing for the project. Their relationship soured over time, particularly after *The quiet man* was finally filmed, and in her memoir O'Hara recounts various incidents of cruel and sometimes bizarre behaviour from Ford, who she characterised as domineering and volatile.

Despite her hopes, she was not offered serious dramatic roles after the success of *How green was my valley*, and instead continued to be cast in either middle-of-the-road fare or outright 'stinkeroos'. Her next film, *To the shores of Tripoli* (1942), was her first in Technicolour. O'Hara would later be declared the 'queen of Technicolour' due to how the process accentuated her red hair, hazel eyes and pale skin. She felt this moniker hindered rather than helped her career, keeping her trapped in 'decorative roles' filmed in Technicolour.

She would appear in over sixty films throughout her long career. Trapped in the studio system for much of that time, she had little choice in the roles assigned to her, many of which she thought were trite and forgettable. In her early years, O'Hara was often consigned to one-dimensional roles as a beauty and felt that her talent was being squandered. She did, however, often enjoy her roles in adventure films. She relished the opportunity to perform her own stunts or brandish a fencing foil in big-budget swashbucklers such as *The black swan* (1942 with Tyrone Power), *At sword's point* (filmed 1949, released 1952) or

Against all flags (1952 with Errol Flynn), and westerns such as *Comanche territory* (1949) for which she mastered the American bullwhip so well she 'could snap a cigarette out of someone's mouth' (*'Tis herself*, 131). Some of her best roles came later in her career, and she enjoyed something of a resurgence in the early 1960s, before retiring from film for two decades from the early 1970s.

The roles she, and critics, rated the most highly from the first part of her career were her first two with Laughton, *Jamaica Inn* and *The Hunchback of Notre Dame*; three of her five films with Ford: *How green was my valley*, *Rio Grande* (1950, her first film opposite John Wayne) and *The quiet man* (her personal favourite); the Christmas classic *Miracle on 34th Street* (1947); *Our man in Havana* (1959) alongside Alec Guinness (while filming on location in Cuba she met Fidel Castro and befriended Che Guevara); the Walt Disney produced smash hit, *The parent trap* (1961); and *Mr Hobbs takes a vacation* (1962), opposite James Stewart.

O'Hara also had aspirations as a singer and performed songs in some of her films as the story required but was passed up for musicals (in her memoir she sorrowfully recounts losing the part of Anna in *The King and I* to Deborah Kerr). During the late 1950s, with the advent of big-name variety television shows, she was frequently invited to sing on the shows of Dinah Shore, Perry Como, Andy Williams and others. She made two albums: *Love letters from Maureen O'Hara* (1960) and *Maureen O'Hara sings her favorite Irish songs* (1963), and she was cast in the lead role of a Broadway musical 'Christine', which closed after just one week in April 1960.

The year before she divorced her estranged husband William Price (August 1952) O'Hara was introduced to banker Enrique Parra while attending the Mexican Film

Festival, and they became romantically involved. They were together for fifteen, mostly happy, years, with O'Hara regularly visiting Mexico City for extended stays, enrolling her daughter in school there. They did not marry (Parra never divorced) and parted company in 1967. In March 1957 gossip magazine *Confidential* published a salacious piece claiming that O'Hara was caught in flagrante with a 'Latin lover' (presumed to mean Parra) in the back row of famed Hollywood cinema, Grauman's Chinese Theater. O'Hara sued the magazine for libel, leading to a high-profile case that was ultimately settled out of court in July 1958 for an undisclosed amount. *Confidential* went out of business shortly thereafter.

After Parra, O'Hara began a relationship with the world-renowned pilot Charles Blair and the two married on 12 March 1968. The couple moved to St Croix in the US Virgin Islands where Blair established a new inter-island airline. O'Hara completed three further films before retiring from the film business: the unsuccessful *How do I love thee?* (1969) with Jackie Gleason; the better performing but still underwhelming, *Big Jake* (1970), her last film with John Wayne; and a made-for-television western, *The red pony* (1973), with Henry Fonda, which she considered among her best performances. She happily left the limelight behind. As well as helping her husband with his business, in 1976 she became publisher of the magazine *Virgin Islander*: 'Life with Charlie on that island had brought me more happiness and joy than all my days in Hollywood ever had' (*'Tis herself*, 265). The couple also bought 'Lugdine' a house in Glengarriff, West Cork, as their Irish bolthole.

In spring 1978 O'Hara was diagnosed with uterine cancer, and after treatment in Los Angeles travelled to

Lugdine with her sister Florrie to recuperate. Blair visited her there but was called away to work, and shortly after was killed in a plane accident. O'Hara was devastated and also suspicious about the circumstances surrounding her husband's death. She believed that his airline, which employed a number of ex-military men, also completed reconnaissance flights over Cuba and that there was perhaps some connection between this activity and his death. The following year in 1979 she lost her closest friend, John Wayne, to cancer.

Following these losses, O'Hara sold the airline (she became president after her husband's death) and magazine, and divided her time between St Croix, Los Angeles and New York, with summers in Glengarriff, where she established the annual General Charles F. Blair and Maureen O'Hara Golf Classic and the Maureen O'Hara Foundation, which focused on film studies. In late 1989, while in New York, she suffered a series of heart attacks and underwent emergency surgery. After making a full recovery, the next year, her seventieth, she returned to the screen as the tough Irish mother to John Candy's character in the well-received *Only the lonely* (1990). Over the following ten years she made a further three popular made-for-television films.

In 2004 Maureen O'Hara published her memoir *'Tis herself* with the assistance of her manager John Nicoletti. In it she depicts herself as a contradictory figure: a tough dame frequently cowed by the men in her life: her first two husbands, John Ford, various film executives. It is peppered with salacious gossip and stories of how she was frequently exploited, betrayed or disappointed by the movie world: a Hollywood story.

After suffering a stroke in 2005 she made Glengarriff her permanent home, and in 2006 power of attorney was granted to her personal assistant, Carolyn Murphy. In 2012 her family and social services responded to accusations that she was being forced to make too many public appearances while in poor health, and that her funds were being misappropriated. At the time O'Hara was suffering short-term memory loss, as well as Type 2 diabetes, and using a wheelchair. The FitzSimons family decided to move the then ninety-two-year-old O'Hara from Cork to Idaho, to be looked after by her grandson, Conor, while a legal battle was waged over power of attorney; a defamation suit was brought by Carolyn Murphy against O'Hara's nephew Charlie FitzSimons. He would ultimately have to pay damages and apologise to Murphy, who he had accused of financial misconduct. In May 2013 O'Hara made a rare public appearance in Winterset, Iowa, for the ground breaking for the new John Wayne Birthplace Museum. The following year, the ninety-four-year-old O'Hara finally received an Oscar in recognition of her long film career.

On 24 October 2015, at her home in Boise, Idaho, aged ninety-five, Maureen O'Hara died in her sleep from natural causes. She is buried at Arlington National Cemetery in Virginia with her late husband Charles Blair. She was survived by her daughter Bronwyn, her grandson Conor FitzSimons (b. 1970) and two great-grandchildren. Bronwyn FitzSimons died in May 2016 in Glengarriff, aged seventy-one.

O'Hara was awarded various honorary accolades over the years. In 1960 she received a star on the Hollywood Walk of Fame, at 7004 Hollywood Boulevard; in 1988 she was awarded an honorary degree by the National University of Ireland, Galway; in 1993 she became a fellow of the British Film Institute and in 2004 she received a lifetime achievement award from the Irish Film and Television Academy; in 2005 she was named 'Irish American of the year' by *Irish America* magazine and was inducted into its hall of fame in 2011; in 2012 she received the freedom of the town of Kells, Co. Meath, where he father had been born, and a sculpture in her honour was unveiled there. She herself was most proud of her dual citizenship, having become the first American citizen to have the nationality 'Irish' as opposed to 'English' recognised in her citizenship paperwork (after a fight); of being the first female president of a scheduled airline company; and of being grand marshal of New York City's St Patrick's Day parade in 1999. Above all, she was proudest of her portrayal of Mary Kate Danaher in *The quiet man*.

In 2020 Maureen O'Hara was rated the top Irish actor of all time by the film critics of *The Irish Times*.

Liz Evers

Sources

General Registry Office (birth certificate); *This is your life*, Ralph Edwards Productions, 27 March 1957; Maureen O'Hara with John Nicoletti, *'Tis herself* (2004); 'Hall of fame 2011: Maureen O'Hara, star of the silver screen', *Irish America*, https://irishamerica.com/2011/01/maureen-ohara/ (accessed 29 April 2021); *Irish Central*, 9 May 2012, https://www.irishcentral.com/ (accessed 29 April 2021); *Irish Examiner*, 21 September 2012; Aubrey Malone, *Maureen O'Hara: the biography* (2013); *Chicago Tribune*, 22 May 2013; *Los Angeles Magazine*, 5 November 2014; *BBC News*, 17 November 2014; *The Irish Times*, 24 October 2015; 27 May 2016; 13 June 2020; *Los Angeles Times*, 24 October 2015; *New York Times*, 24 October 2015; 'Maureen O'Hara and the *Confidential* magazine trial (Fake news: fact-checking Hollywood Babylon)', *You must remember this* (podcast), episode 18, 21 January 2019; 'Maureen O'Hara', Internet Movie Database, www.imdb.com (accessed 29 April 2021); 'Maureen O'Hara', Hollywood Walk of Fame, https://walkof-fame.com/maureen-ohara/ (accessed 29 April 2021); June Parker Beck, 'Maureen O'Hara', *Women's Museum of Ireland*, https://womensmuseumofireland.ie/articles/maureen-o-hara (accessed 29 April 2021)

5. Lives in medicine, science and technology

Introduction

America has always been a place of innovation and invention, and interesting Irish figures have produced significant work in the fields of American medicine, science and technology. These include John Roach (1813–87), known as the 'father of iron shipbuilding in America', who constructed the Harlem Bridge; William Robinson (1840–1921), inventor of the track circuit used in railways throughout the world; John Forrest Kelly (1859–1922), a pioneer of alternating current; William James MacNeven (1763–1841) who, aside from his political activities, is considered the founding figure of American chemistry; and Robert Adrain (1775–1843), one of the foremost mathematicians of his age.

The men and women we have included in this selection contributed to making America, and the world, safer, faster, more technologically advanced and more equitable. James Logan (1674–1751, p. 148) was one of the leading intellectual scientists of his time particularly in the area of botany, however, his most important contribution was not his own research but his role as advisor to others, in particular Benjamin Franklin. John Crawford (1746–1813, p. 151) was a pioneer of the theory of insect-borne disease, something that earned him the scorn of fellow-doctors who believed illness was spread by miasma ('bad air'). He promoted hygiene in the sickroom and was one of the first doctors in America to vaccinate a patient against smallpox. Also in the field of medicine, Gertrude Brice Kelly (1862–1934, p. 162) was one of the first female surgeons in New

York and was politically active on behalf of workers, the cause of Irish independence and universal suffrage.

In the field of technology and science two names stand out: John Philip Holland (1841–1914, p. 157) and Kay McNulty (1921–2006, p. 166). Holland's initial designs for a submarine were rejected by the US navy as the 'fantastic schemes of a landsman', but he eventually succeeded, delivering the prototype for the navy's submarine fleet. McNulty helped to revolutionise modern technology when she and four other women were selected to work on the brand new 'ENIAC' machine in 1945, devising processing routines that established the ways in which artificial intelligence subsequently developed. McNulty is also credited with suggesting the concept of subroutines enabling logical circuits to carry more capacity, though she was not given credit for her work at the time.

NG

James Logan

1674–1751

Public servant and
scientist renowned
for his expertise in
mathematics, natural
history and astronomy,
his library was among
the finest in pre-
independence America.

James Logan was born 20 October 1674 at Lurgan, Co. Armagh, son of Patrick Logan, a schoolmaster and former Church of Scotland clergyman who became a Quaker, and his wife, Isabel Logan (née Hume)—both had moved to Ireland from Scotland to avoid persecution. Educated initially by his father, James Logan was largely self-taught and read voraciously throughout his life. He served a brief apprenticeship with Richard Webb, a Dublin linen merchant, before his family fled back to Scotland during the Jacobite wars. In 1690 his family moved to Bristol and in 1694 he was put in charge of the Friar Meeting House Quaker school there, replacing his father who returned to Ireland. Around 1697–9 Logan attempted to work in the linen trade again, when the Quaker leader William Penn invited him to accompany him to America. His brother William Logan (1686–1757) remained in Bristol where he became a physician; he corresponded regularly with James on scientific matters.

Settled in America, Logan became involved in the fur trade in 1711, using methods that were certainly unscrupulous and bordered on the illegal: he sold rum to Native Americans and left many fur traders in debt. As Penn's secretary, he was closely involved in many of the details of the settlement of Pennsylvania. He was a respected figure in his own right, serving as secretary of the province and clerk of the provincial council of Pennsylvania (1701–17). Other prominent offices followed: he served as mayor of Philadelphia (1722–3), was a chief justice in the supreme court of Pennsylvania (1731–9) and was acting governor of Pennsylvania (1736–7). He was also a founding trustee of the College of Philadelphia, the predecessor of the University of Pennsylvania. Throughout his life he continued to represent the interests of William Penn and his heirs as administrator, lawyer and merchant.

Through his investments in land, and his trade with Native Americans, with whom he was always on good terms despite his practices, Logan became very wealthy. A well-read man, he had an extensive library, and was recognised for his expertise in mathematics, natural history and astronomy. He published numerous scholarly papers on optics and botany, and his pioneering work on the pollination of plants, begun in 1727, marked a breakthrough in plant hybridisation as he recognised that maize reproduced sexually. His most important scientific contribution, however, was not his own research but his role as advisor to others. He tutored the American botanist John Bartram in Latin and introduced him to the famous Swedish botanist Linnaeus. He also advised Benjamin Franklin in his research.

On 9 December 1714 he married Sarah Read, the daughter of Charles Read, a merchant; they had five children. He died 31 October 1751, at Germantown, Pennsylvania. Aristocratic in bearing, and in outlook, Logan is recognised as the leading intellectual scientist of his time. In 1742 he decided to bequeath his vast library to the public, and this request was carried out by his son, James, after his death. First housed at the Bibliotheca Loganiana, the 2,184 volumes are now stored at the Library Company of Philadelphia and are recognised as the finest collection assembled in pre-independence America. Logan's eldest son, William (1718–76), succeeded him as the Penn family advisor.

Patrick M. Geoghegan

Sources

Dictionary of national biography (1885–1901); *Dictionary of American biography* (1928–58); F. B. Tolles, *James Logan and the culture of provincial America* (1957); *Dictionary of scientific biography* (1973); Edwin Wolf II, *The library of James Logan of Philadelphia* (1974); C. A. Elliott, *Biographical dictionary of American science* (1979); Arthur Raistrick, *Quakers in science and industry* (1993)

John Crawford

1746–1813

A pioneer of the theory
of insect-borne disease,
and one of two doctors
who introduced the
smallpox vaccination
into America.

John Crawford was born 3 May 1746 at Ballytromery near Crumlin, Co. Antrim, second son among six children, four boys and two girls, of Thomas Crawford, Presbyterian minister and farmer, and Anne Crawford (née Mackay). Thomas Crawford was the son and grandson of Presbyterian divines noted in their day and was minister in Crumlin from 1724 until his death in 1782.

John Crawford was educated locally, perhaps by his father; he is said to have attended lectures at Trinity College Dublin from about the age of seventeen, but an assertion that he graduated there is unconfirmed. He was probably apprenticed to a Dublin doctor, and between 1772 and 1774 he was surgeon on board the East India Company ship *Marquis of Rockingham* on voyages to Bombay and Bengal; he seems also to have visited China and Saint Helena. In 1772 he published an account of a liver disease fatal in hot climates, which may have been beriberi. He possibly visited Ireland in 1778; around that time he married Mary, daughter of John O'Donnell and Barbara O'Donnell (née Anderson) of Trough, on the border of Co. Clare and Co. Limerick. It is possible that he met her through knowing her brothers in the East India Company: John O'Donnell had an adventurous career in the east before becoming a very prominent merchant in Baltimore, Maryland, and Henry Anderson O'Donnell (b. 1758) married a Persian princess.

Crawford and his wife went to Barbados on his appointment as surgeon to the hospital there. When a hurricane devastated the island in 1780, Crawford could have made a great deal of money from his surviving supplies of food and medicine, but instead gave them away to those in need. His health broke down due to overwork and exposure, and in 1782 he and his wife and two small children travelled to England on furlough, but his wife died on the voyage. Crawford was forced to leave his children behind in England when he returned to Barbados in 1786. In 1790 he became surgeon-major in Demerara, then a Dutch colony, and in 1794, on a visit to Europe, he took his Doctor of Medicine degree in the Dutch university of Leiden; the university of St Andrews had granted him the degree of Doctor of Medicine in 1791.

John O'Donnell, Crawford's brother-in-law, suggested that he and his children should settle in Baltimore, Maryland, and in 1796 he moved there. He found himself among 'more of the branches of the families amidst of which I was born than I have ever seen since I left my native country' (quoted in Wilson, 1942), and was made most welcome. He was friendly with the famous doctor Benjamin Rush, and established a good practice. He enthusiastically studied the natural history of his new environment, as he had done in the tropics; he had a wide knowledge of botany and entomology. Even before 1794, when he discussed his ideas with the medical faculty in Leiden, he had come to the conclusion that insects at various stages of their lifecycles could be vectors of diseases in humans. This had been suggested in outline by earlier authors, but a theory of the role of 'animalculae' in the spread of disease had never found any backing, as it was contrary to the then generally accepted doctrine that fevers and agues resulted from exposure to miasma or from simple contagion. Crawford was first to suggest that insects were involved in the spread of yellow fever. Other medical men poured scorn on his novel ideas, and his practice and reputation suffered.

In 1804 Crawford started publishing a weekly magazine, the *Companion and Weekly Miscellany*, using the pseudonym of Edward Easy, and in 1806 transferred the editorship to his daughter Eliza, who thus became the second woman editor in the United States. In this weekly, retitled *The Observer and Repertory*..., he published during 1806–7 his 'Theory and application to the treatment of disease'. Some notice was taken of his ideas, but he found no adherents. Even in 1811, when he planned a course of lectures on the cause and treatment of diseases, he was not hopeful of convincing his opponents. He wrote to Benjamin Rush that

> my situation can not be made worse by it... My contemporaries may not thank me for the attempt; I know they will not: my great aim is to do good, and I leave the issue to him from whom I have received what I have (quoted in Wilson),

and in the published version of the only lecture that is known to have been delivered he pledged that as long as 'life and health remain, I shall devote myself strictly to the performance of my duty'. A number of palliative and curative measures for use in epidemic diseases, involving *inter alia* rigorous hygiene of the sickroom, were suggested by Crawford on the basis of his theory; some are now established as routine medical practice, though his opposition to any idea of contagion as a means of infection diminishes a few of his recommendations.

As well as his importance as a pioneer of a theory of insect-borne disease, Crawford is recognised as one of the two doctors who first introduced vaccination against smallpox into America. In the summer of 1800, at the same time as Benjamin Waterhouse was also experimenting with cowpox, Crawford received vaccine from London, and apparently successfully vaccinated at least one person. He published nothing on his vaccination work, but rejoiced in 1807 that smallpox had been rendered nearly harmless by the new technique. Crawford was involved with other projects to benefit his fellow citizens in Baltimore: he was one of the founders of Baltimore Library (1798) and of a Society for the Promotion of Useful Knowledge (1800) in the city. He helped to establish a dispensary in Baltimore (1801) and a state penitentiary, and suggested improvements in training military and naval medical men. He was consulting physician to the Baltimore hospital, an examiner in the Baltimore medical faculty, and briefly (1812) held a lectureship in natural history in Baltimore Medical College. He was prominent in the city's Hibernian Society, and was grand master of the Masonic order in Maryland in every year but one from 1801 until his death, which took place on 9 May 1813. He was buried with Masonic honours in Westminster Presbyterian graveyard in Baltimore. Crawford's valuable and important library was bought by the University of Maryland at auction in 1813. The first major book purchase of that institution, it forms the nucleus of what is now known as the Health Sciences and Human Services Library.

Crawford's daughter Eliza survived him. She too had led an adventurous life, having travelled to France as companion to Elizabeth Patterson (1785–1879), first wife of Jérôme Bonaparte (1784–1860). She married first Henry Anderson, probably a relative, then left him and married secondly Maximilian Godefroy, a noted architect. Crawford lived with them from their marriage (1799) until his death. He and his daughter are described by Elizabeth McCalmont (née Barklie) of Larne, Co. Antrim, in memoirs published by Francis J. Bigger. Crawford's son seems to have trained in medicine in London, but may have died of consumption before his father.

Linde Lunney

Sources

F. J. Bigger, *The Magees of Belfast and Dublin, printers* (1916), 33; *Dictionary of American biography* (1928–58); John Rathbone Oliver, 'An unpublished autograph letter from Dr John Crawford (1746–1813) to General William Henry Winder (1775–1824)', *Bulletin of the Institute of the History of Medicine*, iv (1930), 145–51; Julia E. Wilson, 'An early Baltimore physician and his medical library', *Annals of Medical History*, 3rd series, iv (1942), 63–80; Burke, *A genealogical and heraldic history of the landed gentry of Ireland* (4th edition, 1958), 186, 533; Davis Coakley, *Irish masters of medicine* (1992), 47–54; *American national biography* (1999); 'John Crawford 1746–1813', website of Health Sciences and Human Services Library, University of Maryland, www.hshsl.umaryland.edu/resources/historical/crawford/ (accessed October 2020)

This entry has been abridged for publication. The full version is available at www.dib.ie.

John Philip Holland

1841–1914

Inventor of the submarine, his first prototype was funded by America-based Clan na Gael and nicknamed the 'Fenian ram'.

John Philip Holland was born 24 February 1841 at Castle Street, Liscannor, Co. Clare, son of John Holland, a coast guard officer, and his second wife, Mary (née Scanlon). He was educated at St Macreehy's national school, Liscannor, and by the Christian Brothers in Limerick, where his family moved in 1853 after his father's death. During his childhood, a younger brother and two uncles also died.

In June 1858 he entered the Christian Brothers and trained to be a schoolteacher. For many years he taught at schools in Cork, Maryborough (Portlaoise), Co. Laois, Enniscorthy, Co. Wexford, and Drogheda, Co. Louth, becoming known as a maths teacher. Because of ill health, on 26 May 1873 he received a dispensation from the order, releasing him from his initial vows. Sailing for America, he lived first in Boston with his younger brother Michael, a member of the American Fenian Brotherhood who had left for America a few years earlier along with his mother, an elder brother and a sister.

Moving to New Jersey, he became a teacher in a Catholic school in Paterson and continued the experiments that he had begun in Drogheda on the concept of a submarine; a term apparently first coined by Holland himself. His initial interest in the idea stemmed from reading about a pioneering battle between ironclad ships during the US civil war. In February 1875 he offered his patent to the US Navy, but they at first rejected it as 'a fantastic scheme of a civilian landsman'.

In 1876, through his brother Michael's association with Jeremiah O'Donovan Rossa, Holland was introduced to Fenian leaders John J. Breslin and John Devoy. Considering that Britain's mastery of the seas was a great obstacle to Irish independence, Devoy convinced Clan na Gael to use their 'skirmishing fund' to finance Holland's experiments, although there is no evidence that Holland ever joined the revolutionary organisation. With the assistance of Breslin, he gave up teaching in 1876 and worked steadily on the project, mostly at Delamater Iron Works, West 14th Street, New York. He produced his first model, the *Holland I*, in 1878. It was a one-man, 14ft craft, powered by a two-cylinder engine. In summer 1881 he produced a more advanced model, which was 32ft long and could hold a crew of three. A journalist for the *New York Sun* nicknamed this model the 'Fenian ram' and described it as a 'wrecking boat'. It was successfully launched but defective riveting made it unseaworthy when submerged for long periods. Refining his plan, Holland launched a third vessel the following year that weighed nineteen tons. This was capable of prolonged submersion but developed engine problems, and further testing was prevented by its failure to comply with the New York Harbour Board's shipping laws. During 1883 this model was brought to New Haven, Connecticut, where it was kept in storage after its use was forbidden. Later, it was exhibited by Clan na Gael at a bazaar at Madison Square Gardens to raise funds for the families of the 1916 rebels, and then donated to the naval school at Fordham University, New York, before its ultimate relocation to the Paterson Museum in New Jersey.

The total cost of Holland's experiments had been nearly $60,000 and legal issues had also arisen. The Clan therefore tried to assume exclusive ownership of the models, much to the annoyance of Holland who parted their company and began to conduct his experiments privately.

Supported by Edmund L. G. Zalinski, an American military engineer and inventor, Holland developed a fourth vessel, the *Zalinski*, which proved seaworthy but unattractive to investors. Thereafter Holland was forced to work as an engineer to earn a living until financial assistance from E. B. Frost, a wealthy lawyer, allowed him to set up the John P. Holland Torpedo Boat Company in 1893. Two years later, it was contracted by the US Navy to build a submarine, the *Plunger*. This project, however, was dominated by the navy's own engineers who largely ignored Holland's advice. The *Plunger*'s poor manoeuvrability led to it being scrapped by the navy. Holland returned to working on his own design and in 1897 launched the *Holland VI*. This model, which was 53ft long and could hold a crew of six, performed well in tests. It proved capable of reaching speeds of up to 9 knots, diving to a depth of 60ft, and remaining submerged for 40 hours. Utilising compressed air technology, it was armed with a torpedo launcher and an underwater cannon. In April 1900 the US Navy agreed to purchase it for $150,000 and commissioned Holland to build several more. It was named the USS *Holland* and became the prototype for the US Navy's submarine fleet as well as for other forces throughout the world. In 1901, despite Holland's personal reservations, the navy's Electric Boat Company sold the plans to the British admiralty, leading to its creation of the Holland-class submarine. Holland continued to work on improvements to his basic model. In 1910, shortly after his retirement from the submarine business, he was decorated by the emperor of Japan for his work on behalf of the Japanese navy.

A man of considerable versatility and ingenuity, he also worked on developing a viable motor-truck and was an amateur astronomer and musician. He married (January 1887) Margaret Foley, daughter of an Irish immigrant; they had five children. In late 1911, the death of his daughter Julia in her nineteenth year affected him badly.

His own death on 12 August 1914 at 38 Newton Street, Newark, New Jersey, coincided with the start of the first world war, during which the devastating military potential of the submarine was amply demonstrated. He was buried at the Holy Sepulchre cemetery, Paterson, New Jersey.

To mark the centenary of his death a monument was erected, with the support of the Irish Maritime Institute, on the site of the school in which he taught in Drogheda, during a ceremony that was attended by representatives of the American, British and Japanese navies. A limited-edition commemorative coin was also issued by the Central Bank of Ireland, while the school in which he taught in New Jersey was renamed in his honour and a centre dedicated to his life was created in his birthplace of Liscannor.

Aidan Breen and Owen McGee

Sources

Gaelic American, 9, 16 July 1927; D. J. Doyle, 'The Holland submarine', *An Cosantóir*, vii (June 1947), 297–302; William O'Brien and Desmond Ryan (eds), *Devoy's post bag* (2 vols, 1948, 1953), i: 470–1, ii: 514–6, 189, 234, 306–7; Richard K. Morris, *John P. Holland, inventor of the modern submarine: 1841–1914* (1966); Richard K. Morris, 'John P. Holland and the Fenians', *Journal of the Galway Archaeological and Historical Society*, xxxi, nos 1–2 (1964–5), 25–38 (further bibliography, 37–8); J. de Courcy Ireland, 'John Philip Holland: pioneer in submarine navigation', *North Munster Antiquarian Journal*, x, no. 2 (1967), 206–12; K. R. M. Short, *The dynamite war* (1979), 36–7, 168–70; *American national biography* (1999); *Drogheda Independent*, 28 August 2014

Gertrude Brice Kelly

1862–1934

A forgotten radical,
she was one of New
York's first female
surgeons, and a
passionate agitator
for Irish independence.

Gertrude Brice Kelly was born 10 February 1862 near Waterford to Jeremiah Kelly and Kate Kelly (née Forrest), both of whom were teachers and supporters of the movement for Irish independence. She was one of ten children, including notable scientist and political activist John Forrest Kelly (1859–1922), a pioneer of alternating current in electricity. While the family was living in Clonmel, Co. Tipperary, Jeremiah Kelly's involvement in the Fenian movement apparently forced him to emigrate to the United States to escape possible prosecution. His wife and children followed him (1873), and they settled in Hoboken, New Jersey, where Jeremiah became superintendent of schools.

Gertrude Brice Kelly followed her parents into education and became a school principal in New Jersey when still very young. She left teaching to enter the Women's Medical College in New York, and became a demonstrator in anatomy and later a well-regarded surgeon, one of the first female surgeons in the city. She worked in the slums of Newark, New Jersey, and in the tenements of New York's Lower East Side, where she frequently assisted poor patients. Her experience of the poverty and deprivation of the area undoubtedly contributed to the development of her radical political views.

She has been described as a very important but 'forgotten feminist' (McElroy), and while she may have been forgotten, she herself might have regarded the term 'feminist' as too limiting a description of her beliefs. She and her brother John Forrest Kelly were major contributors to the journal *Liberty*. Its founding editor claimed she was one of the most important writers of the movement; Kelly later published a good deal elsewhere in support of natural law beliefs, which were no longer acceptable in *Liberty*, and she supported anarchists such as the Russian prince Kropotkin. She was also an impassioned advocate of Irish independence; in 1914 a donation was accompanied by the hope that it would purchase '$100 worth of bullets for the friends of Queen Mary who may try to defeat the cause of political liberty' (*New York Times*). She was prominent in the efforts to free Jim Larkin from Sing Sing prison, and was president of Cumann na mBan in New York, and of the United Irishwomen. She was friendly with many republicans, including Éamon de Valera, and with Hannah Sheehy Skeffington. Kelly and Sheehy Skeffington both spoke at a meeting in New York on 23 November 1922, when Irish republicans joined forces with the Friends of Freedom for India. She supported other struggling nationalist groups, and with her brother John, 'during the war time was a thorn in the side of the slavish American government' (Magennis, 342).

She was involved on many occasions with pickets and public protests; though in general she escaped arrest because of her popularity as a medical charity worker, she was arrested in December 1919 after a protest about the continued imprisonment of anti-war activists. She and Muriel MacSwiney organised a picket in January 1923 to try to take over the Irish consulate in New York as a protest against the recently established Free State in Ireland. She was injured in a car accident and was an invalid for four years before her death in New York on 16 February 1934. The Irish government was represented at her funeral in Corpus Christi church on 18 February. Two years later, a playground named in her honour was opened by the mayor of New York, Fiorello La Guardia.

James Lunney and Linde Lunney

Sources

New York Times, 17 February 1934; P. E. Magennis, 'One of the faithful few passes', *Catholic Bulletin* (April 1934), 339–43; Joanne Mooney Eichacker, *Irish republican women in America: lecture tours 1916–1925* (2003), 47, 59, 171; Wendy McElroy, 'Gertrude B. Kelly: a forgotten feminist', *Individualist feminism of the nineteenth century. Collected writings and biographical profiles* (2001); Wendy McElroy, 'The non-absurdity of Natural Law', Foundation for economic education website, 1 February 1998 (https://fee.org/articles/the-non-absurdity-of-natural-law/, accessed October 2020); information and assistance (May 2005) from Catherine M. Burns, doctoral student at University of Wisconsin–Madison

Kay McNulty

1921–2006

A pioneering computer programmer whose work helped develop the first general purpose electronic digital computer.

Kathleen Rita ('Kay') McNulty (1921–2006) was born 12 February 1921 in the townland of Feymore, Creeslough, Co. Donegal, the third of six children (three boys and three girls) of James McNulty (1890–1977) and his wife Anne or Annie (née Nelis). Around 1908 James McNulty emigrated from Creeslough to Philadelphia and trained as a stonemason. He returned to Creeslough in 1915 to take part in the struggle for Irish independence and finally returned to Philadelphia in 1923 to join a brother in a construction business; his wife and family, including the infant Kay, followed him to America in October 1924. He was successful in his business, working with John B. Kelly, father of actress Grace Kelly, and was involved in the construction of important government buildings.

The McNulty household in Chestnut Hill, Philadelphia, was Irish-speaking, and Kay first learned English from her two older brothers. She attended the parish grade school and then Hallahan Catholic Girls' High School, where she was an excellent student. Chestnut Hill College offered her a scholarship, and she graduated in spring 1942, having majored in mathematics. By then the US army had a pressing need for mathematicians to produce ballistics calculations and, with a scarcity of trained men, McNulty was one of a number of women taken on to work as 'computers' at the Moore School of Electrical Engineering at the University of Pennsylvania.

Calculating missile trajectories, using the desk calculators and tables then available, took each woman about forty hours, and hundreds of such calculations were required. McNulty and another woman were trained to use a recently-built differential analyser machine (an analogue device, reliant on mechanical operations), which speeded up calculations. A much more sophisticated machine, designed on quite novel principles, using electrical circuits to execute calculations, was being developed in great haste at the army's Aberdeen Proving Ground in Maryland. In June 1945 McNulty was one of five women selected to work on this room-sized ENIAC (Electronic Numerical Integrator and Computer). For the next few months, the women collaborated with the engineers who were still working on the design and construction of ENIAC; there were no manuals, only design blueprints, as the machine was still incomplete. McNulty and others devised the processing routines that enabled the machine to carry out calculations, more or less establishing the ways in which artificial intelligence subsequently developed. ENIAC had no memory capabilities: its programmes had to be input manually, using punch cards and realigning wiring and switches, for each calculation. McNulty is credited with suggesting the concept of subroutines, in which the master programmer element of the instructions to the machine was set to trigger the reuse of sections of code, enabling the logical circuits to carry more capacity. Once they began to perform calculations on the actual machine, McNulty and her colleagues became expert in diagnosing problems and finding where the machine's physical wiring or some of the 17,468 vacuum tubes or 5,000,000 hand-soldered connections had failed, as they did at first every few hours.

The public launch of the ENIAC machine as the first general-purpose electronic digital computer took place on 15 February 1946, causing great excitement in the scientific and business communities, as the potential importance of such machines was already evident. The event, however, relegated the women programmers to the role of hostesses, and official reports and early histories of computing made no mention of female operators. Tellingly, as mid-century America reversed the gains made in wartime by women in employment, science and public engagement, some contemporary observers even regarded the women in the project as 'refrigerator ladies': models employed to stand elegantly in front of machines that they did not understand. Even in 1986, five of the women who had first programmed the 'beast' were not invited to the fortieth anniversary celebration of the birth of the electronic computing age. Kay McNulty was there, and gave an address, but did so as the widow of one of the men who had developed ENIAC. Only as the 1980s ended was the women's contribution to the development of computer systems acknowledged and celebrated.

On 7 February 1948 Kay McNulty married John Mauchly. Her parents were not present, and were deeply upset by her decision to marry a non-Catholic, fourteen years her senior, who had a son and a daughter by a first marriage. John Mauchly was one of the engineers chiefly responsible for designing the hardware of ENIAC; his first wife, also a gifted mathematician, had worked with him, but drowned while on holiday in 1946. Mauchly was also suffering chronic illness, hereditary haemorrhagic telangiectasia (which all but one of his and Kay's five children inherited), necessitating constant vigilance and frequent hospitalisation; he later developed diabetes.

Until her marriage, McNulty had continued to work on ENIAC through 1947 and 1948, testing the device during its re-assembly after a move to the Aberdeen Proving Ground. It is possible she was also involved in its development into a machine with a rudimentary capacity to store an operating system. In her autobiography, Kay noted without comment that her new husband gave her a cookbook on their honeymoon, and that she was thereafter expected to be the family cook; she left paid scientific work on her marriage.

McNulty's possible contribution to developing technology and information systems after her years on ENIAC is now difficult to trace. She may have provided some suggestions in discussions of her husband's pioneering work on the first computer designed for commercial use, UNIVAC, built by his company, Eckart-Mauchly. The couple were, however, increasingly preoccupied by legal tussles over patents (which they lost) and difficulties with Mauchly's security clearance, and spent considerable time in disputes with former colleagues and attempts to establish companies and new projects. For the rest of her life, Kay was bitter about how the industry and the government treated her husband, and ardently defended his work and his claims to priority in the computer revolution. In 2002, she was able to accept John Mauchly's posthumous induction into the National Inventors Hall of Fame.

Kay and John Mauchly had four daughters and a son. While rearing her children, she volunteered in youth and church organisations and did some supply teaching in elementary schools. John Mauchly died on 8 January 1980. Kay married again on 27 December 1985; her second husband was a successful, Italian-born photographer, Severo Antonelli. Her years with him were busy and enjoyable, with travel and social engagements, until he developed Parkinson's disease. He died after two difficult years on 14 December 1995.

In her latter years, Kay McNulty Mauchly Antonelli was lionised as one of the invisible women scientists rediscovered in the late twentieth century, and she developed considerable skills of communication and presentation as she was sought out to attend conferences and functions to discuss and record the role of the women pioneers of information science. Her memoir captures some of the excitement of the wartime work for which she became famous. In April 1999 she and an ENIAC colleague went on a lecture tour in Ireland, and were filmed for a feature documentary, *Oh Kay computer* (1999). She revisited Creeslough for the first time since 1924, and met many of her relatives there. During her visit, a prize for the best student in computer science was established in her honour at Letterkenny Institute of Technology.

In 1997 she and her five female colleagues were inducted into the Women in Technology Hall of Fame. After suffering from cancer, she died on 20 April 2006 in Wyndmoor, Pennsylvania. A computer science building was renamed in her honour at Dublin City University in 2017.

Linde Lunney

Sources

Donegal News, 16 January 1954; 30 April 1999; *The Irish Times*, 30 November 1998; 30 April 1999; Kay McNulty Mauchly Antonelli, *The Kathleen McNulty Mauchly Antonelli Story*, 26 March 2004 (online at https://sites.google.com/a/opgate.com/eniac/Home/kay-mcnulty-mauchly-antonelli, accessed October 2020); Walter Isaacson, *The innovators* (2014); Hayley Williams, 'Invisible women: the six human computers behind the ENIAC', 10 November 2015, www.lifehacker.com.au/2015/11/invisible-women-the-six-human-computers-behind-the-eniac/ (accessed October 2020); 'Kay McNulty, ENIAC superhero', 22 August 2016, codelikeawoman.wordpress.com/2016/08/22/kay-mcnulty-eniac-superhero/ (accessed October 2020); 'Kathleen "Kay" McNulty Mauchly Antonelli', memorial no. 136819670, www.findagrave.com (accessed 29 April 2021)

This entry has been abridged for publication. The full version is available at www.dib.ie.

6. Lives of faith

Introduction

Due to the mass migration of mainly Catholic Irish to America throughout the nineteenth and early twentieth century (it is estimated that nearly half of all immigrants to America in the 1840s were Irish), 'Irish American' has become synonymous with 'Irish Catholic', but this does not account for the significant earlier migrations of non-Catholic Irish to America, from Ulster in particular. Those migrants represented a much broader spectrum of Christianity and helped shape the religious culture of the early colonies, in particular in the different forms of Presbyterianism, as well as the Methodism, Quakerism and Anglicanism, they brought. While we cannot represent them all in this short chapter, we can direct you to the Dictionary of Irish Biography–Ulster Historical Foundation publication, *Transatlantic lives: the Irish experience in colonial America* for a deeper insight into the religious diversity of early emigrants from Ireland to America, when Catholicism was still a minority religion in the colonies.

In our six selected biographies in this chapter, we present three such Irish emigrants who played a foundational role in their respective religious traditions: the Methodist preacher Philip Embury (1728–73, p. 176), who built America's first Wesleyan church at John's Street, New York, and a joint entry for father and son Thomas and Alexander Campbell (1763–1854 and 1788–1866, p. 180), leaders of the 'restoration movement', who together founded a sect broadly titled the Christian Church. The Church has over 3,000 congregations in the United States today.

Among our Catholic contingent, we include Mary O'Connell (Sister Anthony) (1814–97, p. 189), known as 'the Florence Nightingale of America', who saved countless lives in field hospitals during the civil war; and Father Patrick Peyton (1909–92, p. 192), the superstar 'Rosary Priest' who held massive rosary rallies across the country, reinvigorating mid-twentieth-century American Catholicism. We have also included Margaret Haughery (1813–82, p. 185), who went from working for board and lodging with the Daughters of Charity in New Orleans, to establishing several successful businesses, the profits of which she used to finance the charitable work of the sisters. She was one of the first women in America to be commemorated with a statue for her philanthropy.

LE

Philip Embury

1728–73

One of the founders of
Methodism in America
and chief instigator of the
building of the country's
first Wesleyan church.

Philip Embury was one of at least four sons and one daughter of tenant farmer Andreas Imberger, a German Palatine immigrant of 1709. Embury was baptised (29 September 1728) a member of the Church of Ireland in Ballingrane, Co. Limerick. With his cousin Barbara Heck, Embury has been credited with being one of the first properly documented founders of Methodism in America and chief instigator of the building of the first Wesleyan church in North America.

Tradition tells that Embury, a carpenter by trade, was educated in German within the Palatine community in Ballingrane and that he later attended an English school, probably in the town of Rathkeale. He may have first come in contact with John Wesley's teachings in 1749 when Philip Guier, the burgomaster of Ballingrane, established a Methodist society in his home village. Embury converted to Methodism (25 December 1752) and was licensed as a Methodist lay preacher in 1758, by which time a Methodist chapel had been erected in the centre of the village square at Courtmatrix, one of the three original County Limerick Palatine settlements near Rathkeale. Embury is reputed to have done the carpentry for this building.

Embury married Margaret Switzer (1743–1807) on 31 October 1758 in the Church of Ireland, Rathkeale, Co. Limerick. Margaret was one of eight children and the only surviving daughter of Christopher and Elizabeth Switzer, Palatine tenant farmers of Courtmatrix. Philip and Margaret Embury had six children, only two survived to adulthood: Samuel (1765–1853) and Catherine (c.1767–1831).

The Emburys were among twenty-five or more young Palatines forming a company to set up a linen business in North America. In June 1760 they left Limerick for New York on board the *Pery* and arrived on 10 August. In

New York the Emburys lived in Barrack Street and Philip worked as a teacher of reading, writing and arithmetic (in English) while they petitioned for 25,000 acres of land on which he and his friends could set up their linen and hempen manufactory. The Emburys at first attended Trinity Lutheran Church, Rector Street (later Cliff Street), New York, where the first three of their children were baptised between 1761 and 1765. In 1766 the Emburys and others of the Irish Palatine community, including Barbara Heck, became members of the new Lutheran Christ Church, built on the corner of Frankfurt Street and William Street, where Embury and Barbara's husband, Paul Heck, appear on the list of original subscribers.

Between 1760 and 1765 Paul Heck's brothers Jacob and John, and Barbara's brother, Paul Ruttle, arrived with some other Palatines from Limerick, and tradition tells that Barbara was horrified when she came across the newcomers gambling at cards, and implored Embury to preach to them. He began preaching at first in his own home to his family and friends (1766) and then, as his congregation grew, he preached in the city barracks and in a sail-rigging loft on Horse and Cart Street. He is also known to have preached in the Poor House. From 1767 onwards another Irishman, half-pay officer Captain Thomas Webb, assisted him. Dublin Methodists, Charles White and Richard Sause, joined them shortly afterwards. Embury and the other English and Irish Methodists raised subscriptions and in March 1768 purchased a lot in John Street, where they built a chapel, the design of which is said to have been drawn up by Barbara Heck who also, tradition says, whitewashed the interior. This was the first chapel in the world to be named after John Wesley. Embury is reputed to have constructed the pulpit, and he and Paul Heck also carried out other interior woodwork.

On 30 October 1768 he preached his first formal sermon there. The Emburys moved into an old Dutch-style house on the property, which was then used as a parsonage. In November 1769 Wesley sent preachers who formalised the situation and John Street chapel was transferred to Wesley's Methodist Connexion on 2 November 1770, six or seven months after Embury and his compatriots had moved to Camden Valley (present-day White Creek), Charlotte County, New York, where they had leased land from a prominent lawyer of Irish descent. Embury was appointed justice of the peace for Albany County (1770) and for Charlotte County (1772). He was also appointed one of the commissioners of roads for Charlotte County. Embury and a fellow methodist, Thomas Ashton, formed a Methodist Society at Ashgrove and a class at West Camden (1770). For the next three years he continued to preach, sometimes travelling to outlying areas to do so. He died of pleurisy in August 1773, leaving a wife and four children, and is buried in Woodland cemetery, Cambridge, New York. His oldest son Samuel later became a Methodist preacher in Upper Canada.

There are portraits of Philip and Margaret Embury dated 1773 at John Street United Methodist Church, New York.

Vivien Hick

Sources

J. B. Wakeley, *Lost chapters recovered from the early history of American Methodism* (1858); Samuel J. Fanning, 'Philip Embury, founder of Methodism in New York', *Methodist History*, iii (1965), 16–25; Eula C. Lapp, *To their heirs forever* (1977); Arthur Bruce Moss, 'Philip Embury's preaching mission at Chesterfield, New Hampshire', *Methodist History*, xvi (1978), 101–9; Arthur Bruce Moss, 'Philip Embury's Bible', *Methodist History*, xvii (1979), 253–60

Thomas Campbell

1763–1854

Alexander Campbell

1788–1866

This father and son
team were leaders of the
'restoration movement'
in America and founded
the Christian Church,
which today has 3,000-
plus congregations across
the country.

Thomas Campbell, son of a soldier, Archibald Campbell, and his wife Alice McNally, was born 1 February 1763 at Sheepbridge, Co. Down. Archibald Campbell was born Catholic but joined the Church of Ireland, while his son joined the seceding branch of the Presbyterian church and studied at the University of Glasgow (graduating MA in 1786, it is said, although he does not appear in the published records of the university). He became a teacher but was determined to become a minister, and studied in the Anti-Burgher Divinity Hall in Whitburn, West Lothian (or the Seceder Theological Seminary in Whithorn, Wigtownshire, according to another source) for two months each year for five years. He was ordained minister in the seceding congregation of Ahorey, Co. Armagh, probably in 1798. Although at first a member of the anti-burgher party in his church, Thomas Campbell began to believe that divisions between and within denominations were prejudicial to true Christianity. He wrote a report (1804) suggesting that burgher and anti-burgher Presbyterians in Ireland should unite; when this was vetoed in 1805 by the General Associate Synod of Scotland, Campbell (then moderator of the Irish Seceding Synod) initiated an unsuccessful move to seek independence from Scottish control. His experiences with church authorities undoubtedly increased his belief in the need to rediscover the scriptural basis of religion, freed from man-made creeds.

In 1804 Campbell set up an academy at Richhill, Co. Armagh. He was one of the founders (1798) of the Evangelical Society of Ulster in which clergymen from differing sects cooperated, but resigned when this enterprise was frowned on by seceding authorities.

In poor health in 1806, Thomas Campbell resigned from Ahorey, and went (1807) to the United States, where he preached in small congregations around Washington, Pennsylvania. He was soon accused of doctrinal unsoundness, of disciplinary laxity and of administering the sacraments to non-Presbyterians; his appeal to the Associate Synod of North America was unsuccessful, and in 1809 he ceased to be a minister of the seceder church. His liberal views on Christian unity and on the paramount importance of the bible attracted supporters, and in 1809 they founded the Christian Association of Washington. Campbell published a *Declaration and address* in which he set out the principles of this body. His followers claimed it represented a 'second reformation' or a 'restoration'; it forms the basis of the doctrine of what became America's most important indigenous religious development, and is regarded as significant in the history of the wider ecumenical movement. He published a great many other tracts and articles. Thomas Campbell died, in Bethany, West Virginia on 4 January 1854.

Thomas had married Jane Corneigle in 1787 and their eldest son Alexander was born 12 September 1788, probably near Shane's Castle, Co. Antrim, in his grandmother's house, or in Broughshane, Co. Antrim, where his father was teaching. His parents intended him for the ministry, and he received a good education, partly from his father, and religious training from both parents; he was greatly influenced by his strongminded and pious mother. In October 1808 his family set sail for America to join his father; the ship was wrecked on the island of Islay, off Scotland. All on board were saved, partly thanks to Alexander's strength and leadership. Rather than continuing the voyage by other means, Alexander spent eight months in the University of Glasgow to prepare himself for the ministry.

In the summer of 1809 the family finally arrived in Pennsylvania, among many emigrants from Ulster. On 1

January 1812 Alexander was ordained as a minister of the Christian Association, and quickly took over the leadership of the fledgling church. By 1812 most of their followers, thenceforth often called Campbellites, had undergone baptism by immersion; a union with the Baptist denomination resulted, but did not survive after 1830, by which date Campbell's work on a translation of the Greek New Testament had convinced him that baptism was unscriptural. Controversy between the two groups continued for many years.

A very able preacher and debater, whose public discussions attracted much attention, Alexander Campbell attacked the creeds and governance of established churches. In 1823 he founded the journal the *Christian Baptist*. Subsequently in 1830, after the break with the Baptists, he started the *Millennial Harbinger*. Both periodicals were largely written by Campbell and his father, Thomas, and were widely influential. He was convinced that church unity would usher in a millennial age of peace and harmony; primitive Christianity was thus to bring about a utopian future. His book *Christianity restored* (1835; then as *The Christian system* in 1839) was widely read, in Britain as well as in America. In 1826 a translation of the Greek New Testament was printed by Campbell's press in Bethany, West Virginia; largely based on recent translations by others, it nonetheless contains variant readings by Campbell and furthered his aim of providing followers with authoritative texts on which to base their beliefs. In 1841 Alexander Campbell founded Bethany College, West Virginia, and was its president until his death (in Bethany, 4 March 1866), when he left it $10,000 and a large library.

In 1832 several fledgling churches joined the Campbellites and formed a new body called the Christian Church, or Disciples of Christ, which today has over

3,000 congregations in the United States. The two guiding principles of the lifelong beliefs of the Campbells were in the end irreconcilable. An emphasis on the literal interpretation of scripture allowed believers to form beliefs at variance from those of co-religionists, and neither Alexander Campbell's great authority in the denomination nor Thomas Campbell's emphasis on the need for church unity were enough to prevent the fissions inevitable in a church that so strongly opposed man-made creeds. There are now at least six major divisions of the Church of Christ, one of several alternative names.

On 2 March 1811 Alexander Campbell married Margaret Brown, and thenceforth derived his income from the large farm that had belonged to her family. They had eight children, who all died in their father's lifetime. Margaret Brown Campbell died on 22 October 1827. On 31 July 1828, in fulfilment of his wife's dying request, the widower married the English-born Selina Huntington Bakewell, and had six children with her. Four of those children survived him; Selina Campbell wrote a memoir of her husband, published in 1882, and lived until 1897.

Linde Lunney

Sources

Robert F. West, *Alexander Campbell and natural religion* (1948); David Stewart, *The Seceders in Ireland* (1950), 233–4; David M. Thompson, 'The Irish background to Thomas Campbell's *Declaration and address*', *Journal of the United Reformed Church History Society*, iii, no. 6 (1985), 215–24; Alfred R. Scott, 'Thomas Campbell's ministry at Ahorey', *Restoration Quarterly*, iv, no. 29 (1987); *Dictionary of Scottish church history and theology* (1993); Claude Cox, 'The Campbell–Stone movement in Ontario', *Studies in American Religion*, 62 (1995); *Dictionary of evangelical biography* (1995); Eva Jean Wrather, *Alexander Campbell: adventurer in freedom, a literary biography*, vol. 1 (2005); Lester G. McAllister, *Thomas Campbell: man of the book* (1954, republished 2012)

Margaret Haughery

1813–82

This self-made businesswoman-turned-philanthropist supported orphanages in New Orleans, and was one of the first women in America commemorated with a statue.

Margaret Haughery was born on Christmas Day 1813 in Carrigallen, Co. Leitrim, fifth of six children to William Gaffney, tenant farmer, and his wife Margaret (née O'Rourke). In 1818 the Gaffneys moved with their three younger children to America, leaving the three eldest with an uncle. After a gruelling six-month journey at sea, they landed at Baltimore, Maryland, where the youngest girl died shortly afterwards. Further tragedy followed when, during the 1822 yellow fever epidemic, both of Haughery's parents succumbed to the disease. Shortly afterwards her older brother Kevin disappeared. Only nine-years-old, orphaned and alone, Haughery was taken in by a Welsh family named Richards who employed her as a domestic servant. There was no money or time for school, so she grew up illiterate.

In 1835 she married Irishman Charles Haughery and the couple had a daughter named Frances. When Charles fell ill they moved to New Orleans, but again tragedy awaited. Within a year Haughery had been widowed and her small daughter was dead. These early tragedies left her with a strong charitable drive. She never remarried but dedicated the rest of her life to the poor. After a brief period as a laundress at Saint Charles Hotel, she moved into an orphanage run by the Daughters of Charity and worked as a volunteer in exchange for food and board. Feeling she could be more useful working in the outside world, she never became a nun, although she lived with the Daughters for the next twenty-three years and financed their charity all her life.

Arranging a loan through the parish priest, she bought two cows to provide milk for the orphanage children and began selling the excess from a cart. This enabled her to buy more cows; she discovered that she had entrepreneurial ability and within a few years she owned a dairy of forty cows. Her milk cart was a daily sight in New Orleans and as she did her rounds, she begged spare vegetables for the children and collected subscriptions on their behalf. With her help, $36,000 was raised between 1838 and 1840 to build a new orphanage and in 1843 the New Orleans Female Orphan Asylum was opened, housing over one hundred orphans.

Haughery invested her money smartly and was able over the next decades to contribute to the building of new orphanages and 'houses of industry' for older children. Her only regret was that running the dairy left her little time to devote to the children; she did, however, nurse many of them through the yellow fever epidemic of 1853.

Her next major enterprise was the takeover of a failing bakery in New Levee Street. She sold her dairy and finally moved out of the orphanage into a small flat above the bakery. Hers was the first steam bakery in the southern states, and it soon extended over four buildings and employed forty people. She also co-invented a more efficient oven and created a method of packaging crackers that kept them fresh for weeks. She distributed bread to the poor, opened a soup kitchen and during the civil war forced her way through army lines to get flour, which she used to feed confederate and, occasionally, union soldiers. Despite these handouts, her business prospered, and she was respected throughout New Orleans for her acumen. Seated in her widow's weeds in the doorway of her bakery, she freely dispensed business advice. Unfailingly modest, she was amazed to receive a crucifix from Pope Pius IX.

Her death on 9 February 1882 at the Hôtel Dieu hospital was announced in specially black-edged newspapers as a public calamity. Funeral mass was celebrated in Saint

Patrick's Church and her pallbearers included the current and former governors of Louisiana, the mayor of New Orleans and the archbishop. All stores and offices were closed for the day and the city was thronged with mourners. She was buried in Saint Louis cemetery in the same plot as Sister Francis Regis Barret, the nun with whom she had started her first charity work.

Haughery's philanthropy continued after her death; she left large bequests to all the city orphanages, regardless of colour or creed, although she left the bulk of her estate to the Daughters of Charity. Her will was signed with an 'X'. The idea of erecting a statue to her memory was raised immediately, and on 9 July 1884 a marble statue by Alexander Doyle was unveiled in a small park named Margaret Place. Although not the first statue erected to a woman in the US, it is the first publicly erected one, the first monument to a female philanthropist and the only known statue of a baker. A Margaret Haughery Club was founded in New Orleans in 1948 and revived in 1992. Its members are women of Irish Catholic descent, its aims are charitable, and it also selects the New Orleans candidate for the annual 'Rose of Tralee' title.

Bridget Hourican

Sources

Catholic World, xliii, no. 853 (April 1936), 153–4; Raymond J. Martinez, *The immortal Margaret Haughery* (1956); Edward F. Murphy, *Angel of the Delta* (1958); Mary Lou Widmer, *Margaret, friend of orphans* (1996); *Catholic encyclopedia* at www.newadvent.org (accessed October 2020); *The Irish Times*, 10 February 2017

Mary O'Connell (Sister Anthony)

1814–97

Known as 'the
Florence Nightingale
of America', Sister
Anthony served
in field hospitals
during the civil war,
pioneering battlefield
triage techniques that
saved countless lives.

Mary O'Connell was born 15 August 1814 in Limerick, daughter of William O'Connell and Catherine O'Connell (née Murphy). After the death of her mother (1825), the family emigrated to America; Mary was raised by an aunt in Maine, while her father worked in Boston. Educated at the Ursuline Convent, Charlestown, Massachusetts, she entered the Sisters of Charity in Emmitsburg, Maryland (June 1835). There she took the name Sister Anthony, by which she is now remembered. Working at St Peter's orphanage, in 1852 she became a founding member of the newly independent Cincinnati Sisters of Charity. Involved in running the order's hospital, Saint John's Hospital and Hotel for Invalids (the city's first medical hospital), in 1854 she decided to train as a nurse, and the following year became head of St John's.

The outbreak of the American civil war in 1861 thrust her to national prominence. Volunteering to help the ill and wounded, she initially served at Camp Dennison near Cincinnati. Establishing a reputation as 'the Florence Nightingale of America', she pioneered battlefield triage techniques that saved countless lives. She reinforced her image as the 'angel of the battlefield' after the battle of Shiloh in April 1862, one of the bloodiest of the war, in which almost 23,000 union and confederate soldiers were wounded. Sister Anthony tended to the fallen, making no distinction between federal and rebel, black and white, Catholic and Protestant. She was present at many of the key battles in the western theatre, and served for twenty-eight months at general hospital no. 14, a field hospital in Nashville, Tennessee. Through her work as a field nurse, and her long hours on the riverboat hospitals, she befriended many leading figures, including union generals William T. Sherman and Ulysses S. Grant, as well as the confederate president, Jefferson Davis.

After the end of the war (1865) she was discharged and returned to Cincinnati. There she built a larger hospital, the Good Samaritan Hospital, which was open to all religions. In 1873, despite some controversy, she established a shelter for unwed mothers, the Saint Joseph Infant and Maternity Home. Both institutions were run by Sister Anthony until her retirement, possibly because of pressure from the local bishop, in 1880.

She died 8 December 1897 in Cincinnati and was buried at Mount Saint Joseph cemetery. Her courageous work throughout the civil war is credited with bringing about a degree of rapprochement between Catholics and Protestants in the Midwest, and her piety and devotion earned many tributes before and after her death. Praised for her extraordinary generosity and caring, she was 'reverenced alike by the blue and the grey, by Protestant and Catholic' (quoted in *American national biography*).

Patrick M. Geoghegan

Sources

Dictionary of American biography (1928–58); Sister Marie Emmanuel, 'Angel of the battlefield', *Saint Anthony Messenger* (April 1962), 8, 10–12; *Notable American women* (1971); David R. Collins and Haris Petie, *Great American nurses* (1971); Kit and Cyril Ó Céirín, *Women of Ireland: a biographic dictionary* (1996); *American national biography* (1999); Peter F. Stevens, 'Sister Mary Anthony: the Boston Irish Florence Nightingale', in *Hidden history of the Boston Irish* (2008); Michael O'Sullivan, 'Mary Ellen O'Connell—heroine of the American civil war', *Lough Gur District Historical Society Journal*, no. 15 (2009), 8–13

Patrick Peyton

1909–92

Endorsed by Hollywood's
Catholics, the 'Rosary
Priest' held massively
popular rallies across
America preaching
'the family that prays
together, stays together'.

Patrick Peyton was born 9 January 1909 in Carracastle, near Ballina, Co. Mayo, sixth of the nine children of John Peyton (1868–1934), county road repair worker, and Mary Gillard Peyton (1871–1939) of Rathreedane, Bonniconlon, Co. Mayo. Peyton was educated at Bofield and in Bonniconlon, but left school aged fifteen and returned to work on the family farm. While he was drawn to a vocation and applied to the Redemptorists, Capuchins and to the Society of African Missionaries in Cork, he lacked sufficient schooling to be admitted to the seminary. With no chance to pursue his vocation and little other opportunity for employment, Peyton and his brother Thomas sailed for America in 1928 to join their sisters who had emigrated earlier to Scranton, Pennsylvania.

Through his sister Ellen (Nellie), Peyton met Monsignor Paul Kelly, rector of Saint Peter's Cathedral, Scranton, who employed him as a sexton and encouraged him to reconsider his vocation. With Kelly's support Peyton and his brother Thomas enrolled at Saint Thomas High School in Scranton where they completed their freshman year. In early 1929 the brothers met a group of visiting priests from the Congregation of the Holy Cross and decided to continue their education at the Holy Cross Minor Seminary at Notre Dame, Indiana, enrolling there in September 1929 with the warm endorsement of Monsignor Kelly.

The brothers professed their temporary vows with Holy Cross in 1933 and commenced studying for Bachelor of Arts degrees at Notre Dame University, followed by theological studies at the Holy Cross College on the campus of the Catholic University of America in Washington, DC in 1937. In October 1938 Peyton was diagnosed with advanced tuberculosis and became seriously ill. He recovered in time to be ordained with his brother at Notre

Dame on 1 June 1941. He credited his recovery to the Virgin Mary (to whom he prayed regularly) and vowed to devote his life to restoring the custom of the family rosary.

In his first assignment as chaplain to the Holy Cross brothers and Sisters of Mercy who taught at the Vincentian Institute in Albany, New York, he enlisted student help in starting his Family Rosary organisation. Believing that radio was the best medium for a national family rosary crusade, Peyton convinced Elsie Dick, director of religious programming at the Mutual Broadcasting Company, to give him a half-hour programme. It was launched on 13 May 1945, the day President Harry S. Truman declared a day of national thanksgiving to mark the end of the war in Europe. Peyton built on that success by recruiting prominent Catholics to recite the rosary on air, including Bing Crosby and the Thomas F. Sullivan family of Waterloo, Iowa, who had lost their five sons aboard the *Juneau* at Guadalcanal (11 November 1942). Expanding his programming to radio theatre, Peyton broadcast on 13 February 1947 the drama 'Flight from home' featuring Loretta Young and Don Ameche; it was the first in a twenty-year series. He recruited other Hollywood personalities when he moved into television and film; a young James Dean made his film debut in Family Theatre's *Hill Number 1*. After Peyton completed a series of fifteen films about the mysteries of the rosary, a project largely funded by communities of American nuns, Pope Pius XII wrote to him commending him on their 'apostolic character'.

In 1947 Peyton started organising prayer rallies in support of the Rosary Crusade in the US and Canada. Through his friendship with Loretta Young and her husband Thomas H. A. Lewis, an advertising executive with Young and Rubican, Peyton met the copywriter Al

Scalpone who created the Crusade slogans 'The family that prays together, stays together' and 'A world at prayer is a world at peace'. Peyton brought his Crusade to Europe (1952, 1953), Australia (1953), Southeast Asia (1954, 1959), Africa (1955) and Latin America (1959, 1960–64). When he brought the Crusade to Ireland in 1954, the meeting in Knock drew 20,000 people. His 1985 Crusade in the Philippines attracted two million participants.

In Latin America, the Crusade had something of an anti-communist agenda. Peyton had long been outspoken against communism, which came to the notice of the CIA, through Peyton's friend and benefactor J. Peter Grace. Grace made the case that the Catholic church, through Peyton's work, could steer Latin American countries away from nascent communism and secured US government funding for the Crusades throughout the early 1960s. The Congregation of Holy Cross became worried about the Crusade's reliance on this funding and the potential reputational damage in Latin America should it become public knowledge. In 1966, after consultation with Pope Paul VI, Holy Cross officials demanded that the arrangement come to an end.

Peyton, who called himself 'Our Lady's salesman', chronicled his Crusade in his 1967 autobiography *All for her*. He had bypass surgery in 1978 for coronary artery disease, and in his later years, lived in the Little Sisters of the Poor retirement centre in San Pedro, California. He was named Mayo Man of the Year in 1987. On 15 August 1990, RTÉ aired a documentary on his life and work made during one of his visits to Mayo. He died 3 June 1992 at the age of eighty-three and was buried in the community cemetery at Stonehill College, North Easton, Massachusetts.

In October 1998 the Father Peyton Memorial Centre was opened in Attymass, Co. Mayo, to house Peyton memorabilia and photographs. In March 2019 RTÉ broadcast a documentary *Guns & rosaries*, which considered his involvement with the CIA in Latin America. *Pray: the story of Patrick Peyton,* a documentary by Family Theater Productions, was released in 2020.

Father Peyton's cause for sainthood was officially opened by Cardinal Sean Patrick O'Malley on 8 December 1992, citing his 'heroic virtues'. Pope Francis named him as 'venerable' on 18 December 2017. Richard Gribble CSC (Congregatio a Sancta Cruce), wrote Peyton's official biography, *American apostle of the family rosary, the Life of Patrick J. Peyton* (2005). Peyton's papers are at Stonehill College, Easton, Massachusetts.

Deirdre Bryan and Maureen O. Murphy

Sources

Patrick Peyton, *The ear of God* (1954); *Irish Catholic*, 11 March, 29 April, 3 May 1954; Patrick Peyton, *All for her; the autobiography of Father Patrick Peyton, CSC* (1967); Jeanne Gosselin Arnold, *A man of faith* (1983); *A world of prayer. The vision of Father Patrick Peyton* (1987), video; *RTÉ Guide*, xiv, no. 33 (10 August 1990), 8; M. Charles ('A Trappist Monk'), *Father Peyton's rosary prayer book* (1991); *Catholic Herald and Standard*, 12 June 1992; *Mayo News*, 14 October 1998; Michael Glazier (ed.), *The encyclopedia of the Irish in America* (1999); Richard Gribble, 'Anti-communism, Patrick Peyton, CSC, and the CIA', *Journal of Church and State*, Summer 2003, 535–58; Richard Gribble, *American apostle of the family rosary, the life of Patrick J. Peyton* (2005); information from Delia Ginley, director, Father Peyton Memorial Centre; 'Father Patrick Peyton CSC' website, www.fatherpeyton.org (accessed October 2020)

7. Lives of conscience

Introduction

As emigration from famine-stricken Ireland to America soared in the mid-nineteenth century, so too did anti-Irish sentiment in the country they arrived in, particularly from so-called 'nativists'. As is the experience of migrant groups the world over, past and present, these Irish arrivals experienced discrimination and cruel stereotyping, while having their labour exploited—often being underpaid and overworked—or being excluded from workplaces altogether. To counter this hostility, the Irish became adept at organising themselves: developing benevolent societies and fraternal and cultural organisations, and ultimately unionising.

The Irish were involved in the development of the labour movement in America from its beginnings in the late eighteenth century. In particular, the actions of Irish canal workers in the 1820s and 1830s (which led to the first intervention of the US Army in labour disputes) and of Pennsylvania anthracite miners from the 1840s to 1870s were influential in directing the consciousness of workers toward unionisation. Leading Irish figures in the union movement include Mary Harris Jones ('Mother Jones') (1837?–1930, p. 200) who worked tirelessly for the rights of American mine, textile and steel workers among others; and Joseph Patrick McDonnell (1846–1906, p. 212) a radical of the International, who helped develop new laws on child and convict labour and workplace safety, and first introduced Labor Day. Our selection of lives also includes Charlotte Grace O'Brien (1845–1909, p. 209) who campaigned successfully on both sides of the Atlantic for the cause of Irish emigrant women. There were also those who worked to improve the lot of African Americans and other minority groups, such as the influential John Boyle O'Reilly, editor of the Boston newspaper the *Pilot* (1844–90, p. 203), and later Paul O'Dwyer (1907–98, p. 219), one of America's leading civil-liberties and civil-rights attorneys from the 1940s to the 1970s.

Irish American history also includes many ignoble records, however. Many Irish Americans participated in the persecution of more vulnerable groups, in particular African Americans. Slave-ownership and involvement in lynching are the among the worst expressions of this. Many African Americans migrated to cities from the mid-nineteenth century, leading to intense competition for jobs and housing between them and urban-dwelling Irish immigrants at the bottom rungs of society's ladder. Some Irish-dominated unions refused membership to African Americans, or at least limited the numbers allowed to join, while the infamous 'draft riots' saw many unionised Irishmen engage in a rampage of looting and violence against African Americans during a four-day shutdown of New York in July 1863. In the twentieth and twenty-first century, many controversial social and political commentators of Irish heritage have used the airwaves to spread racist and xenophobic views and other prejudices.

LE

Mary Harris Jones ('Mother Jones')

1837?–1930

A symbol for feminists, socialists and the American labour movement, 'Mother Jones' remained active in the labour movement and radical causes into her nineties.

Mary Harris Jones ('Mother Jones') was, according to baptismal records, born in July 1837 in Cork city; however, the year is disputed. Many details of her life come from *The autobiography of Mother Jones* (1925; 1974). She emigrated to North America as a young girl with her father, Richard Harris, a railway labourer, possibly during the famine. She lived in the US and Canada, where she attended and later taught in a Catholic school in Toronto. In the US she taught in a convent school in Michigan and worked as a seamstress. In 1861 she married George Jones, an iron-moulder and labour union member in Memphis, Tennessee. After the death of her husband and their four children in a yellow fever epidemic in 1867, Jones relocated to Chicago, Illinois, where she became involved with an early industrial union, the Knights of Labor. Her seamstress shop was destroyed by the great Chicago fire of 1871.

In the 1890s she became known as 'Mother Jones' and began a long association with socialist causes and the United Mine Workers of America. She attended the founding convention of Social Democracy of America, later known as the Cooperative Brotherhood, in 1897, and in the same year organised support and publicity for striking bituminous coal miners in West Virginia, including a children's march and parades of farmers delivering food to the miners' camp. These types of defiant mass action became her trademark. Notable activities included organising women in support of an 1899 anthracite coal strike in eastern Pennsylvania; directing strikes of young women working in textile mills; a 1903 'children's crusade' against child labour, which included a ninety-mile march from Philadelphia to New York City; participating in 1905 in the founding convention of the Industrial Workers of the World, a radical labour union committed to the organisation of unskilled workers; campaigning for the release of Mexican revolutionaries imprisoned in American jails; and testifying in 1915 in congressional hearings against the abuse of corporate power by Rockefeller interests.

Jones reportedly met with James Connolly, Irish socialist and labour organiser, in New York City in 1910. She was arrested for the first time for violating a federal injunction during a miners' strike in West Virginia in 1902, and in 1904, during a Colorado miners' campaign, had to avoid the authorities to escape possible deportation. During a 1914 strike in Ludlow, Colorado, she was imprisoned without trial for nine weeks. In 1919 she was arrested in Pennsylvania during a steelworkers' strike for defending freedom of speech and the right of workers to organise unions. Jones remained active in the labour movement and radical causes into her nineties. She died on 30 November 1930 and was buried in the coal miners' cemetery in Mount Olive, Illinois.

Alan Singer

Sources

M. F. Parton (ed.), *Autobiography of Mother Jones* (1925; 1974); D. Fetherling, *Mother Jones, the miners' angel* (1974); E. M. Steel (ed.), *The speeches and writing of Mother Jones* (1988); P. Long, *Where the sun never shines: a history of America's bloody coal industry* (1989); Elliott J. Gorn, *The most dangerous woman in America* (2001); Rosemary Feurer, 'Mother Jones. A global history of struggle and remembrance: from Cork, Ireland, to Illinois', *Illinois Heritage* (May 2013)

John Boyle O'Reilly

1844–90

As a public figure, and as editor and proprietor of Boston's *Pilot*, he mobilised support for Land League and home rule efforts back home, while his social justice advocacy in the US foreshadowed American Progressivism.

John Boyle O'Reilly was born 28 June 1844 in Dowth, Co. Meath, third child among three sons and five daughters of William David O'Reilly and Mary O'Reilly (née Boyle). He attended the local national school where his father was the head teacher. O'Reilly entered the newspaper business at the age of eleven, when he was apprenticed to the *Drogheda Argus*. Then, on emigrating to England in 1859, he worked as a compositor and reporter for the *Preston Guardian* before returning to Ireland in 1863, when he joined the 10th Hussars regiment of the British army on 1 July in Dublin.

Recruited into the IRB by John Devoy, he eventually brought eighty fellow soldiers into the Fenian movement. O'Reilly was arrested and convicted by court martial of conspiracy to incite military mutiny in July 1866. Along with sixty-one other Fenians, he was transported to Western Australia in 1867, where he served as a probationary constable at the Bunbury prison labour camp. In March 1869 O'Reilly made a daring escape from the penal colony on the New Bedford whaler, the *Gazelle*, eventually arriving in Philadelphia in November. He quickly established contact with American Fenians, enrolling in the 1st Battalion of the Legion of Saint Patrick and attending the April 1870 Fenian convention in New York, but the ill-conceived and futile Fenian raid from Saint Albans, Vermont, on Canada the following June, in which he participated and covered for Boston's *Pilot* newspaper, precipitated his resignation from the Fenian movement. Nonetheless, O'Reilly remained friendly with his former colleagues, especially Jeremiah O'Donovan Rossa and John Devoy, with whom he organised the Clan na Gael-sponsored rescue of six Fenians from Western Australia in 1876 on the New Bedford whaling ship, the *Catalpa*.

O'Reilly enjoyed a rapid advance in his chosen career, becoming editor in 1874 and two years later co-owner of the *Pilot*, the country's foremost Catholic newspaper. Under his editorship the paper had a national weekly circulation of 103,000, providing timely news on Irish political developments to its subscribers, the majority of whom were recent Irish immigrants. As a popular orator, prolific journalist and especially as editor (1874–90) of the *Pilot*, O'Reilly championed the cause of Irish nationalism. While rejecting Fenian methods on pragmatic grounds, O'Reilly remained faithful to the republican, non-sectarian principles of the movement throughout his life. His enthusiasm for land reform was reflected in the support and detailed coverage the paper gave to the organisation and activity of the Irish Land League (1879–82). He welcomed Michael Davitt to Boston on three occasions and commissioned him to submit articles on the land question and Irish politics for the *Pilot*. O'Reilly was consulted on and approved the 'New Departure' arrangements worked out by Devoy and Davitt in 1878 to provide American support for the land agitation and the political efforts of Charles Stewart Parnell. He supported the land agitation chiefly for its utility in strengthening the national political cause rather than for any specific programme of land reform.

After Parnell's election as president of the Irish National Land League in late 1879, in January 1880 O'Reilly officially welcomed him to New York and presided at a very successful Boston meeting, one of sixty in the Irish leader's American tour. O'Reilly helped organise and chaired the first national convention of the American Land League in New York city on 18–19 May 1880. He admired Parnell's sisters Anna and Fanny for their efforts on behalf of Irish tenants and published a number of Fanny's poems, including her famous 'Hold the harvest'. Over the next few years, his vigorous and articulate espousal of the home rule cause in print and on public platforms mobilised the American Irish community in Boston and beyond.

O'Reilly's literary interests generated friendships with some prominent American literary figures such as Henry Wadsworth Longfellow, Ralph Waldo Emerson and T. W. Higginson, who gained a new respect for Ireland, its people and the nationalist cause from knowing him. The invitation that O'Reilly received to compose and read a poem for the dedication of Plymouth Rock in 1889 was a sign of the great esteem Boston's Brahmin elite had for him, as well as of his effectiveness in promoting better relations between them and the burgeoning Irish immigrant community in the city. Notwithstanding his deep commitment to the freedom of his homeland, O'Reilly urged his fellow Irishmen and other immigrants to integrate into mainstream American political and civic life.

O'Reilly's greatest contribution as a journalist and poet rests on his recognition of the negative consequences of rapid industrialisation and urbanisation. He was a passionate advocate for the downtrodden and all victims of racial, ethnic, class and religious discrimination and oppression. A full decade before the publication of *Rerum Novarum* (1891) by Pope Leo XIII, O'Reilly urged his readers, and especially the Roman Catholic clergy, to reject a complacent acceptance of poverty and human misery based on laissez-faire economics and Spencerian notions of evolutionary determinism. O'Reilly defended labour's right to organise, and frequently called for legislation providing for minimum wages, compulsory arbitration and stronger factory inspection procedures to ensure safety and limits on child and female labour.

As a firm believer in the equality and dignity of each individual, O'Reilly in his editorials railed against the injustice and discrimination experienced by Black Americans, which he witnessed in the country's south. As he did with his fellow Irish immigrants, he urged Black Americans to mobilise politically and to acquire as much education as possible to take full advantage of their rights as citizens and to realise their full human potential. O'Reilly was a fierce critic of religious prejudice of any kind, readily condemning Catholic as well as Protestant intolerance, as shown by his outrage over Catholic attacks on parading Orangemen in New York in July 1870. O'Reilly's passionate pleas for social justice, clean government and prison and asylum reform, and his acceptance of some government intervention to improve urban environmental conditions, foreshadowed initiatives associated with American Progressivism at the century's end.

Between 1873 and 1886 O'Reilly published four books of poetry, the last of which, *In Bohemia* (1886), is considered his best. In 1878 his novel *Moondyne*, a romantic adventure based on his Australian experience, was serialised in the *Pilot* and later published in numerous editions. Like many of his former Fenian colleagues, O'Reilly valued athletics for their character-building potential, and in 1888 he published *Ethics of boxing* and *Manly sport*. The public renown O'Reilly earned was reflected in his presidency of the Boston Press Club, his honorary degrees from Notre Dame University (1881) and Georgetown University (1889), as well as his induction into Phi Beta Kappa at Dartmouth College (1881). His unexpected death at age forty-six from an accidental overdose of sleeping medicine on 10 August 1890 in Hull, Massachusetts, generated scores of tributes and testimonials from prominent Irish and American politicians, leading Catholic churchmen as well as notables in the literary establishment (President Benjamin Harrison, Patrick A. Collins,

Archbishop John J. Williams, Cardinal James Gibbons, Oliver Wendell Holmes). O'Reilly was buried at Holyhood cemetery in Brookline, Massachusetts.

He married (15 August 1872) in Charlestown, Massachusetts, Mary, daughter of two Irish immigrants, James Murphy of Co. Fermanagh and Jane Murphy (née Smiley) of Co. Donegal. They had four daughters together. Mary shared her husband's literary interests and took a leading role in editing his poems and speeches after his death. The John Boyle O'Reilly memorial on Boston's Fenway, which features a bust of O'Reilly surrounded by carved Gaelic interlace, was funded by public subscriptions collected shortly after his death. A similar memorial with Gaelic-revival motifs was erected in his native Dowth in 1903. The Burns Library at Boston College holds a small collection of his papers as well as a bust of O'Reilly. Other repositories containing limited O'Reilly material are the Boston Public Library, Houghton Library of Harvard University and the archives of the archdiocese of Boston. A slim volume of unpublished poems written during his Australian sojourn and dedicated to the Reverend Patrick McCabe, the priest who arranged his escape, was discovered more recently and is at the Battye Library in Perth, Australia.

Catherine B. Shannon

Sources

Pilot, 1870–90; James Jeffery Roche, *The life of John Boyle O'Reilly, together with his complete poems and speeches, edited by Mrs John Boyle O'Reilly* (1891); Katherine E. Conway, *Watchwords of John Boyle O'Reilly* (1891); William O'Brien and Desmond Ryan (eds), *Devoy's post bag, 1871–1928* (2 vols, 1948, 1953); William G. Schofield, *Seek for a hero: the story of John Boyle O'Reilly* (1956); Francis G. McManamin, *The American years of John Boyle O'Reilly, 1870–1890* (1976); A. G. Evans, *Fanatic heart: a life of John Boyle O'Reilly* (1999); Ian Kenneally, *From the earth a cry: the story of John Boyle O'Reilly* (2011)

Charlotte Grace O'Brien

1845–1909

She campaigned
successfully on both
sides of the Atlantic
for the cause of Irish
emigrant women.

Charlotte Grace O'Brien was born 23 November 1845 at Cahirmoyle (Cahermoyle), Co. Limerick, younger daughter of the Young Ireland leader, William Smith O'Brien, and his wife Lucy Caroline, daughter of Joseph Gabbett of High Park, Co. Limerick. She lived in Cahirmoyle until 1861, except for a period between 1854 and 1856, when the family were in Brussels. She spent much of the time from 1861 until his death in 1864 accompanying her father on his travels. She then returned to Cahirmoyle, then her brother Edward's home, and from the death of his wife in 1868 until 1878 cared for his children. She then moved into a little house near Mount Trenchard on the Shannon.

O'Brien's principal cause was that of Irish emigrant women and the hazardous conditions under which they travelled to America—from the grim, overpriced boarding houses at Queenstown (Cobh) pre-departure, to the awful conditions onboard ships, to the dock slums and exploitation they arrived to. She vividly portrayed these dangers in her influential May 1881 article for the *Pall Mall Gazette* on the 'Horrors of the immigrant ship'. She campaigned successfully on both sides of the Atlantic on these issues, and to the dismay of the shipping lines she established a boarding house at Queenstown (Cobh) and was able to give advice to thousands of emigrants on the best way to travel to America.

O'Brien actively opposed the coercive legislation of 1881 and was a supporter of the Land League. Later she was an enthusiast for the Gaelic League. In spite of increasing deafness she was an avid traveller in later life. She became a Catholic in 1887 and died on 3/4 June 1909 at home in Co. Limerick.

She wrote for the *Nation* and *United Ireland* and published a number of works of literature including *A drama and lyrics* (1880). Her most noted work was a novel, *Light and shade* (1878), which attempts to foster a positive relationship between landlord and tenant through mutual goodwill, and offers an explanation of the circumstances that sustained secret societies and led to agrarian outrages. Thus at the end of the novel, which was 'received with a chorus of praise by the critics of all manner of politics' (Katharine Tynan), the Fenians are seen as tragic examples of a lost opportunity for conciliation, a sad reflection on Ireland's troubled history.

James H. Murphy

Sources

Charlotte Grace O'Brien: selections from her writings and correspondence, with a memoir by Stephen Gwynn (1909); James H. Murphy, *Catholic fiction and social reality in Ireland, 1873–1922* (1997); *Oxford dictionary of national biography* (2004)

Joseph
Patrick
McDonnell

1846–1906

A friend of Marx and
Engels, this union leader
helped develop new laws
on child and convict
labour, and on workplace
safety. He is also credited
with the introduction of
Labor Day.

Joseph Patrick McDonnell was born 27 March 1846 in Smithfield, Dublin, son of Peter McDonnell, baker's foreman. Educated at Marlborough Street national school (1853–8) and St Paul's Academy, Arran Quay (1858–60), he grew into a man of slight build with red, curly hair and a somewhat oval face. By 1861 he had enrolled in the Catholic University but he would be threatened with expulsion twice because of his extra-curricular activities. Becoming involved with the National Brotherhood of Saint Patrick (NBSP), he started giving lectures, expressing opposition to a visit by the Prince of Wales and complaining that entrants to Maynooth College were expected to take an oath to inform against secret societies. In February 1863 he abandoned his studies to assume an editorial position with James Daly's *United Irishman and Galway American*, a short-lived radical paper (1862–4). He also became joint secretary of the NBSP with C. G. Doran who was probably responsible for inducting him into the Irish Republican Brotherhood (IRB). He became a frequent contributor to its paper, the *Irish People* (established November 1863), and championed its call to exclude priests from politics. As a confidant of the IRB leader James Stephens, in August 1864 McDonnell resigned from the council of the NBSP to establish IRB branches in London and to arrange secret arms importation into Dublin.

As a cover for these activities, in April 1865 he set up a rope and twine firm at 52 Henry Street, Dublin that soon relocated to 36 New Row West. Following the government's suppression of the *Irish People* (September 1865), he edited a short-lived underground sheet called the *Fenian Times* but was arrested at his father's home, 40 North Brunswick Street. He found prison life unbearable and so offered to give information in return for his release.

He subsequently chose to leave the movement rather than act as an informer. In April 1867 he took over a Dublin tobacconist shop owned by his future father-in-law (who had left for London), but the business soon collapsed, reputedly due to constant police supervision of its customers. His police record prevented him from acquiring further employment in Dublin. With the assistance of a priest, in November 1867 he moved to Mullingar to manage a new Catholic bookshop, but it closed after three months because the police raided the premises several times expecting to find secret IRB documents (none were found). In March 1868 McDonnell left for London, never to return to Ireland. He lived with the family of his girl-friend Mary McEvatt in Peckham. The couple married on 15 March 1870 in the local Franciscan church.

Through Irish connections in London, McDonnell started working as a journalist with the *Universal News* and the *Evening Standard* and acted as secretary of an Irish mutual benefit society. In February 1869 he was made a local secretary of the Amnesty Association, which was set up to campaign for the release of Fenian prisoners. He acted as a public lecturer and was made the principal speaker at a monster rally at Hyde Park (24 October 1869). After editing *New Ireland*, a short-lived journal (June–September 1870), on 20 October 1870 he was charged at Bow Street police court with attempting to organise a brigade of Irishmen to take part in the Franco-Prussian war. A fund to organise his defence was launched by the *Irishman* newspaper in Dublin, but he was convicted and imprisoned in Clerkenwell and subsequently Newgate prison until late February 1871.

After his release he became involved in groups that were sympathetic to the Paris Commune. This led to his introduction to Friedrich Engels and Karl Marx (June 1871). On 4 July 1871 he was appointed to the general council of the International, becoming 'corresponding secretary for Ireland' on 1 August. He had advised Marx that, together with Fenian exiles in New York such as John Devoy and Jeremiah O'Donovan Rossa, he could organise a significant Irish segment of the International, provided it tolerated Irish nationalist goals. He founded eight of the nineteen short-lived branches of the International in England, in Bradford, Sheffield, Liverpool and Middlesbrough, as well as four in London. During the spring of 1872 he sent men to establish branches of the International in Cork and Dublin, but these were short-lived due to hostility from both the clergy and the IRB. After establishing a 'propaganda fund for Ireland' in April 1872, he co-wrote a pamphlet with Marx that accused the Royal Irish Constabulary (RIC) of perpetually intimidating the public and running rebels out of employment. After attending the Hague conference of the International (8 September 1872), he wrote a protest on behalf of the International to the British prime minister regarding the treatment of Fenian prisoners (1 October 1872) and spoke before 30,000 people at a rally at Hyde Park (3 November 1872). As the branches of the International he had founded were already disbanding, however, McDonnell and his wife decided to follow his father-in-law to New York, arriving on 1 January 1873.

After witnessing the appalling conditions on cheap transatlantic steamships, McDonnell issued protest letters regarding the American steamship companies to President Ulysses S. Grant and Richard O'Gorman, judge of the superior court of New York and a former Young Ireland rebel. McDonnell then attempted to act as a champion of the New York immigrant community by writing for the New York *Herald* and *Griffin's Guide to America*, a popular journal for immigrants. He continued to work for the International, however, and in February 1873 he became corresponding secretary of its New York council. He remained a correspondent of Engels for many more years (he was writing letters of introduction to Engels as late as 1892). In January 1875 he established a new branch of the International called the 'Association of United Workers of America' and in April 1876 became editor of the New York Marxist journal, the *Socialist*, before attending the last conference of the International in Philadelphia (15 July 1876).

In 1877 after a split in the American labour movement, the *Socialist* was renamed the *Labor Standard* (New York) and as editor, McDonnell abandoned the use of inter-nationalist rhetoric. Thereafter he rose in significance as an activist in American labour politics. In the summer of 1878, following the outbreak of a textile workers' strike in Paterson, New Jersey, he was fined $500 for writing articles that advocated the intimidation of those who abandoned the strike. Local workers paid the fine on his behalf. In October he relocated the *Labor Standard* to Paterson and lived there while his wife remained with her father's family in New York. He was charged again on the same offence during a subsequent bricklayers' strike and was sentenced to two months imprisonment on 12 February 1880. On his release (1 April), he was made the subject of a free-speech demonstration of 20,000 people and received a presentation on behalf of the workers of New Jersey.

Although he was associated with the International Labour Union (1878–83), McDonnell soon became committed to engaging directly with congressmen to forward the labour interest. This made him a close friend of American labour leaders Samuel Gompers and Terence Powderly. As chairman of the legislative committee of the Federation of Organized Trades and Labor Unions of New Jersey (1883–91), he drafted labour reform bills that were sent to the state legislature through non-partisan channels. Mostly through his efforts, legislation was introduced to restrict child labour, improve safety standards in the workplace, limit weekly work hours, restrict the use of convict labour, and introduce compulsory education for children. He also encouraged New Jersey to become the first American state to make 'Labor Day' a legal holiday. Upon his being appointed as the official factory inspector for the state in 1887 (his first salaried job in America), his wife joined him in Paterson. In 1892, after affiliating his New Jersey trade federation with the American Federation of Labor (AFL), he served as a general organiser of the AFL. He was also appointed to the New Jersey state board of arbitration. Ill-health, caused by a long-term inflammation of the kidneys, forced him to retire from active politics in 1895. Thereafter his wife took over the management of the *Labor Standard*.

On 24 May 1897, at the request of C. G. Doran, he was made an honorary member of the 1798 Centenary Committee in Dublin in recognition of his past rebel career, although he played no role in its activities. His last political action was to attempt to launch a campaign to oppose an alleged rise of American imperialism in the wake of the Spanish–American war of 1898, but the AFL refused to endorse his efforts. By the early 1900s he was effectively an invalid. He died on 16 January 1906 in his house at High Mountain Road, Haledon, just outside

Paterson, New Jersey. His wife survived him, but they had no children. His papers were later donated to the State Historical Society of Wisconsin.

Owen McGee

Sources

Irish Daily Independent, 26 May 1897; *Irish World*, 27 January 1906; Cormac O'Grada, 'Fenianism and socialism: the career of J. P. McDonnell', *Saothar*, i, no. 1 (1975), 31–41; P. Quinlivan and P. Rose, *The Fenians in England* (1982), 144–6; Sean Daly, *Ireland and the First International* (1984); L. A. O'Donnell, 'Joseph Patrick McDonnell (1847–1906): a passion for justice', *Éire–Ireland*, xxii, no. 4 (1987), 118–33; R. V. Comerford, *The Fenians in context* (2nd edn, 1998), 81, 185

Paul O'Dwyer

1907–98

Described as 'the conscience of New York politics', he was one of America's leading civil-liberties and civil-rights attorneys from the 1940s to the 1970s.

Paul O'Dwyer was born 29 June 1907 in Lismirrane (Lismiraun), Bohola, Swinford, Co. Mayo, youngest of eleven children of Patrick O'Dwyer, native of Tullylease, Co. Cork, national school teacher, and Bridget O'Dwyer (née McNicholas) of Lismirrane, assistant teacher. From his father, an organiser for the Irish National Teachers' Organisation, he derived pro-trade union and anti-clerical attitudes.

Educated at Bohola national school and Saint Nathy's college, Ballaghaderreen, Co. Roscommon, he attended University College Dublin for one year before following four of his elder brothers to America, settling in New York city (1925). He worked successively as a stock clerk in an automobile garage, an elevator operator, and a shipping clerk in a textile factory, and studied in the Fordham University evening pre-law course (1925–6). While attending evening classes in Saint John's College law school, Brooklyn (1926–9), he worked as a checker on the Brooklyn docks and as a seaman on summer runs to Latin America; he held a longshoreman's union card for the remainder of his life. After successfully sitting the New York state bar examination on special petition (owing to his status as an alien), he worked as a legal clerk (1929–31). Naturalised a US citizen and admitted to the bar (1931), he entered a Brooklyn law firm, becoming a partner in 1934. While participating in all aspects of the firm's general practice, he was deeply involved in cases concerning trade union organising rights, defending strikers and pickets against court injunctions, and opposing deportation orders against foreign-born activists.

Becoming in time senior partner of the firm (O'Dwyer and Bernstein), which moved in 1939 to offices on Wall Street, Manhattan, over the next half-century he was one of America's leading civil-liberties and civil-rights attorneys. Asserting as fundamental the democratic principles of freedom of conscience and of political association, he was prominent in efforts of the National Lawyers' Guild to withstand the witch-hunting, red-scare hysteria of the later 1940s. Chairman of the guild's civil rights committee, president of its New York chapter (1947), and member of its national board of directors (1948–51), he defended teachers and other public employees dismissed from employment for alleged 'disloyalty', and represented writers, entertainers and fellow attorneys under investigation by the House Un-American Activities Committee. He endured persistent charges of unpatriotic and communist sympathies, especially by Catholic and Irish American publications and personalities. A strenuous advocate of a Jewish state in Palestine, he arranged illegal arms shipments to the Irgun resistance movement for its armed struggle against the British mandate (which he equated with the British presence in Ireland), coordinated with Irish politician Robert Briscoe to facilitate smuggling of arms and volunteers through Irish ports, and lobbied for recognition of the state of Israel by the US and UN. Despite criticism by several Jewish American trade unionists opposed to the Irgun's reactionary, anti-labour policies, he welcomed Irgun leader Menachem Begin to New York (December 1948). Thereafter he distanced himself from internal Israeli politics, while remaining a conspicuous supporter of Israeli foreign policy.

Perceived as the 'radical younger brother' of leading New York politico William O'Dwyer, who served as the city's mayor from 1946 to 1950, Paul O'Dwyer was a persistent candidate for public office, being twice elected to the New York city council, but losing many bids for election to the US senate, US house of representatives and the New York mayoralty. During a two-year term on the city council as Manhattan councilman-at-large (1964–5), O'Dwyer succeeded in raising the city's minimum wage.

He litigated widely in racial integration cases, represented civil-rights activists in court proceedings in hostile southern states, and successfully argued before the US supreme court for the right of citizens educated in public schools in Puerto Rico to sit the New York voter literacy test in Spanish. In 1951 his litigation on behalf of tenants of the Metropolitan Life Insurance company stimulated municipal and federal legislation against racial discrimination in housing. He worked closely with the Mississippi Freedom Democratic Party (MFDP) to challenge the institutionalised exclusion of African Americans from the voting register and the political process. An early opponent of the Vietnam war, he helped launch the Coalition for a Democratic Alternative, through which he supported the anti-war candidacy of Senator Eugene McCarthy for the 1968 Democratic presidential nomination. A delegate to the turbulent national convention in Chicago, he marched with anti-war demonstrators on the streets, and denounced the Johnson administration's Vietnam policy on the convention floor. He served on the legal defence team of the 'Harrisburg seven', an anti-war group that included Father Philip Berrigan and other Catholic religious, on trial on bizarre charges of plotting to kidnap presidential adviser Henry Kissinger and to blow up government buildings (1971–2).

O'Dwyer's tenure as president of the New York city council (1974–7) was dominated by a severe fiscal crisis threatening municipal bankruptcy. While conceding the necessity for sweeping cutbacks in expenditure to restore the city's solvency, he opposed local and state initiatives that effectively transferred social policy to non-elected officials and private institutions. He secured the establishment of a records and information service to manage the city archives, and alteration of the date on the city seal from 1664 (when the Dutch colony was surrendered to British arms) to 1625 (when New Amsterdam was founded by Dutch settlers). He was appointed Manhattan borough historian (1986) and helped engineer the election of David Dinkins as New York's first African American mayor (1989). Named city commissioner to the United Nations (1990), he boycotted the UN cafeteria for anti-union policies, and soon resigned so as not to impede his freedom to criticise human rights abuses in member states.

Throughout his career O'Dwyer promoted numerous Irish cultural and charitable activities, and stoutly advocated the Irish nationalist interest in America. As national coordinator in the 1950s of the American League for an Undivided Ireland, he lobbied unsuccessfully for a congressional resolution urging a thirty-two county plebiscite to determine the constitutional status of Northern Ireland. He was active in founding and served as first president (1956) of the Irish Cultural Institute. A supporter of the Northern Ireland civil rights campaign (1968–9), thereafter he consistently refused to condemn the political violence of the Irish Republican Army, citing the 'causative violence' of sectarian discrimination, poverty and official repression. He represented Irish defendants in political and immigration cases in American courts, including leaders of the Irish Northern Aid Committee (NORAID) jailed for contempt after refusing to testify before a federal grand jury investigating alleged gun-running (1972). After opposing the 1985 Anglo–Irish agreement, he was

instrumental in initiating and facilitating the involvement of American president Bill Clinton in the Northern
Ireland issue. He lobbied to secure the granting of a US
entry visa to Sinn Féin president Gerry Adams, whom
he welcomed on his arrival in New York (1994), and he
endorsed the 1998 Good Friday agreement. A frequent
visitor to Ireland, he established and funded the O'Dwyer
Cheshire home for physically disabled adults on the old
family homestead in Bohola, Co. Mayo, and established
the O'Dwyer Forestry Foundation.

O'Dwyer was fiercely browed and florid of face, with
a dark-eyed glare under a shock of prematurely white
hair. His sharp-tongued public persona was mellowed
by his private warmth and tolerance of individual diversity. Described as 'the conscience of New York politics'
(*Newsday*, 25 June 1998), he was courageous in his consistent commitments to freedom of conscience, and to social
and racial inclusion, and in opposition to various episodes
of American overseas military intervention; he nonetheless
refused to censure physical force Irish republicanism or
militarist aspects of the Zionist movement.

Named Mayoman of the year in 1974, he was awarded
an honorary doctorate by Saint Thomas University,
Minnesota. He published an autobiography, *Counsel for
the defense* (1979), and edited the memoirs of his brother
William, *Beyond the golden door* (1986). He married first
(1935) Kathleen Rohan (d. 1980), an Irish American of
Galway ancestry; they had three sons and one daughter.
He married secondly (1984) Patricia Hanrahan, chief of
the New York state women's division, who survived him;
they had no children. After living at several addresses in
Brooklyn before and after his first marriage, in 1939 he
moved his family to 350 Central Park West, Manhattan,

his residence for many years. A country retreat in Goshen, New York, overlooking the Hudson river valley forty miles from the city, became his final permanent residence. After suffering a series of strokes from 1993, he was confined to a wheelchair in his last years. He died 24 June 1998 in Goshen; his ashes were scattered at his birthplace in Bohola. His papers are deposited in Saint John's University, Long Island, New York.

Lawrence William White

Sources

Connacht Tribune, 8 March 1974; *The Irish Times*, 21 June 1978; 16 June 1994; 25 June, 13 July 1998; Paul O'Dwyer, *Counsel for the defense* (1979); William O'Dwyer, *Beyond the golden door* (1986); Chris McNickle, *To be mayor of New York: ethnic politics in the city* (1993); *New York Times*, 25, 28 June 1998; *Newsday*, 25, 28–9 June 1998; *Ireland on Sunday*, 28 June 1998

8. Lives of art and architecture

Introduction

It is said that the Irish built America. While it was most definitely not a single-handed effort, there was undoubtedly a considerable Irish presence on the labour gangs who built the country's early railroads and canals, its roads and sewers, and later its skyscrapers and suburbs. To quote Dan Mulhall, Irish ambassador to the US (2017–21), the 'nation's infrastructure bears an indelible Irish imprint'.

Not only did Irish labour help build the nation, Irish minds contrived some of its cornerstone buildings. In our selection we feature James Hoban (c.1762–1831, p. 230), who designed what is arguably America's best-known building: the White House (as well as the state department and the war department offices). We also present Charles Donagh Maginnis (1867–1955, p. 245), perhaps the most prolific architect in America of the early twentieth century: numerous chapels, seminaries and other church buildings were built to his designs across twenty states.

Here too we celebrate the contribution of Irish-born artists to American culture, featuring sculptors Augustus Saint-Gaudens (1848–1907, p. 238), the country's preeminent sculptor of the nineteenth century, who produced over 150 works in marble and bronze, and Jerome Connor (1874–1943, p. 250) who contributed to or created some significant American commemorative works; and painter John Mulvany (c.1844–1906, p. 233), who created the iconic 'Custer's last rally'. Painted shortly after Custer's catastrophic defeat in the battle of Little Bighorn, Mulvany's masterpiece rendered the general's loss as a tragically noble one and established the artistic convention of the last 'rally' or 'stand' in battle paintings.

Though not included in our final selection, honourable mentions are due to a number of Irish artists for their contribution to art in America. John James Barralet (c.1747–1815) produced popular engravings of George Washington and served as professor of drawing from the antique at the Academy of Art in Philadelphia. He is thought to have invented a ruling machine for engravers and improved the ink used for copperplate prints. William Alexander Coulter (1849–1936) was an influential maritime painter whose work provides a visual chronicle of pre-mechanised shipping and of San Francisco as a thriving frontier port. Thomas Hovenden (1840–95) painted grand historic American scenes as well as intimate scenes of rural domestic life, and painted African American subjects with a dignity and individuality rare for the times.

LE

James Hoban

*c.*1762–1831

Architect who designed
the first US president
George Washington's
residence, the White
House, as well as the
state department and the
war department offices.

James Hoban was born in Callan, Co. Kilkenny, son of Edward Hoban and Martha Hoban (née Bayne). From 1779 he was educated at the Dublin Society's School of Drawing in Architecture where he studied under Thomas Ivory, receiving a medal in 1780 for his work. Employed as an artisan in Dublin, he worked on the Royal Exchange, the bank of Glendowe, Newcomen & Co. and James Gandon's Custom House, before deciding to emigrate to the newly independent United States of America.

Advertising his services in Philadelphia in 1785, he described himself as someone who 'can execute the joining and carpenter's business in the modern taste'. He later moved to South Carolina, where he designed the Charleston County Courthouse, built on the ruins of the former South Carolina Statehouse, as well as other public buildings. On his tour of the south, President George Washington admired Hoban's work.

Returning to Philadelphia in 1792, Hoban met Washington and was persuaded to enter the open competition to design public buildings. On 17 July his design for the president's house won first prize, beating an anonymous submission by Thomas Jefferson, and winning him a lot in what would become Washington, DC, as well as $500. His drawing incorporated details from a plate by James Gibbs, and also showed the influence of Leinster House in Dublin, leading to speculation that the building was copied from that design. The original president's house, which would later be called the 'executive mansion', and finally the White House, was a simple Georgian mansion in a classic Palladian style. Enlisted by the federal government to supervise the building of his design, Hoban was present at the laying of the foundation stone by Washington (13 September 1793). A freemason, he organised a masonic lodge in the federal city, and served as master. Recognised as one of the leading architects in the capital city, he was also employed as a superintendent on the construction of the Capitol building, designed the Great Hotel (1793–5), and built the Little Hotel (1795). In 1799 he became a captain in the Washington artillery, and in 1802 was elected to the city council, on which he served until his death.

Hoban's greatest achievement, the White House, was burned by the British under Robert Ross in 1814 and almost completely destroyed. Reconstruction work began once the war ended, with Hoban again employed, and it was completed in 1829. He also designed and built the state department and war department offices. Described as 'a very ingenious mechanic and draughtsman', he achieved great respect in America, and Washington, DC, in particular, for the quality of his architectural work. He died 8 December 1831 in Washington, DC.

He married (1799) Susannah Sewell; they had ten children. His son (and namesake) served as a United States attorney for the District of Columbia.

Patrick M. Geoghegan

Sources

Marcus Whiffen and Frederick Koeper, *American architects, 1607–1976* (1981); *Dictionary of American biography* (1928–58); Henry Boylan, *A dictionary of Irish biography* (3rd edn, 1998); *American national biography* (1999)

John Mulvany

*c.*1844–1906

Mulvany painted the
iconic 'Custer's last
rally', a hugely popular
patriotic painting
that reimagined a
humiliating defeat as a
victory of grit and spirit.

John Mulvany was born to a farming family in Moynalty, Co. Meath. Details of his life until the latter 1860s are sketchy and often contradictory; some sources place his birth as early as 1839. Educated locally, he emigrated to the US—reputedly alone and at age twelve—where he worked as a towpath drover along the Erie canal, and at various odd jobs in New York city. While he was working as a students' model and general errand boy at the National Academy of Design (NAD), his chalk and charcoal sketches of scenes and characters along the canal were noticed by an instructor, who gave him informal training in watercolour and photographic colouring. By 1861 he was practising the latter trade in Chicago and doing freelance artwork for Irish newspapers. While serving in the US army during the civil war (1861–5), he also worked as a frontline sketch artist.

In the second half of the 1860s he journeyed to Europe, joining the considerable number of American art students then active in Munich. Admitted to the prestigious Bavarian Royal Academy of Fine Arts, he received a medal of honour for excellence. With a keen interest in military art, he studied briefly in other European centres, including Düsseldorf, Antwerp and Paris, under masters noted for battlefield pieces. Visiting Ireland, he sketched in the Kells area and elsewhere. Returning to America in the early 1870s, he was active in St Louis, Cincinnati and Chicago (where he lost his studio and its contents in the great fire of 1871), before moving to the Iowa–Nebraska frontier, where he began to concentrate on western subjects. A painting in this genre, 'The preliminary trial of a horse thief', was exhibited at the NAD and sold for an impressive $5,250 (1876).

Based in Kansas City, Missouri, Mulvany worked for two years (1879–81) on his most famous work, 'Custer's last rally', one of the earliest artistic renderings of the comprehensive defeat of the US 7th cavalry regiment under the command of General George Armstrong Custer by warriors of the Lakota and Cheyenne peoples under the leadership of Tasunka Witko ('Crazy Horse') at the Little Bighorn river on 25 June 1876. Seeking historical verisimilitude, he visited the battlefield and sketched the terrain, interviewed battle veterans on the Lakota reservation, obtained portraits and descriptions from military associates of Custer and his officers, and painstakingly researched Native American and US cavalry dress, weaponry and tactics. On the resulting massive canvas, measuring 20ft by 11ft, he depicted Custer as the central figure in a scene of vivid, crowded, swirling action, revolver in one outstretched hand and sabre in the other, ringed by his beleaguered, dismounted troopers, with Native American riders circling through clouds of dust in the background. Mulvany transformed a recent and humiliating defeat for the American army (owing in large measure to the reckless bravado of a vainglorious commander) into a visitation of the heroic sublime. Widely exhibited for over a decade to paying audiences throughout America and in Europe, its influence was enormous. Walt Whitman's effusive laudation encapsulated the general response: 'nothing in the books like it, nothing in Homer, nothing in Shakespeare; more grim and sublime than either, all native, all our own, and all a fact' (Taft (1953), 138–9). Probably viewed and discussed by more people than any other American painting, the work firmly established the largely speculative tradition that the battle—from which not a single white survivor returned—culminated in a heroic last 'rally' or 'stand', the imagery generating a vast progeny in art, popular literature and cinema.

In the late 1890s the painting was purchased by business magnate Henry J. Heinz, who, it is rumoured, commissioned Mulvany to paint a duplicate for its continuing public exhibition, though only one painting is known to be in circulation. After its time on tour ended, it reportedly found a home on the wall of Heinz's corporate headquarters. Notable later exhibitions include in the 1950s when it was exhibited at the Museum of Science and History in Memphis and in the 1960s at the Amon Carter Museum in Fort Worth, Texas. It has been bought and sold an unknown number of times since then, and has occasionally reappeared in public for special exhibitions. In 2020 the painting again emerged for sale, valued at $23 million. It was sold at auction in July 2020 for an undisclosed sum.

Mulvany's numerous landscapes and vignettes of western life include 'Scouts of the Yellowstone', exhibited alongside the Custer painting in Chicago in 1882. Notable among his paintings of American civil war subjects is 'Sheridan's ride from Winchester', depicting a dramatic moment in the 1864 Shenandoah valley campaign of General Philip Sheridan.

Mulvany was an adroit and prolific portraitist, his subjects including Mormon leader Brigham Young, Robert Emmet and Tatanka Iyotanka ('Sitting Bull'). A staunch Republican in American politics, he was close to Fenian leader John Devoy and active in Clan na Gael. Commissioned by the Irish American Club of Chicago in 1883, he visited Ireland, England and France to research 'The battle of Aughrim', depicting the decisive battle of the Williamite war in 1691. Conceived as the first in a series (ultimately aborted) of Irish historic battle scenes, the painting was executed in Paris, where it was first exhibited and then subsequently in Dublin, where it proved hugely popular among nationalists. The painting's location was unknown for many years, until it resurfaced for sale in 2010, misidentified as an American battle scene.

Despite the erstwhile extent of his popular acclaim and commercial success, by 1900 interest in Mulvany's work had waned considerably. In 1897 he moved to Greenpoint in Brooklyn, New York, close to his sister. Succumbing to alcoholism, he spent his last years in dereliction and penury, becoming homeless in his final weeks. He was found drowned in the East River, New York city, in May 1906. In his pockets there were reportedly news clippings from his heyday, some recent rejection letters and a tragic love poem. As a consequence, his death was presumed to be suicide. He was buried in Calvary cemetery in Queens, New York.

Lawrence William White

Sources

Samuel Isham, *The history of American painting* (1905); Thomas P. Tuite, 'John Mulvany: great Irish painter…', *Gaelic American*, 6 March (photo), 3, 10 April 1909; Robert Taft, 'The pictorial record of the old west, iv: Custer's last stand—John Mulvany, Cassilly Adams, and Otto Becker', *Kansas Historical Quarterly*, xiv, no. 4 (November 1948), 361–90; William O'Brien and Desmond Ryan (ed.), *Devoy's post bag 1871–1928*, ii (1948); Robert Taft, *Artists and illustrators of the old west 1850–1900* (1953); William H. Goetzmann and William N. Goetzmann, *The west of the imagination* (1986); Harold McCracken, *Great painters and illustrators of the old west* (1988); Corey Kilgannon, 'Over a century later, an Irish painter's Brooklyn renaissance', *New York Times* (15 March 2017); *Invaluable* (fine art auction website) 'Lot 101: "Custer's Last Rally", Randall Hill Auctioneers, Dallas, Texas', 11 August 2020, www.invaluable.com/catalog/j8nwv0bsgo (accessed November 2020); website of Kansas State Historical Society, www.kshs.org/kansapedia/custer-s-last-rally-lithograph/10121 (accessed November 2020)

Augustus Saint-Gaudens

1848–1907

The preeminent
American sculptor of the
nineteenth century, he
produced over 150 works
in marble and bronze.

Augustus Saint-Gaudens was born 1 March 1848 at 35 Charlemont Street, Dublin, eldest of three surviving sons of Bernard Saint-Gaudens, shoemaker, of Aspet, Gascony, France, and Mary Saint-Gaudens (née McGuiness), a plasterer's daughter, of Ballymahon, Co. Longford. His parents had met in a Dublin shoe factory where both worked; two elder brothers born in Dublin died before Augustus's birth. When six months old he was brought by his parents to the US (September 1848), settling in New York, where Bernard soon opened a thriving shop making and selling French-style ladies' boots and shoes. Augustus was educated in New York public schools until age thirteen, then apprenticed as a cameo cutter (1861–7), studying evenings at the Cooper Institute art school and the National Academy of Design. Supporting himself with cameo work, he trained in sculpture in Paris (1867–70), initially at the Petite École, then at the prestigious École des Beaux-Arts.

While working in Rome (1870–75) he carved cameos, portrait busts and copies of classical statues for wealthy tourists, and executed two original full-size marbles. There, he became engaged to Augusta Fisher Homer, a painting student from Boston. Returning to New York (1875–7), he sought a lucrative commission that would allow their marriage. Contracted to execute a memorial to the American civil war naval commander David Glasgow Farragut, he married Augusta (June 1877) and immediately embarked with her for Paris, where his studio became a gathering place for expatriate American artists (1877–80). Unveiled in 1881 at Madison Square Park, New York, the Farragut monument—a bronze figure atop a carved bluestone pedestal and bench—was immediately hailed by artists and critics alike as a breakthrough in American art, revolutionary for its dynamic realism combined with allegory, and for the unity of its conception. It was the first of numerous collaborations with architect Stanford White; the careful attention to site, landscaping and architectural detail in creating a comprehensive artistic environment would be characteristic of Saint-Gaudens's subsequent career.

Based in New York (1880–97), Saint-Gaudens held a place among the most renowned artists in America. His *oeuvre* (over 150 works in marble and—his forte—bronze) established his reputation as the preeminent American sculptor of the nineteenth century. Notable amongst his public monuments are those honouring civil war leaders: the standing figure 'Abraham Lincoln: the man' (1884–7; Lincoln Park, Chicago); the seated figure 'Abraham Lincoln: the head of state' (1897–1906; Grant Park, Chicago); the imposingly situated equestrian monument to General and US Senator John A. Logan (1894–7; Grant Park/Michigan Avenue, Chicago); 'General Sherman led by Victory' (1892–1903; Central Park, 59th Street entrance, New York), a gilded bronze equestrian, both resplendent and terrifying, of the conqueror of Georgia, set upon a pink granite base. Two works widely popularised in later reductions were 'The puritan' (1883–6; Springfield, Massachusetts), a paradigmatic representation; and the nude 'Diana' (second version 1892–4, latterly in Philadelphia Museum of Art) in gilded copper atop the tower of old Madison Square Garden, New York, which weathered scandalised commentary to become one of the city's foremost landmarks (until the building's demolition in 1925).

Perhaps the most moving of his works are two in contrasting modes. As an image of self-sacrifice in service to human emancipation and the inclusive, multi-racial democratic ideal, the Robert Gould Shaw/54th Massachusetts memorial (1884–97; Boston Common) transcends the platitudes of military commemoration. A bold medley of high and low relief and sculpture-in-the-round, the work depicts a mounted white commanding officer amid the marching infantry of the first regularly constituted black regiment in the union army. Working from live models, Saint-Gaudens rendered one of the first dignified, thoroughly realistic, depictions of black people in American art, which theretofore had been dominated by racist caricature. For the Adams memorial (1886–91; Rock Creek cemetery, Washington, DC), commissioned by historian Henry Adams after the suicide of his wife, Saint-Gaudens drew on Japanese Buddhist models and Michelangelo's Sistine sibyls to create an enigmatic, shrouded figure, androgynous and contemplative, regarded as a harbinger of the modernist temper.

Saint-Gaudens sculpted over 100 portraits in various media of family, friends and patrons, exhibiting remarkably subtle skills of drawing and modelling and a masterful facility for realistic representation while capturing character and mood. A version of an 1887–8 portrait became the basis for the famed Robert Louis Stevenson memorial in St Giles cathedral, Edinburgh (1899–1904). A leading personality of the American 'gilded age', Saint-Gaudens moved among statesmen, financiers and socialites, fulfilling their commissions for portraits, house decoration and funerary memorials. A generous mentor of young talent, especially encouraging to women students, he taught at New York's Art Students League (1888–97) and was co-founder of the American Academy in Rome (1894). Seeking wider recognition in Europe, he moved to Paris (1897–1900), where, through the promotion of Auguste Rodin, he exhibited an unprecedented fifteen works at the 1898 Salon de la Société Nationale des Beaux-Arts and won the Grand Prix at the 1900 Paris Exposition Universelle. Three months later he was diagnosed with colon cancer and returned to America for surgery. For his remaining seven years (1900–07) he lived and worked at Cornish, New Hampshire, his summer home since 1885. An adviser to the Macmillan commission for the redesign and park planning of Washington, DC (1901–4), he fulfilled a request by President Theodore Roosevelt and designed a new American gold coinage (1905–7). A rare foreign recipient of the French Légion d'honneur (1901), he received honorary degrees from Princeton (1897), Harvard (1897) and Yale (1905) universities and was elected to the National Academy of Arts and Letters (1904).

His last completed major work was the Dublin monument (1903–7) to Charles Stewart Parnell. With his characteristic attention to detail, he studied photographs and drawings of Parnell, ordered an entire suit of clothes from Parnell's former Dublin tailor, and constructed a scale model of the proposed site in Upper Sackville Street/Rutland Square. Hoping to capture 'the commanding spirit of Parnell, and the nobility and calmness of his bearing' (quoted in O'Keefe, 17), and mindful of Parnell's legacy as a formidable parliamentary debater, he chose to depict his subject in the act of speaking, with right arm outstretched in the characteristic pose of the orator in classical Roman statuary. In September 1904 John Redmond, prime mover of the monument project, visited Saint-Gaudens's Cornish studio and inspected the near-completed plaster work. A fortnight later the 'Parnell' was all but destroyed in a devastating studio fire, from which the head alone was rescued. With Saint-Gaudens suffering worsening health, most of the resumed work was done by his chief assistant, Henry Hering. Redmond suggested the quotation from a Parnell speech as an inscription, with Saint-Gaudens himself proposing the addition of a line in Irish language and lettering. Saint-Gaudens intended going to Dublin to oversee the installation, but a month after the bronze casting was shipped to Ireland, he died in Cornish on 3 August 1907. The work was finally unveiled on 1 October 1911 to mark the twentieth anniversary of Parnell's death. A bronze relief portrait plaque of Saint-Gaudens was installed in the pavement facing the monument in 2007 to mark the centenary of the sculptor's death, but was subsequently removed to accommodate tracks of the LUAS light-rail line; at time of writing (November 2020) the plaque is in storage pending possible reinstatement in a suitable Dublin location.

Saint-Gaudens and his wife had a son, Homer Saint-Gaudens (1880–1968), who edited and amplified *The reminiscences of Augustus Saint-Gaudens* (1913) and became director of the Carnegie Institute Museum of Art, Pittsburgh. Another son, Louis Clark, was born to his long-time mistress and model, Davida Johnson Clark. The sculptor's brother, Louis Saint-Gaudens (1854–1913), also a sculptor and assistant to his brother over many years, executed original work, notably the statuary in Boston Public Library and in Union Station, Washington, DC. Saint-Gaudens's widow (d. 1926) developed their home at Cornish as a memorial and museum, latterly administered by the National Park Service as the Saint-Gaudens National Historic Site, the only such site to an American artist. As well as materials at the Saint-Gaudens National Historic Site, a Saint-Gaudens collection is held by the

Baker Library, Dartmouth University, Hanover, New Hampshire. The Friends of Saint-Gaudens Memorial host an illustrated online database of the artist's work at www.sgnhs.org.

Lawrence William White

Sources

Louise Hall Tharp, *Saint-Gaudens and the gilded era* (1969); Richard Benson and Lincoln Kirstein, *Lay this laurel* (1973); John H. Dryfhout, *The work of Augustus Saint–Gaudens* (1982); Timothy J. O'Keefe, 'The art and politics of the Parnell monument,' *Éire–Ireland*, xix (spring 1984), 6–25; New York Architectural Book Publishing Company, *A monograph of the works of McKim, Mead and White 1879–1915* (1985); Burke Wilkinson, *The life and works of Augustus Saint Gaudens* (1992); Robert Hughes, *American visions: the epic history of art in America* (1997); *American national biography* (1999); *Augustus Saint-Gaudens 1848–1907: a master of American sculpture* (1999, exhibition catalogue); Gregory C. Schwarz, Ludwig Lauerhass and Brigid Sullivan, *The Shaw memorial: a celebration of an American masterpiece* (2002 edition); information from Saint-Gaudens National Historic Site (September 2000; Gregory C. Schwarz, chief of interpretation) and Heritage Office, Dublin City Council (November 2020)

This entry has been abridged for publication. The full version is available at www.dib.ie.

Charles Donagh Maginnis

1867–1955

Perhaps the most
prolific architect of the
early twentieth century,
numerous chapels,
seminaries and other
church buildings were
built to his designs
across twenty states.

Charles Donagh Maginnis was born 7 January 1867 in Derry city, son of Charles Maginnis and Bridget Maginnis (née McDonagh). He attended local schools there before entering Cusack's Academy, Dublin. A period in the South Kensington Museum School of Art in London followed, and in 1883 he won the Queen's prize in mathematics. He was offered a British civil service post but chose instead to emigrate with his mother, brothers and sister to North America. Accounts of his early years in America are vague, but it would appear that he spent some time in Toronto, Canada, before joining the architectural firm of William P. Wentworth in Boston, Massachusetts, in 1888.

By 1891 he was working as a designer in another Boston architectural firm, that of Edmund M. Wheelright, where he gained much experience in drawing plans, in various architectural styles, for buildings such as the new Boston fire department. Around 1895 he was appointed as a teacher of pen and ink drawing at the Cowles Art School, Boston, and published an instructional work, *Pen drawing* (1898), which ran to several editions. In 1898 he also formed a partnership with Matthew Sullivan and Timothy F. Walsh, establishing the company of Maginnis, Walsh & Sullivan. He had recently written an article on the construction of small parish churches and on foot of this was asked to design Saint Patrick's church in Whitinsville, Massachusetts. It was the beginning of a long association with the Catholic church, and he devoted much of the rest of his career designing ecclesiastical architecture while also designing collegiate buildings for church-administered universities. An early example of his work was Saint John's Seminary chapel in Brighton, Boston (1899–1902).

In 1906 he published a pamphlet, *Catholic church architecture*, in which he called for a return to the simple styles of medieval Italian brick churches. The church of Saint Catherine of Genoa in Somerville, Massachusetts (1907–16) followed these principles and was constructed to a medieval design. When Sullivan left the firm in 1908 it was renamed as Maginnis & Walsh. During a career spanning over fifty years, numerous chapels, shrines, seminaries and other church buildings were built to Maginnis's designs in twenty states and also in Canada, Mexico and China. He was largely responsible for a rebirth of interest in the Spanish mission style, his most notable example of this type of architecture being his design for the Carmelite convent of Santa Clara, California (1926–7). The American Institute of Architects (AIA) awarded him their gold medal (1925) for this design. A further gold medal followed (1927) for his design for Trinity College chapel, Washington, DC, which was constructed in what he termed a 'Roman basilican' style. In 1942 he designed the bronze doors, the altar and the baldacchino (altar canopy) for Saint Patrick's cathedral, New York. Best known as an exponent of the Spanish mission and Gothic styles of architecture, he also used a wide variety of other styles, including Byzantine, Italian renaissance and English collegiate.

Maginnis is usually associated with ecclesiastical architecture but he also designed many collegiate buildings. These included buildings for the University of Chicago (1892) and Princeton University (1909). He was responsible for the designs for long-term building programmes at Boston College's Chestnut Hill campus (1909–59) and the University of Notre Dame (1929–53). Other colleges for which he designed buildings included the Catholic University of America in Washington, DC, the College of the Holy Cross in Worcester, Massachusetts, and Fordham

University, New York. He was awarded the AIA gold medal for outstanding achievement in 1948; the firm was renamed as Maginnis, Walsh & Kennedy in 1954. His work has often been overlooked by architectural historians who have preferred to focus on modernist architectural designs. Maginnis preferred well-established styles, as he realised that they were both functional and aesthetically pleasing. He was, without doubt, one of the most prolific architects of the early twentieth century.

Throughout his career he played a prominent role in numerous professional and cultural associations. He was a member of the Boston Society of Architects from 1900 and served a term as its president (1924–6). In 1901 he joined the AIA; he was elected a fellow in 1906 and later served as vice-president (1932) and president (1937–9). He was the first president of the Liturgical Arts Society (1932). In 1932 he was elected president of the Charitable Irish Society, and in 1935 he became president of the Catholic Alumni Sodality.

He served as president of the fifteenth international congress of architects in 1939. His connections with many cultural associations included the Art Commission of the City of Boston, the Massachusetts State Art Commission and the Boston Museum of Fine Arts, among others. The National Academy of Design elected him as an academician (1942), and in 1944 he was elected to the National Institute of Arts and Letters. Awarded Notre Dame's Laetare medal (1924), he also received honorary degrees from Boston College (1921), Holy Cross College (1925), Tufts College, Boston (1945), and Harvard University (1949). The American Irish Historical Society and the Eire Society of Boston awarded him gold medals. In 1945 he was elected a Knight of Malta. He died in Brookline, Massachusetts, on 15 February 1955.

He married (1907) Amy Brooks; they had five children. A large collection of his writings and drawings is held in the Boston Public Library.

David Murphy

Sources

Times (London), 16, 17 February 1955; John J. Delaney and James Edward Tobin, *Dictionary of Catholic biography* (1962), 733–4; *Dictionary of American biography*, supplement 5 (1977), 462–3; Adolf K. Placzek, *The Macmillan encyclopaedia of architects* (1982); Kenneth T. Jackson, *The encyclopaedia of New York city* (1995); *American national biography* (1999); Norval White and Elliot Willensky (eds), *AIA guide to New York city* (revised edn, 2000)

Jerome Connor

1874–1943

Sculptor, craftworker
and graphic artist who
contributed to and
created many significant
sculptural monuments in
America before returning
to Ireland where his
career faltered, and he
ultimately died destitute.

Jerome Connor was born 23 February 1874 in Coumduff, Anascaul, Co. Kerry, youngest among six surviving children (four sons, two daughters) of Patrick Connor, farmer and housebuilder, and his second wife, Margaret Connor (née Currane), both of Anascaul. Educated locally, in 1888 he emigrated with his family to Holyoke, Massachusetts, where his eldest brother Timothy had settled *c.*1878. Trained in the Springfield, Massachusetts area as stone carver, machinist and sign painter, he moved to New York *c.*1896, financed by prize-fighting winnings (as 'Patrick J. O'Connor'). He learned bronze-casting and assisted with Roland Hilton Perry's 'Fountain of Neptune' (Washington, DC, 1898). When working on the collaborative Dewey victory arch project (New York, 1899), fellow sculptors noted his ability.

About January 1899, when staying with a patron, Bill Spear, at Quincy, Massachusetts, he was recommended to arts-and-crafts promoter Elbert Hubbard and joined his Roycroft community at East Aurora, New York. There he helped with several crafts, produced competent book illustrations, and fired his first sculptures (signed 'Saint Gerome') in terracotta. Despite his later claims to be self-taught, this work, visibly influenced by Augustus Saint-Gaudens (p. 238), indicates a formal training. He exhibited, initially as 'Jerome (Stanley) Conner' (Pennsylvania Academy of the Fine Arts, 1900, 1902–4, 1906, 1908, 1915–16, 1919–21; Art Institute of Chicago, 1916). In 1902 Connor left Roycroft 'to direct the Fine Arts' at Gustav Stickley's United Crafts, Syracuse, New York, a major arts-and-crafts centre. The movement's ideals were embodied in a Whitman memorial proposal, incorporating 'The labourers', a celebration of the dignity of craftsmanship, which won Connor immediate critical approval. An early commission, the Kirkpatrick memorial fountains (Syracuse, 1904)—life-studies of Onondaga Iroquois braves—led the Onondaga to honour him, and he participated for some years in their ceremonies.

After 1903, with his wife Anne, a fellow Roycrofter, he made an extended study visit to Italy, perhaps funded by sculptor and art patron Gertrude Vanderbilt. The Connors then moved from Syracuse, New York, to Washington, DC, c.1910. Major commissions followed for memorials to Irish American general James Shields (Carrollton, Missouri, 1910); to university founder Archbishop John Carroll (1735–1815) (Washington, 1912); to Robert Emmet (Washington, 1917; also San Francisco; Emmetsburg, Iowa; Dublin); and for war memorials: 'The supreme sacrifice' (Washington, marble, 1921), 'The angels of the battlefield' (US civil war nursing nuns, Washington, 1924), and 'Victory memorial' (the Bronx, New York city, 1925). His 1920 portrait of Éamon de Valera is a unique historical record.

American victims of the 1915 *Lusitania* sinking included Elbert Hubbard of Roycroft, and Gertrude Vanderbilt's multi-millionaire brother Alfred. Their families, with politicians including Franklin Roosevelt, formed the Lusitania Peace Memorial Committee to honour the dead at Queenstown (Cobh), Co. Cork, appointing Connor sculptor. In 1925 he moved with his family to Dublin. In 1929 they returned to America, but travelled regularly between the US and Ireland until the outbreak of war in 1939.

In Dublin, Connor's reliefs of government ministers William T. Cosgrave, Kevin O'Higgins, Desmond FitzGerald, Ernest Blythe and John Marcus O'Sullivan, and bust of George Russell (all 1926), Irish coinage submissions (1927), and 'The patriot', a 1916 memorial proposal (1929), won recognition. He exhibited at the Royal Academy (1929–32) and British Empire Academy (1930), and his 2 North Circular Road studio became a recognised meeting-place for artists and writers, but he received no state commissions.

After completing a companion Hubbard memorial (East Aurora, 1930), he addressed the *Lusitania* project, now delayed by briefing changes. Reflecting committee-member Gertrude Vanderbilt's shifting tastes, an initial allegorical angel was replaced (*c.*1930) by mourning fishermen. In 1934 a design incorporating both concepts was approved. He had personally cast the 'Fishermen' (the first large *cire-perdue* bronze attempted in Ireland) and completed the plaster 'Angel of peace' and the stonework when work stalled owing to lack of further funds (September 1936).

Before the depression Connor had hoped to erect memorials in his native Kerry. Alternative 'Liberty' (*c.*1930) and 'Pikeman' (1931) proposals for Tralee remained unrealised, but a Killarney 'Kerry poets memorial' ('Éire in mourning', evoking Whitman's poem 'Old Ireland') seemed viable, with his businessman brother Timothy covering part of the fee. Then local payments stopped (March 1932) amid claims that the design was 'pagan'. After a standoff, Connor was judged in breach of contract, and obliged to return all advances (July 1936).

Although many questioned this judgement, it precipitated Connor's bankruptcy (December 1938), eviction from his Dublin studio (February 1939), and subsequent poverty. He continued exhibiting (Royal Hibernian Academy 1937–8, 1941–3), however, now developing a late style, marked by an increasingly free use of clay—evident when contrasting the 1931 Tralee 'Pikeman' maquette with the near-expressionist 'Pikeman' study commissioned *c.*1941 by John Reihill. Another supporter, James Digby, provided him with a studio apartment (15 Crampton Court, his last address). By mid-1943, however, without a wartime fuel ration, he was unable to cast further bronzes. Admitted to the Adelaide Hospital suffering from malnutrition, he died of heart failure, 21 August 1943. In 1945 sculptor Domhnall Ó Murchadha helped save the main studio plasters. He completed the *Lusitania* memorial (1968) and 'Éire' (Dublin, 1976), designed Connor's Dublin gravestone and a memorial for Anascaul, and (with local help and the support of the Connor estate) set up the Jerome Connor Trust collection of Connor sculptures, intended for display at Anascaul once a gallery was built there for the purpose. A permanent exhibition space was finally opened in April 2014. Connor's fourth 'Emmet' bronze, recovered in the US, was erected in St Stephen's Green, Dublin, in 1968.

Connor is represented in the following collections: Dublin: Áras an Uachtaráin, Hugh Lane Municipal Gallery of Modern Art, National Gallery of Ireland (NGI), National Museum of Ireland (NMI); East Aurora, New York: ScheideMantel House; Frankfort, Kentucky: Old Capitol Building; Limerick: City Art Gallery; New York: Metropolitan Museum of Art; Washington, DC: Woodrow Wilson House; and Waterford: Municipal Art Collection.

Contemporaries admired Connor's work for its unflinching realism and sensitivity to individual character. His monuments gave historic events immediacy, his models embodying ideals of heroism, spirituality and sorrow. Catholic, nationalist Irish America found him an eloquent advocate, communicating their values to a wider society by his sophisticated use of contemporary secular imagery. In Ireland, such imagery was unappreciated, and

Connor was reduced to penury, his achievement preserved for the nation only by the timely action of a dedicated few.

Connor married (1901) fellow Roycroft craftworker Anne Bowen Donohue, daughter of Dr Thaddeus Donohue of Memphis, Tennessee (born Tralee, Co. Kerry; surgeon, 110th Regiment US Colored Infantry, 1864–6), and Anna Elizabeth Donohue (née Chase), of a southern planter family. The Connors had one child, Marjorie ('Peggy') Connor.

Giollamuire Ó Murchú

Sources

US Department of Commerce, Bureau of the Census, *12th census of the United States, population* (1900), Holyoke, MA, and East Aurora, NY, entries (courtesy Donna Reid Hotaling); Lorado Taft, *History of American sculpture* (1903); Frances B. Sheafer, 'A sculptor of the people', *Appleton's Booklover's Magazine* (June 1903), 623–8; H. N. Kirwan, 'An Irish-American sculptor—Mr Jerome Connor', *The Crystal* (May 1926), 100–01; *Daily Express* (London), 10 August 1929; *Kerryman*, 7 March 1931; Arthur Power, 'Irish sculpture', *Irish art handbook* (1943), 1–8; *The Irish Times*, 23 August 1943; J. D. Riley, 'Stephen MacKenna in New York, an anecdote and some extracts', TS (*c*.1955), Thomas MacGreevy papers, TCD MS 8115/96, courtesy Susan Schreibman; J. D. Riley, 'Stephen MacKenna in New York', *Dublin Magazine* (October–December 1955), 28–30; Máirín Allen, 'Jerome Connor', *Capuchin Annual 1963*, 347–68; *1964*, 357–69; *1965*, 365–90; Dermot McEvoy, 'Roving eye', *Hibernia*, 23 November 1978; Charles F. Hamilton, *Roycroft collectibles* (1992); Giollamuire Ó Murchú, *Jerome Connor, Irish American sculptor 1874–1943* (1993); Giollamuire Ó Murchú, 'General James Shields', Gorry Gallery, *An exhibition of 18th, 19th and 20th century Irish paintings*, Dublin (November 1993), 22, catalogue; Giollamuire Ó Murchú, 'The sculpture of Jerome Connor', *Kerry Magazine*, no. 5 (1994), 29–30; Marie Via and Marjorie B. Searl (eds), *Head, heart and hand: Elbert Hubbard and the Roycrofters* (1994); information from George Chase, Waco, Texas (7 March, 6 April 1994), and Colleen Becker, Whitney Museum of American Art (25 September 1997); Giollamuire Ó Murchú, 'Connor, Jerome', Günther Meißner (ed.), *Allgemeines Künstlerlexikon*, xx (1998); Smithsonian American Art Museum Art Inventories, *Connor, Jerome* and *Dewey Arch*, http://siris-artinventories.si.edu (accessed March 2021); annascaul.org (accessed March 2021)

9. Lives in print

Introduction

To capture the scope of the involvement of Irish immigrants in American publishing, journalism and literature, we have curated a diverse range of figures from the eighteenth to the twentieth century. We have done this not only with an eye to the Irish contribution to America's political, publishing and literary histories (John Dunlap, p. 260, Margaret Maher, p. 274, Richard Kyle Fox, p. 277, Carmel Snow, p. 282), but also to how Irish immigrants (of the famine generation in particular) communicated Irishness (Mary Anne Sadlier, p. 263, Michael J. Logan, p. 268). This helped a dislocated community deal with its traumas and retain the sense of national and religious identity that still underpins today's Irish American community. With the inclusion of *New Yorker* columnist Maeve Brennan (p. 288), we hope to capture the shift toward a more sophisticated and reflective articulation of the Irish American experience in the twentieth century.

John Dunlap (1746/7–1812) is known primarily as the printer of both the declaration of independence (1776) and the US constitution (1787), but he is also a significant figure in American newspaper history. He started his first paper, the *Pennsylvania Packet* in 1771, which, when it became a daily publication in 1784, was the first of significance in the country. Richard Kyle Fox (1846–1922), pioneered another type of publication: the tabloid. His enormously popular *National Police Gazette* mixed sports with sensationalism and was instrumental in popularising boxing in America.

Margaret Maher (*c.*1845–1924) and Carmel Snow (1887–1961) both made critical contributions to American literature, but in very different ways. Maher, a domestic servant, is credited with preserving the poetry of Emily Dickinson; while Snow, as editor of *Harper's Bazaar*, fostered the talent of American and Irish writers including Frank O'Connor, Sean O'Casey, Eudora Welty and a young Truman Capote.

Mary Anne Sadlier (1820–1903) was a prolific famine-generation novelist who documented the Irish immigrant experience. In her moralistic tales, she portrayed the plight of poor Irish men, women and children in workplaces, public institutions and within corruptive urban environments, and expressed the perceived dangers for the Irish who ascended to the American upper classes. Michael J. Logan (1836–99), known as the 'father of the Gaelic language movement' in America, believed the language 'should be cultivated in order to maintain Irish ideas and Irish nationality in their integrity'. His bilingual journal, *An Gaodhal (The Gael)*, is thought to be the first anywhere to carry material printed in Irish, including beginners' lessons in the language.

Maeve Brennan (1917–93) was the daughter of writer and diplomat Robert Brennan (1881–1964), and wrote as much about her childhood in Dublin as she did about her adulthood in America. She was recruited to *Harper's Bazaar* by the above-mentioned Carmel Snow as a fashion writer known for her chic personal style, before moving to the *New Yorker* and expanding her repertoire as a social diarist. While she appeared at ease in literary New York, her short stories were preoccupied with Ireland, a place of melancholy and emotional paralysis, reminiscent of the country depicted by fellow emigrants (or exiles) Joyce and Beckett.

LE

John Dunlap

1746/7–1812

War of independence
veteran and printer
to the Continental
Congress who printed
the Declaration of
Independence (1776)
and the first public
version of the US
Constitution (1787).

John Dunlap was born in what is now Meetinghouse Street, Strabane, Co. Tyrone, a younger son among probably three sons and four daughters of John Dunlap, saddler, and Sarah Dunlap (née Ector). He may have been apprenticed to learn the printing trade in Gray's of Strabane; when he was about ten, he was sent to assist his uncle William Dunlap, who had earlier emigrated to America. William Dunlap had married Benjamin Franklin's niece and was a printer and bookseller; Franklin appointed him postmaster of Philadelphia (1757), but in 1764 he was replaced by another Franklin relative. Partly as a result, William Dunlap got into financial difficulties. In 1766 he gave up bookselling to enter the ministry of the Church of England, and in 1768 John Dunlap, who had completed his apprenticeship, bought his uncle's printing business. He at first had to sleep under the counter in the printing shop. The following year he reprinted an English political satire and attributed it to Benjamin Franklin to increase sales.

In November 1771 Dunlap started a weekly newspaper, the *Pennsylvania Packet*; on 21 September 1784 it became the first newspaper of significance in America to be published daily. Around 1777 he was also publishing the *Maryland Gazette*. In 1774 Dunlap published a reprint of Thomas Jefferson's *Summary view of the rights of British America*; he was also official printer to the Continental Congress which met in Philadelphia. On 4 July 1776 that body formally adopted the declaration of independence, which was thereupon printed overnight by Dunlap for distribution to the colonial assemblies; surviving copies of this document are regarded as historical and bibliographical treasures of the United States. In September 1777, when Philadelphia was taken by the British, Dunlap moved his press to Lancaster, Pennsylvania, where he printed material for the revolutionary Pennsylvania assembly and also printed the journals of the continental congress. He was the first printer to re-establish business in Philadelphia in July 1778. Dunlap and his partner also printed the constitution of the United States in 1787.

Dunlap, one of the founders in 1774 of the 1st troop of Philadelphia City Cavalry, saw active service in the war of independence in 1776–7; in 1780 he subscribed £4,000 to found the National Bank for the United States to provide supplies for the new country's army. He was a major in command of the cavalry during the Pennsylvania 'whiskey insurrection' of 1794. From 1789 to 1792 he was a member of the common council of Philadelphia. Dunlap helped several of his relations to emigrate from Ireland, was charitable and fair-minded, and somewhat intemperate. He retired in 1795 a very wealthy man; he had speculated in land and owned 98,000 acres in several states. He married (4 February 1773) Elizabeth Ellison (née Hayes), a widow from Liverpool, and they had five daughters and three sons; two of the sons died in infancy. Dunlap died on 27 November 1812 of apoplexy and was buried with military honours in the graveyard of Christ Church, Philadelphia, Pennsylvania.

Linde Lunney

Sources

Dictionary of American biography (1928–58); George W. Corner (ed.), *The autobiography of Benjamin Rush: his travels through life together with his commonplace book for 1789–1813* (1948), 319; Leonard Labaree (ed.), *The papers of Benjamin Franklin,* xiii (1969), 84n; William B. Willcox (ed.), *The papers of Benjamin Franklin,* xvi (1972), 62; Frederick R. Goff, *The John Dunlap broadside: the first printing of the declaration of independence* (1976) (portrait, c.1803); Public Records Office Northern Ireland, August 1998, material from website on the Dunlap papers (T1336); genealogical information from Virgil D. White, *Genealogical abstracts of revolutionary war pension files* (1990–92) and from John T. Humphrey, *Pennsylvania births: Philadelphia county* (1994), supplied by Oscar Dunlap (family historian) of Texas; information from Ken Dunlap (family historian)

Mary Anne Sadlier

1820–1903

Influential writer
on the emigrant
experience, her novel,
*New lights; or Life
in Galway* (1853)
was the first fictional
description of the
famine to be published.

Mary Anne Sadlier was born 31 December 1820 in Cootehill, Co. Cavan, daughter of Francis Madden, a successful merchant who educated his daughter at home after the early death of his wife, whose name is unknown. Mary evidenced writing talents at a young age and in 1839 had verse published in an English literary periodical, *La Belle Assemblée*. Soon after this her father's business suffered financial setbacks, which seem to have contributed to his death in 1844. Later that year Mary emigrated to Montreal, Canada, where she experienced the difficulties of being an impoverished immigrant without family. She had stories published in papers such as the *Literary Garland*. Recent critics have speculated that she worked briefly as a domestic servant, given her later concern for and identification with this class in her novels; however, she was reticent about her early life and there is no proof of this. In 1845 her first book, *Tales of the olden time: a collection of European traditions*, appeared in serial form in the *True Witness*. The following year she married (November 1846) James Sadlier, co-owner with his brother Denis of a leading New York Catholic publishing house, D. & J. Sadlier. The couple remained in Montreal for fourteen years and during that time Sadlier had six children, adopted one more, and wrote six novels. *New lights; or Life in Galway* (1853) was the first fictional description of the famine and describes 'souperism' (the provision of food to the Catholic poor on condition they receive Protestant religious instruction) in lurid terms. *The Blakes and the Flanagans: a tale illustrative of Irish life in the United States* (1855) paints a black and white world of upstanding Catholics against sinful Protestants and is censorious about the effects of American public education on immigrants' faith. Her novels drew on the ready-made audience of Irish immigrants and were all bestsellers, contributing greatly to the success of her husband's publishing firm.

In 1860 the Sadliers moved to New York, where they were leading figures in conservative Catholic circles, hosting weekly receptions at their house on East Broadway and in their summer home in Rockaway, a popular Irish seaside resort. Friends included Archbishop John Joseph Hughes of New York and the Irish poet and politician Thomas D'Arcy McGee. Her politics were nationalist and she apparently donated stories to like-minded journals. When McGee moved to Canada in 1867, the Sadlier firm bought his paper, the *American Celt*, and, changing its name to the *Tablet*, continued to publish it for many years with Mary Sadlier as editor. She continued to write prolifically, often using themes suggested by her husband. Her most enduring work is *Bessy Conway; or the Irish girl in America* (1862), which depicts a pious immigrant servant defending her Catholic beliefs in a Protestant household, then returning to Ireland to save her family from eviction and marrying the landlord's son, who has converted to Catholicism.

Her husband died in 1869 and Sadlier took over running his share of the business. She wrote fewer novels, concentrating on Catholic readers for schoolchildren, on translations of religious works from French and on short dramas. After McGee's assassination (1869), she edited a volume of his poems, and on the death of her Jesuit son, Francis Xavier, she composed *Purgatory: doctrinal, historical and poetical* (1886). She spent much of her time in philanthropic works, particularly sponsoring Catholic alternatives to Protestant welfare institutions, such as a foundling asylum, an old people's home and a home for friendless Catholic girls. The publishing firm started to run into difficulties in the 1880s, due to increased competition and her real-estate speculation; nevertheless, after the death of her brother-in-law (1885), Sadlier continued to run the firm single-handed from Montreal, where she returned that year to be near her children. Her control of the company ended ten years later when her nephew, William Sadlier, took over only to sell outright to P. J. Kennedy & Sons, who bought up all the copyrights and reprinted Sadlier's novels—a new wave of Irish immigrants having refreshed the demand. Sadlier, however, gained no royalties from these reprints, and the remainder of her life was troubled by financial problems. Friends established a fund in her name and arranged a blessing from Pope Leo XIII. In 1895 she received the Notre Dame University Laetare medal for her services to the Catholic faith. She died 5 April 1903 in Montreal, having written around sixty books, and was survived by four of her children, including the novelist Anna Sadlier (1854–1932).

Sadlier's work is of sociological interest as an indicator of the reading material of Irish immigrants, but it has been largely dismissed as sentimental, contrived and marred by excessive didacticism. Some recent critics have, however, commended her for honestly depicting immigrant problems of poverty and alcoholism, and feminist critics have uncovered a strain of radicalism—though Sadlier always arranges marriages for her heroines, few of the married women are happy; and though she encourages submission, she sets up a conflict of duty between husband and God. Her life contradicted her work, since she preached that a woman's place was in the home but was herself a highly resourceful and energetic breadwinner.

There is a Mary Anne Sadlier archive on the University of Virginia website containing a full bibliography of her works and the text of *Bessie Conway*.

Bridget Hourican

Sources

T. P. Slattery, *The assassination of D'Arcy McGee* (1968); Terence N. Brown, 'Sadlier', in Edward T. James *et al.* (eds), *Notable American women, 1607–1950* (1971); Michele Lacombe, 'Frying pans and deadlier weapons: the immigrant novels of Mary Anne Sadlier', *English Canadian Writing*, xxix (1984); Paul and Jane Schlueter, *An encyclopedia of British women writers* (1988); Michael Glazier (ed.), *Encyclopedia of Irish Americans* (1999); Anne Commire (ed.), *Women in world history* (2001), xii; Liz Szabo, 'My heart bleeds to tell it: women domestics and the American ideal in Mary Anne Sadlier', University of Virginia (1995, https://www.xroads.virginia.edu/~Hyper/SADLIER2_OLD/Sadlier/Intro.html, accessed October 2020); Rolf Loeber and Magda Loeber, *A guide to Irish fiction 1650–1900* (2006), 1155–63; The Mary Anne Sadlier Archive, University of Virginia: http://xroads.virginia.edu/~Hyper/SADLIER/Sadlier.htm (accessed October 2020)

Michael J. Logan (Micheál Ó Lócháin)

1836–99

In his effort to preserve native culture and language among Irish immigrants, Michael J. Logan's newspaper *The Gael* helped forge the 'Irish American' identity.

Michael J. Logan (Micheál Ó Lócháin) was born 29 September 1836 at Currach Doire (Curraghderry), Baile an Mhuilinn (Milltown), near Tuam, Co. Galway, son of Patrick Logan, a small farmer. Michael's mother was one of the Oisins (Hessions) from Garraí Mór an tSléibhte (Garrymore Mountain), Co. Mayo, and spoke only Irish. Logan was raised in an area where Irish was the everyday language.

He was probably educated at a local hedge school or may have attended one of the independent schools established by Archbishop John MacHale (1791–1881). It is said that one of his teachers was a Maynooth seminarian, possibly Ulick Bourke (1829–87), a passionate advocate of the Irish language. Logan reported that he left school at eighteen in 1854, but nothing else is known about his life until 1871 when he emigrated to New York at the age of thirty-five with his family (his wife Margaret and four of their five children). He may have been a schoolteacher in Ireland in those intervening years, given he became principal of Our Lady of Victory school in Brooklyn within a year of arriving in America. He worked as a teacher for five years then opened a real-estate agency in Brooklyn in 1878, which enjoyed some success.

On 25 May 1872, a year after leaving Ireland, Logan wrote a letter signed 'The Gael' to the *Irish World* (an English-language newspaper), criticising the Irish-speakers living in America who denied their nationality and cultural heritage by abandoning their own language. Logan argued that a national language was essential to national identity. He followed with letters urging that classes be offered in the Irish language, and he himself taught it at his home in Brooklyn and in a local hall.

Logan was not the first person to promote the Irish language in America. A branch of the Ossianic Society had been established in New York in 1858; its interests were primarily in Irish manuscripts and literature, however, not in Irish as a vernacular language. Logan's appeal struck a chord, and by 1886 his letters and those of supporters had inspired Irish Americans to establish some fifty Irish-language organisations, beginning with the Philo-Celtic Society of Boston (28 April 1873). Logan's learners' group developed into the Brooklyn Philo-Celtic Society, founded 12 December 1874. The next year, across the river in Manhattan, the New York Gaelic Society was founded. They began offering classes in Irish in May 1878.

In October 1881 Logan founded *An Gaodhal (The Gael)*, which described itself as 'a monthly journal devoted to the preservation and cultivation of the language and anatomy of the Irish nation'. It was the most significant development in encouraging the language movement in America, and had an almost equal impact on Ireland. Logan's first editorial explained his purpose: 'We place *The Gael* before the Irish people; it will give lie to those ignorant or envious persons who would try to make it appear that the Irish people had no cultivated language, insinuating thereby that they were uncivilised and unlettered.' He claimed that it was the first newspaper in the world to carry material printed in Irish, and it used Irish typeface. Logan was editor of *An Gaodhal*; the publishers were the Nolan Brothers of Fulton Street, Brooklyn. After three issues the paper was making a loss and the backers wanted to stop publication, but Logan was determined to continue and became sole proprietor. Not only that, to cut costs, he had to learn how to set up type and print. By June 1882 Logan had taken over the typesetting and printing. By the end of the first year, *An Gaodhal* had 1,257 subscribers; the editor declined an offer of a $5,000 subvention 'because those supplying the money would naturally expect a share of its control' (*An Gaodhal*, 1882, 54). The number of subscribers increased to 2,800, but Logan continued to print and distribute every issue and never took any profits from the project.

Logan's concern about control no doubt reflected his sense of purpose for *An Gaodhal*: he wanted no dilution of its dedication to the Irish language. To that end, he published Irish lessons for beginners based on *Easy lessons; or Self instruction in Irish, part 1* (1860) by Ulick Bourke (Uilleog de Búrca), and he printed letters, essays and poems in the Irish language. *An Gaodhal* was in every sense pioneering; it provided beginners with lessons before language textbooks were widely available. Learners would have to wait until 1894 for *Simple lessons in Irish* by Father Eugene O'Growney (1863–99).

Logan served as secretary of his parish temperance society, arguing that drink impeded the progress of the Irish in America and freedom in Ireland. After Douglas Hyde and Eoin MacNeill founded the Gaelic League in Ireland in 1893, Logan supported the work of that organisation in *An Gaodhal*, featuring the leaders and workers in a series of profiles, and covering the activities of League branches. In 1898 he served as secretary of the Gaelic League of America. Logan supported some aspects of Irish nationalism, though distancing himself from the extremist 'gasbags of the Irish-American political societies' (*Leader*, 10 October 1942, 210). He made a clear distinction between obeying the pope on spiritual matters and opposing him on political issues such as the land war and the Plan of Campaign (*An Gaodhal*, 1888, 807), and he was unforgiving about what he regarded as the Irish hierarchy's favouring of the English language over Irish

(1892, 188). In 1890 Logan endorsed the Boycott League, an organisation pledged to fight England by boycotting English goods. Publishers of Irish or Catholic books and journals were the main advertisers in *An Gaodhal*, and in 1898 Logan began to import a selection of Irish books, primarily Irish-language texts.

An Gaodhal also encouraged other Irish-language newspapers and journals such as *The Irish Echo* (Boston) and the *Gaelic Journal* (Dublin). Articles, stories and poems from *An Gaodhal* were carried in Irish papers and journals. *An Gaodhal* featured Irish literature, music, history and items on the arts. Logan's readers found prosperity and respectability in Irish America at the turn of the century, but in some cases for the first time realised that they had something of their own that was of value when Logan invited his readers to send poetry, stories and folklore in Irish or in English to *An Gaodhal*. By showing that he valued the contributions of Irish readers, Logan helped develop their pride in their own oral traditions. He has been credited with having been the first to visualise the possibilities of an Irish Ireland, and certainly his work helped form Irish America.

Logan published *An Gaodhal* up to his sudden death on 10 January 1899 from apoplexy near his home at 267 Kosciusko Street, Brooklyn. He was survived by his wife, two sons and two daughters; his eldest daughter, Mary, predeceased him in 1892. He is buried in Brooklyn's Holy Cross cemetery. Publication of *An Gaodhal* continued until 1904 with Geraldine Haverty as editor, assisted by members of the Gaelic League.

Maureen O. Murphy

Sources

'Deaths from the cold', *Brooklyn Eagle*, 10 January 1899; S. Ó Laighin, 'Cailleadh Mhichil Uí Lócháin', *An Gaodhal*, xviii, no. 1 (1899); Tadhg Ó Donnchadha ('Torna'), 'Tuireadh Mhichíl Uí Lógáin', *An Gaodhal*, xviii, no. 5 (1899); 'Ramrod', 'Irish Ireland born in America', *Leader*, 10 October 1942, 209–11; Breandán Ó Buachalla, '*An Gaodhal* i Meiriceá', in Stiofán Ó hAnnracháin (ed.), *Go Meiriceá Siar* (1979); Maureen Murphy, '*The Gael*, 1881–1904', *An Gael*, ii, no. 2 (spring 1984), 20, 22; Fionnuala Uí Fhlannagáin, *Mícheál Ó Lócháin agus An Gaodhal* (1990); *Beathaisnéis 1882–1982*, iii, 114–15; Philip O'Leary, *The prose literature of the Gaelic Revival 1881–1921. Ideology and innovation* (1994); Kenneth E. Nilsen, 'The Irish language in New York, 1850–1900', in Ronald H. Baylor and Timothy J. Meagher (eds), *The Irish in New York* (1996), 252–74; Ronald H. Baylor, *The New York Irish* (1997), 268–70; Úna Ní Bhroiméil, *Building Irish identity in America, 1870–1915. The Gaelic revival* (2003)

This entry has been abridged for publication. The full version is available at www.dib.ie.

Margaret Maher

*c.*1845–1924

Described by the poet
Emily Dickinson as
'warm and wild and
mighty,' she served the
family for thirty years
and is credited with
preserving Dickinson's
poetry.

Margaret 'Maggie' Maher was born in Killusty, Co. Tipperary, the third of four children, to Michael and Mary Maher. About 1865 she emigrated to America with her older sister Mary, her brother Michael and possibly their youngest sibling, Thomas. Soon after their arrival, Mary married Thomas Kelley and the family settled in Amherst, Massachusetts. Maher returned to Tipperary and brought her parents back to Amherst with her. Initially Maher worked for a family called Boltwood and, when the Boltwood children left for school, she intended to follow her brother Thomas to California. In February 1869, however, she was engaged by the Dickinsons, one of the foremost Amherst families, and the most eccentric. Edward Dickinson was an authoritarian lawyer, his wife was a semi-invalid and their eldest daughter, the poet Emily Dickinson, was a recluse who did not leave the house after 1866.

Maher stayed thirty years with the family and was loyal, hard-working and equal to their eccentricities. She was rewarded by the solicitude of all the family, especially Emily—who wrote Maher amusing letters when she was sick with typhoid and supported her when her brother died in 1881. Emily Dickinson described Maher warmly in her correspondence: 'Maggie, good and noisy, the north wind of the family' (Dickinson, *Letters*, 690); 'Maggie, with us still, warm and wild and mighty' (827). The evidence from Maher's letters—misspelled, ungrammatical but dignified and heartfelt—bears out the poet's description. On her own directions for her funeral, Emily Dickinson was borne to her grave by the six Irishmen who had worked on her father's grounds, with Maher's brother-in-law Thomas Kelley as chief pallbearer. The story that Maher saved Dickinson's poems by refusing to burn them after her death as she had requested, comes from the poet's niece Martha, who recalled a tearful scene where Maher sought the advice of Austin and Susan Dickinson about the conflict caused by her promise to burn the poems. Although possibly apocryphal, what is certain is that the poems were kept in Maher's trunk, and were preserved for posterity.

Maher remained with the family until Emily's younger sister Lavinia died in 1899. During that period she also cleaned and cooked for Mabel Loomis Todd the editor who posthumously published Dickinson's poetry. Maher also provided Todd with the only known daguerreotype of the poet, an image she had kept despite the family hating it. She died in 1924 and her correspondence is held in the Detroit public library and in Harvard University.

Bridget Hourican

Sources

Jay Leyda, 'Miss Emily's Maggie', *New World Writing*, iii (1953), 255–67; Thomas H. Johnson (ed.), *Letters of Emily Dickinson* (1958); Jay Leyda (ed.), *The years and hours of Emily Dickinson* (1970); Richard B. Sewall, *Life of Emily Dickinson* (1974); Polly Longsworth, *Austin and Mabel* (1984); Aífe Murray, 'Miss Margaret's Emily Dickinson', *Signs*, vol. 24, no. 3 (spring 1999), 697–732

Richard Kyle Fox

1846–1922

A pioneer of tabloid
journalism, Fox's hugely
popular *National Police
Gazette* mixed sports
with sensationalism and
was instrumental in
popularising boxing in
America.

Richard Kyle Fox was born on Albertbridge Road, Belfast, on 12 August 1846. Fox's father James was a carpenter and mason, and his mother Mary (née Kyle) was the daughter of Henry Kyle, a Belfast presbyterian minister. As a teenager Fox worked as an office boy for the *Banner of Ulster* before later working at the *Belfast News Letter* for ten years. He emigrated to the United States in September 1874.

Continuing his trade in America, Fox landed a position at the *Commercial Bulletin* of New York within days of his arrival at the immigration station at Castle Garden. He subsequently became business manager at the then foundering *National Police Gazette* and by late 1876 had taken ownership of the publication in lieu of back wages, transforming it into a profitable business.

Years before Joseph Pulitzer's *New York World* and William Randolph Hearst's *New York Journal* managed to master and monopolise the techniques of 'yellow journalism', Richard Kyle Fox had been a pioneer. Printed on pink paper, and usually featuring frolicking females on its cover, the *National Police Gazette* provided an assortment of crimes, scandalous tales, extraordinary endeavours and the latest sports news. Wherever men gathered, from barrooms to hotel lobbies, the 'bible of the barbershop', as it became known, could be found.

Following the *Gazette*'s coverage of a fight between Tipperary native Patrick Ryan and Joe Goss of England in 1880, circulation rose from 150,000 to 400,000 copies a week, prompting the Belfast proprietor to engage in the promotion of prize fights. By the mid-1880s, Fox's publication had skyrocketed in circulation, with sporting coverage (particularly boxing) featuring on two or more pages of illustrations.

It was Fox's ongoing feud with the popular 'Boston strong boy', John L. Sullivan, that proved a convenient sales strategy for the former's weekly publication. The lively and profitable discord between Fox and Sullivan is said to have originated at Harry Hill's saloon in New York, when an inebriated Sullivan refused an invitation to join Fox at his table. The more likely story is that Sullivan, who had presented himself at the *Police Gazette* offices following his easy victory over Steve Taylor, conducted himself in an impertinent manner during a visit to Fox's office. Though less than impressed by the brass-necked Bostonian, Fox initially agreed to back him against Patrick Ryan until Sullivan later declared that he had never authorised Fox to make a match on his behalf and declined his offer.

Over the next couple of months Fox's determination to humble the insolent Sullivan allowed the Belfast man to master the art of boxing promotion by becoming one of the first to sponsor ring matches with belts, cash and other prizes and use his publication to fight against laws banning prize fighting. When the fight was eventually organised, Ryan, who Fox had declared *Police Gazette* champion in order to coax Sullivan into fighting, had his colours displayed in the barbershops and saloons whose proprietors were regular subscribers to the *Gazette*. Fox's publication even went so far as to reassure those intending to travel to the Sullivan–Ryan fight that, despite the state of Louisiana's attempt to hasten a legislative bill in order to prosecute those involved in prize fighting, the bout should be over by the time the law was enacted. The fight occurred on 7 February 1882, not in Louisiana, but in Mississippi. Sullivan easily dispatched his opponent in the ninth round prompting Fox to immediately declare that he would put up $5,000 for a rematch (which produced a similar result).

In March 1883 Fox opened his new premises on the corner of Franklin Square and Dover Street, overlooking the final stages of the construction of the Brooklyn Bridge. Describing his new premises as a 'veritable palace of journalism, unequalled by any newspaper establishment in New York', the 'Fox building', as it became known, occupied seven floors and was replete with the finest furnishings of that era. The building included ten printing presses on the ground floor and a museum of sports and sensationalism. When the Brooklyn Bridge finally opened on 24 May, Fox's decision to send out 10,000 invitations ensured that the building was packed with journalists, dignitaries and some of the leading athletes of the day. This was as good as it was going to get for Richard Kyle Fox, though his publication continued to promote all manner of sports and unusual physical endeavours, including Frank Samuelson and George Harbo's 1896 crossing of the Atlantic in an eighteen-foot rowboat.

In many ways Fox became a victim of his own ingenuity when many of the leading daily newspapers of the day had, by the end of the nineteenth century, adopted the *Gazette*'s penchant for featuring sport and sensationalism. By the early twentieth century the *National Police Gazette* had become little more than a purveyor of old news and quaint raciness in an increasingly more relaxed and modernist society. It was the adoption of the eighteenth amendment that was detrimental to the *Gazette*, for it cut off its entire barroom circulation. The new speakeasies that replaced the barrooms had little interest in the *Gazette*, and when women began to adopt the flapper hair style, which required that they frequent male barbershops, it was no longer acceptable to have Fox's publication for viewing pleasure.

Leaving behind assets well in excess of $3,000,000, Richard Kyle Fox died on 15 November 1922 following a long battle with pneumonia and is buried at Woodlawn Cemetery in the Bronx, New York, in an elaborate mausoleum. He was posthumously inducted into the International Boxing Hall of Fame (IBHF) in June 1997, along with fellow boxing promoter, Don King. Fox is described by the IBHF as having done more to popularise boxing in the United States than anyone else in the nineteenth century.

Liam Barry-Hayes

Sources

National Police Gazette, 10 March 1883; *Belfast News Letter*, 29 November 1922; Edward Van Every, *Sins of New York as exposed by the Police Gazette* (1930); Frank Luther Mott, *A history of American magazines, 1741–1930* (1958); Elliott J. Gorn, *The manly art: the lives and times of the great bare-knuckle champions* (1989); Guy Reel, *The National Police Gazette and the making of the modern American man, 1879–1906* (2006); Christopher Klein, *Strong boy: the life and times of John L. Sullivan, America's first sports hero* (2015)

Carmel Snow

1887–1961

Editor of *Vogue* and
Harper's Bazaar who
published for 'well-
dressed women with
well-dressed minds'
and showcased some
of America's finest
young writers.

Carmel Snow was born 27 August 1887 in Dalkey, Co. Dublin, one of six children to Peter White (1850–93), businessman, and his wife Anne (née Mayne), daughter of Thomas Mayne, an MP for the Irish Home Rule Party from 1883 to 1890. Snow's father was managing director of the Irish Woollen Manufacturing and Export Company and a member of the Irish Industries Association. When he died unexpectedly while organising the 'Irish village' concession for the World's Fair in Chicago in 1893, his widow took over the project, which proved a huge success. Anne White decided to remain in Chicago, opening a shop of Irish handicrafts, and in 1895 sent for Carmel and her sister, who had been living with their maternal grandparents in Terenure, Dublin.

Carmel was educated at the prestigious Dearborn Seminary in Chicago, a boarding school in Winnetka, Illinois, and a convent finishing school in Brussels, Belgium. By this time her mother had married a New York retailer, Edward Van Pelt Douglass, and taken over a well-known New York custom dressmaking firm, T. M. & F. M. Fox, which produced Parisian haute couture for the American market. Anne White was imposing, managerial and hardworking and made the firm ever more successful; the family lived comfortably, with frequent holidays in Ireland. Carmel spent her formative years helping her mother supervise the shop and workroom, which employed 250 fitters and seamstresses, and accompanying her on buying trips to Paris.

During the first world war Snow went to Paris with the Red Cross and proved so efficient and hardworking, that she was put in charge of all Red Cross female personnel in the city. At the end of the war she returned to New York with a reference from her employers stating that she was 'indefatigable and smart as a tack' (Snow, 35). While preparing for a buying trip to Paris, she was asked by a fashion columnist to report on the collections. Her copy was so good that she began writing a syndicated fashion column for the *New York Times* and was given a letter of introduction to Edna Woolman Chase, editor of *Vogue*. In 1921 she was brought on to the *Vogue* staff as assistant fashion editor, where her verve, charm and creativity compensated for her lack of magazine experience. Her personal view of fashion was also developing, encapsulated in such aphorisms as 'Buy only what you need. Buy the best quality you can afford' (Snow, 57). Snow also led an active social life and on 11 November 1926, at the age of thirty-nine, she married socialite George Palen Snow. He had a seat on the New York stock exchange and was independently wealthy but preferred to spend his time at sport and gardening. She gave birth to three daughters in quick succession, and a son who died at birth, but pregnancy did not slow her down: she reportedly only took one week off for each of the births.

In 1929 Snow was made American editor of *Vogue* but she was increasingly frustrated by the magazine's stuffy and exacting approach and by its emphasis on fashion and society, to the exclusion of culture and literature. She was also chaffing beneath the domineering and inflexible authority of Woolman Chase and, when an opportunity arose to jump ship, she did so, taking the role of fashion editor at William Randolph Hearst's *Harper's Bazaar*. Hearst's publications were in direct competition with *Vogue* and the two publishers had made an informal agreement not to poach each other's staff. Snow's defection caused immense bitterness and *Vogue*'s publisher Condé Nast never spoke to her again, although she was godmother to one of his children.

Appointed editor of *Harper's Bazaar* in 1935, Snow finally had full freedom to exercise her talents. Her first priority was to improve its look. Her eye for talent was legendary—she considered it her greatest gift—and she quickly assembled a dynamic team. Graphic designer Alexey Brodovitch was appointed art director, and soon the magazine had a fresh, bold, modernist format where text and pictures interacted. She took a leap into the unknown with Diana Vreeland, a socialite with no magazine experience but whose highly original sense of style was admired by Snow—eventually editor of *Vogue*, she was one of the icons of the twentieth-century fashion world. Snow also persuaded a little-known Hungarian photographer, Martin Munkacsi, to leave Berlin and join *Harper's* although he had no previous experience in fashion. His first assignment made history when he produced the first action fashion picture, a swimsuit-clad model running on a beach. But Snow's ambitions for her readers went beyond fashion; she wanted 'well-dressed women with well-dressed minds' (Snow, 172). She appointed the brilliant but mercurial writer George Davis as literary editor, and *Harper's* became a showcase for good writing, featuring for example the work of Frank O'Connor, Katherine Anne Porter and Evelyn Waugh. The magazine also helped discover Truman Capote and introduced the waspish drama critic Kenneth Tynan to American readers. During the second world war she published photographs smuggled out of occupied France to show Americans how destructive the war was.

Once they were hired, Snow allowed her staff full creative freedom; her own strong organisational abilities and sharp decisiveness kept them in order. Within a few years *Harper's* circulation had increased threefold. It was a byword for style and innovation in the industry, and its small, slim, impeccably dressed editor became a legend. She crossed the Atlantic every year for the Paris collections, and her nod was enough to get a designer started. In appreciation of her help in reviving the postwar French fashion industry she was awarded the Knight's Cross of the Légion d'honneur in 1949. The Italian government awarded her the Stella della Solidarietà. She brought the designers Christian Dior and Cristóbal Balenciaga to prominence in the US, and in later life was invariably dressed in Balenciaga suits.

Ireland also benefited from her fame and influence; she never lost her Irish identity nor her accent and was known as the 'Irish pixie' in reference to her throaty voice, her slimness and her famed intuition. One of her discoveries in the 1950s was the Irish tweed and linen designer Sybil Connolly, and in 1953 she arranged for a group of American fashion designers to accompany her to Ireland; *Vogue* and *Life* responded by featuring Connolly and the Irish model Ann Gunning. Two years later, when *Harper's* devoted twelve pages of an issue to British fashion, Snow insisted that four of them went to Ireland.

Her devotion to *Harper's* was all-consuming: her children were mainly brought up by nannies and she and her husband lived increasingly separate lives. Though some accused her of ruthlessness, most of her staff appreciated her humour, warmth and willingness to take risks. Known for her love of a three-martini lunch, Snow remained as editor well past the usual retirement age and became increasingly erratic and demanding. She was eventually ousted in 1957 and replaced with her niece, Nancy White, whom Snow had dismissed for years as insufficiently tough for the publishing world. Her departure marked the end of an era.

After retirement Snow spent three years living in Rossyvera House in Clew Bay, Co. Mayo, but the move was not a success. Her friends visited infrequently, and she found the isolation and climate too much to bear. She returned to New York and died in her sleep on 7 May 1961. Her funeral was so well attended that it had to be moved from the Lady Chapel to the main body of Saint Patrick's Cathedral. Carmel Snow was buried, in a red brocade Balenciaga suit, in Cold Spring Harbour, Long Island, New York.

Bridget Hourican

Sources

Dictionary of American biography (1928–58); *New York Times*, 9 May 1961; Carmel Snow and Mary Louise Aswell, *The world of Carmel Snow* (1962); Bettina Ballard, *In my fashion* (1960); Diana Vreeland, *D. V.* (1984); Gerald Clarke, *Truman Capote* (1988); *Sunday Independent*, 21 February 1999; Robert O'Byrne, *After a fashion* (2000); Penelope Rowlands, *A dash of daring* (2005); *The Irish Times*, 12 March 2019

Maeve Brennan

1917–93

Fiction writer and
New Yorker columnist
known-as the 'Long-
winded lady', Brennan
was almost unknown in
Ireland until her work
was revived to critical
acclaim in the late 1990s.

Maeve Brennan was born in Dublin on 6 January 1917, second of four children of the nationalist journalist Robert ('Bob') Brennan (1881–1964), and his wife, Una (née Anastasia Bolger, 1888–1958), both of whom she portrayed in successive stories. As Una Bolger, her mother was active in Maud Gonne's Inghinidhe na hÉireann and in Cumann na mBan; she was probably the author of a series of feminist articles in the *Enniscorthy Echo* in 1908–9.

The Brennans married in July 1909; their daughter Emer (1910–86), was followed by a son who died in infancy. Both parents took part in the 1916 rising in Enniscorthy, and Robert was in prison in England when Maeve was born some nine months later. She became known as a '1916 baby', leading to confusion about her birth year. When she was young her father was often on the run from the British, and later from Irish Free State forces.

In late 1921, as the Anglo-Irish Treaty was negotiated in London, the Brennans bought and moved into 48 Cherryfield Avenue, Ranelagh, Dublin. This modest terraced house, where they remained until 1934, is the setting for almost half of Brennan's forty published short stories. 'The day we got our own back' (1953), describes an armed raid there in 1922, when Robert was in hiding elsewhere.

The meticulously detailed descriptions in Brennan's fiction of day-to-day life in the Ranelagh house and garden represent her life-long turning away from the political and public issues that had dominated her childhood. Along with stories set in rural and urban Wexford, they offer unique portraits of middle-class Irish interiors and domestic life. Her work rises far above the local, however, to evoke the texture and minutiae of unsatisfactory intimate relationships, and show solitary women and men negotiating both private and public space.

Brennan attended Saint Mary's national school, Belmont Avenue, and Muckross Park primary school, both near her home, and from September 1929, a convent boarding school. 'The devil in us' (1954), describes Cross and Passion College in Kilcullen, Co. Kildare. Two years later, she and her younger sister transferred to the Irish-speaking Scoil Bhríde in Dublin. Set up by the French-born-and-educated nationalist Louise Gavan Duffy (1884–1969), who rejected violence, Scoil Bhríde nurtured Brennan's cultural nationalism along with her appreciation of theatre and literature in English and French.

In 1934 Taoiseach Éamon de Valera appointed Robert Brennan as secretary of the Irish legation in Washington, DC, and Brennan, who had finished her secondary schooling, moved to the US with her family. She attended Immaculata Seminary in Washington, followed by American University, where she was active in student literary societies and graduated BA in June 1938. She studied library science at the Catholic University of America, also in Washington, and in 1940 or 1941 moved to New York. She lived first at the Holley Hotel on Washington Square, and worked at the New York Public Library (NYPL) in central Manhattan.

Brennan left the NYPL when Carmel Snow (p. 282), Irish-born editor of *Harper's Bazaar*, invited her to join the magazine. From 1943 to 1949 she wrote fashion copy for *Harper's* and for its wartime offshoot, *Junior Bazaar*, and completed her pitch-perfect novella 'The visitor' before the end of 1945. Her striking, glamorous image— dark lipstick, high heels and hair piled up—dates from this period, while trained observation of fabric, cut and colour later lent characteristic detail to all her short fiction and essays. She lived mostly in Greenwich Village, met members of the Abbey Theatre and other visiting artists, and often accompanied photographers on assignment for the magazine. They included Karl Bissinger, who famously photographed her in 1948, when she escorted the playwright Denis Johnston to a session with him.

In 1949 William Shawn recruited Brennan to the *New Yorker*, to write unsigned fashion notes and book reviews. In December 1950 *Harper's Bazaar* published her story 'The holy terror'. In April 1952 'The poor men and women' followed: the first of many stories, in two cycles about contrasting, yet similar, couples, in which she probes the walls where she grew up for the codes they imposed. Beginning in December that year, the *New Yorker* fiction editor William Maxwell, later a trusted friend, published all of her further stories of Dublin, alternating them with another series set in an exclusive community on the Hudson River, which she called Herbert's Retreat. The Irish-born domestic servants she places there are surprising and memorable, drawn in many dimensions with ferocious sympathy and Brennan's keen awareness of household politics and registers of language. Throughout the 1950s and 1960s, her 'Long-winded lady' pieces also appeared regularly among the mostly male voices in *New Yorker*'s most-read section, 'Talk of the town'.

Colleagues at her new office admired Brennan's appearance, mordant wit and especially her writing; many appreciated her impulsive kindness. Several men's names were linked to hers, not always accurately, but in 1954 she married charming, talented, fellow staff-writer St Clair McKelway, who was addicted to alcohol and three times divorced, and went to live with him in Snedens Landing, the original of Herbert's Retreat. The marriage lasted until 1959, when she moved back to Manhattan.

Brennan never owned a house or apartment, although ideas of home permeate almost everything she wrote. In the 1960s she spent winters in East Hampton, Long Island, alone but for her black Labrador, Bluebell, and several cats. Later, she lived by the sea in Massachusetts. In summer she usually returned to Manhattan, where she rented or borrowed apartments, or stayed at the Algonquin Hotel; she made trips to Ireland and Europe by ocean liner.

Intimidatingly acerbic and helplessly compassionate, Brennan worked compulsively to capture the human realities behind the depictions of Irish domesticity in the 1937 constitution and popular writing. Her first fiction collection, *In and out of Never-Never Land*, and her own selection, *The long-winded lady*, appeared in the US in 1969. Critics hailed both, but she had begun to suffer writer's block, and bouts of mental illness.

Brennan's longest and most powerful story, 'The springs of affection', went through many versions before appearing in the *New Yorker* on 18 March 1972. Set in County Wexford, and based on her family, it caused hurt, and estranged her from some relatives. The magazine published only two more of her stories. It continued to pay her, and she wrote book reviews, but spent little time there in the years that followed.

During a series of artist's residencies at the MacDowell Colony (now MacDowell) in New Hampshire in the 1970s, Brennan wrote agonised, occasionally humorous, letters to Maxwell about her difficulties with money and her writing. She spent months at a time with relatives, first in Dublin, then, after a disturbing incident at the *New Yorker* offices and a spell in a psychiatric hospital, at her brother's home in Peoria, Illinois. Hinting at disarray, the publication date of her second fiction collection, *Christmas eve*, was June 1974.

Brennan's books were not reprinted, nor were they published in Ireland or Britain. Between periods spent in hospital, she lived in run-down hotels, or slept at the *New Yorker* offices, rejecting old friends who tried to help her. Unknown to them, however, and to most readers, she had made new, supportive friendships at MacDowell with Tillie Olsen (1912–2007) and Edith Konecky (1922–2019), feminist writers from eastern European Jewish backgrounds, whose outsider experience chimed with her own. She stayed at Konecky's New York apartment for weeks at a time, and wrote an encouraging meditation during one of Olsen's writing 'silences' that both Olsen and Konecky later placed above their desks. Konecky's second novel, *A place at the table*, features Brennan herself as the much-loved, fascinating, frustrating Irish writer, 'Deirdre'.

Brennan's last *New Yorker* piece, 'A blessing', appeared on 5 January 1981. The magazine's management found her a nursing home in Arverne, New York, but declined to give information on her whereabouts to anyone outside the organisation, so that family and friends lost contact with her. She died of heart failure there on 1 November 1993.

Editor Christopher Carduff had already begun to read all of Brennan's stories, selecting and arranging them in effective sequences. He commissioned a moving introduction by William Maxwell for the first of two new volumes, which appeared in 1997 and 2000, and produced a new, expanded edition of *The long-winded lady* in 1998. He discovered 'The visitor', in a university archive and edited it for publication in 2000. Brennan became known to a new generation of readers in the US, while in Ireland, a secular, liberal, Irish society embraced these four books as classics of twentieth-century writing.

A number of critics on both sides of the Atlantic, from backgrounds in feminist studies, urban studies and 'the body', as well as literature and history, have searched out previously unknown correspondence and published illuminating and persuasive readings of Brennan's work, while writers of popular non-fiction have seized on her story to illustrate their themes.

Amplified by this new work, her reputation was consolidated in 2017, when the centenary of her birth brought new Irish editions of her work, with introductions by Anne Enright and Belinda McKeon, and numerous events and publications in her honour.

Angela Bourke

Sources

Edith Konecky, *A place at the table* (1989); Maeve Brennan, *The rose garden: short stories* (2000); Roddy Doyle, *Rory and Ita* (2002); Angela Bourke, *Maeve Brennan: homesick at the* New Yorker (2004); Maeve Brennan, *The visitor* (2014); Maeve Brennan, *The springs of affection: stories of Dublin* (2016, first published 1997); Maeve Brennan, *The long-winded lady: notes from the* New Yorker (2017, first published 1998)

Bibliography

ARCHIVES

American Battlefield Trust
Alexander Brown & Sons papers, Library of Congress, Washington, DC
Brown Brothers & Company papers, New York Historical Society
Brown, Shipley & Company papers, Liverpool Public Library (copies held)
Mathew Carey papers, Historical Society of Pennsylvania
Mathew Carey papers, Library Company of Philadelphia, Pennsylvania
John Crawford Collection, Health Sciences and Human Services Library, University of Maryland
General Register Office (Republic of Ireland)
Thomas MacGreevy papers, Trinity College Dublin
Public Record Office of Northern Ireland
Mary Anne Sadlier Archive, University of Virginia
Smithsonian American Art Museum Art Inventories, http://siris-artinventories.si.edu
United States Census Bureau, www.census.gov

COMMEMORATIVE WEBSITES AND PUBLICATIONS

'Annie Moore revisited' website, https://anniemoore.net/home.html
'Belinda Mulrooney—the richest woman in the Klondike', Smithsonian National Postal Museum, https://postalmuseum.si.edu/
'Father Patrick Peyton CSC' website, www.fatherpeyton.org
'Special issue: Ireland, America and Mathew Carey', *Early American Studies*, vol. 11, no. 3, Fall, 2013.

REFERENCE

Allgemeines Künstlerlexikon, www.degruyter.de/akl
Biographical directory of the United States Congress, https://bioguideretro.congress.gov/
Catholic encyclopedia, 1913–, newadvent.org/cathen
Film Reference, www.filmreference.com
Find a Grave, www.findagrave.com

Internet Broadway Database, www.ibdb.com
Internet Movie Database, www.imdb.com
Irish Theatre Institute: Irish playography, www.irishplayography.com
Lortel Archives: The Internet Off-Broadway Database, www.lortel.org
Primetime Emmy® Award Database, www.emmys.com

Dwan, Martin (dir.), 2006 *The people's tenor*. Documentary. Zampano
Productions.

Boylan, Henry, 1998 *A dictionary of Irish biography* (3rd edn). Dublin. Gill
& Macmillan.
Burke, Sir John Bernard, 1958 *A genealogical and heraldic history of the
landed gentry of Ireland* (4th edn; first published 1899). London. John
Burke family *et al.*

Cameron, Nigel M. de S. 1993 *Dictionary of Scottish church history and
theology*. Downers Grove, IL. Intervarsity Press.
Collier Hillstrom, Laurie and Lofting, Claire (eds), 1997 *International
directory of film and filmakers*, ii: *Directors* (3rd edn). Detroit and London.
St James Press.
Commire, Anne (ed.), 2001 *Women in world history: a biographical encyclo-
pedia*. Detroit. Gale Group.
Concannon, John Joseph and Cull, Francis Eugene (eds), 1984 *The Irish
American who's who*. Baltimore, MD. Ancient Order of Hibernians. Port
City Press.

Delaney, John J. and Tobin, James Edward, 1962 *Dictionary of Catholic
biography*. London. R. Hale.

Garraty, J. A. and Carnes, M. C. (eds), 1999 *American national biography.*
New York. Oxford University Press.
Gillespie, Charles Coulston, 1973 *Dictionary of scientific biography*. New
York. Scribner.
Glazier, Michael (ed.), 1999 *The encyclopedia of the Irish in America*. Notre
Dame, IN. University of Notre Dame Press.

Hanrahan, Brenda, 1982 *Donegal authors: a bibliography*. Dublin. Irish
Academic Press.
Hobson, Bulmer (ed.), 1934 *The Gate Theatre Dublin*. Dublin. Gate Theatre.

Isham, Samuel, 1905 *The history of American painting*. New York. Macmillan.

Jackson, Kenneth T., 1995 *The encyclopedia of New York city*. New Haven, CT. Yale University Press.

James, Edward T. *et al.* (eds), 1971 *Notable American women, 1607–1950*. Cambridge, MA. Belknap Press of Harvard University Press.

Johnson, Allen and Malone, Dumas (eds), 1928–58; reissue 1955–64 and supplements, *Dictionary of American biography*. New York and London. Scribner.

Kunitz, Stanley J. and Haycraft, Howard (eds), 1964 *American authors, 1600–1900*. New York. The H. W. Wilson Co.

Lewis, Donald M. 1995 *Dictionary of evangelical biography*. Oxford. Blackwell.

Loeber, Rolf, Stouthamer-Loeber, Magda and Mullin Burnham, Anne, 2006 *A guide to Irish fiction 1650–1900*. Dublin. Four Courts Press.

Matthew, H. C. G. and Harrison, Brian (eds), 2004– *Oxford dictionary of national biography*. Oxford. Oxford University Press.

Ó Céirín, Kit and Ó Céirín, Cyril, 1996 *Women of Ireland: a biographic dictionary*. Galway. Tír Eolas.

O'Donoghue, D. J., 1970 *The poets of Ireland: a biographical and bibli-ographical dictionary of Irish writers of English verse* (facsimile reprint). New York. Johnson Reprint (first published Dublin and London, 1912.)

Placzek, Adolf K., 1982 *The Macmillan encyclopaedia of architects*. New York. Free Press.

Stephen, Sir Leslie and Lee, Sir Sidney, 1885–1901 and supplements, *Dictionary of national biography*. London and New York. Macmillan.

Schlueter, Paul and Schlueter, Jane, 1988 *An encyclopedia of British women writers*. New York. Garland.

Whiffen, Marcus and Koeper, Frederick, 1981 *American architects, 1607–1976*. Cambridge, MA. MIT Press.

White, Norval and Willensky, Elliot (eds), 2000 *AIA guide to New York city* (revised edn). New York. Three Rivers Press.

Wilmeth, Don B. (ed.), 2007 *Cambridge guide to American theatre*. Cambridge. Cambridge University Press.

Newspapers and periodicals

Advocate (New York)
American Cinematographer
American Historical Review
An Cosantóir
An Gael
An Gaodhal
Annals of Medical History
Appleton's Booklover's Magazine
Belfast News Letter
Brooklyn Eagle
Bulletin of the Institute of the History of Medicine
Canadian Journal of Irish Studies
Capuchin Annual
Catholic Bulletin
Catholic Herald and Standard
Catholic World
Chicago Tribune
Connacht Tribune
Cork Examiner
The Crystal
Daily Express (London)
Daily Telegraph (London)
Decies: Waterford Archaeological and Historical Society
Donegal News
Drogheda Independent
Dublin Magazine
Éire–Ireland
English Canadian Writing
Gaelic American
Guardian (London)
Hibernia
Illinois Heritage
Independent (London)
Ireland on Sunday
Irish America
Irish Catholic
Irish Central
Irish Daily Independent

Irish Echo (New York)
Irish Examiner
Irish Independent
Irish Law Times and Solicitors' Journal
Irish Political Studies
Irish Press
Irish University Review
Irish World (Boston)
Journal of American History
Journal of Church and State
Journal of the Galway Archaeological and Historical Society
Journal of the United Reformed Church History Society
Kansas Historical Quarterly
Kerry Magazine
Kerryman
Leader (Boston)
Longford Leader
Los Angeles Magazine
Los Angeles Times
Mayo News
Methodist History
Moberly Weekly Monitor
Musical Leader
National Police Gazette (New York)
New World Writing
New York Herald
New York Mirror
New York Times
Newsday
North Munster Antiquarian Journal
Observer (London)
Pilot (Boston)
Record Collector
Restoration Quarterly
San Francisco Chronicle
Saothar
Signs
Studies
Studies in American Religion
Sunday Independent

Syracuse Herald
Tennessee Historical Magazine
The Irish Times
Times (London)
Washington Post
Western People (Mayo)
Yakima Herald (Washington)

BOOKS AND ARTICLES

Appleby, John C., 1991 'Women and piracy in Ireland: from Gráinne O'Malley to Anne Bonny', in Margaret MacCurtain and Mary O'Dowd (eds) *Women in early modern Ireland*, 59–63. Edinburgh University Press.

Armstrong, Nevill A. D., 1936 *Yukon yesterdays: thirty years of adventure in the Klondike*. London. J. Long.

Arnold, Jeanne Gosselin, 1983 *A man of faith*. Hollywood, CA. Family Theater.

Asbury, Herbert, 1927 *Gangs of New York*. New York. Garden City Publishing Company.

Athearn, Robert G., 1949 *Thomas Francis Meagher: an Irish revolutionary in America*. Boulder, CO. University of Colorado Studies.

Bair, Deirdre, 1978 *Samuel Beckett*. London. Cape.

Ballard, Bettina, 1960 *In my fashion*. London. Sheed & Ward.

Bartleme, Tony, 2018 'The true and false stories of Anne Bonny, pirate woman of the Caribbean', *The Post and Courier* (South Carolina), 21 November.

Barton, Ruth, 2014 *Rex Ingram: visionary director of the silent screen*. Lexington, KY. University Press of Kentucky.

Baylor, Ronald H., 1997 *The New York Irish*. Baltimore, MD. Johns Hopkins University Press.

Beck, June Parker, n.d. 'Maureen O'Hara', *Women's Museum of Ireland*, https://womensmuseumofireland.ie/articles/maureen-o-hara (accessed 29 April 2021).

Bell Jr, Malcolm, 1987 *Major Butler's legacy: five generations of a slaveholding family*. Athens, GA. University of Georgia Press.

Benson, Richard *et al.*, 1973 *Lay this laurel*. New York. Eakins Press.

Berton, Pierre, 1960 *Klondike: the life and death of the last great gold rush*. London. W. H. Allen.

Bigger, F. J., 1916 *The Magees of Belfast and Dublin, printers*. Belfast. W. & G. Baird.

Blanton, DeAnna, 1993 'Women soldiers of the civil war', *Prologue Magazine* (spring), vol. 25, no. 1. Available at: https://www.archives.gov/publications/prologue/1993/spring/women-in-the-civil-war-1.html (accessed 30 April 2021).

Blanton, DeAnna and Cook, Lauren M., 2002 *They fought like demons: women soldiers in the American civil war*. Baton Rouge, LA. LSU Press.

Bourke, Angela, 2004 *Maeve Brennan: homesick at the* New Yorker. Berkeley, CA. Counterpoint.

Brands, H. W., 2005 *Andrew Jackson: his life and times*. New York. Anchor Books.

Bradsher, Earl L., 1966 *Mathew Carey, editor, author and publisher: a study in American literary development* (first published 1912). New York. AMS Press.

Brennan, Maeve, 2000 *The rose garden: short stories*. Washington, DC. Counterpoint.

Brennan, Maeve, 2014 *The visitor*. London. Atlantic Books.

Brennan, Maeve, 2016 *The springs of affection: stories of Dublin* (first published 1997). Dublin. Stinging Fly Press.

Brennan, Maeve, 2017 *The long-winded lady: notes from the* New Yorker (first published 1998). Dublin. Stinging Fly Press.

Bric, Maurice J., 2008 *Ireland, Philadelphia and the re-invention of America 1760–1800*. Dublin. Four Courts.

Brown Brothers and Company, 1919 *Experiences of a century, 1818–1918*. Philadelphia.

Brown, John Crosby, 1909 *A hundred years of merchant banking*. New York. Arno Press.

Callow, Simon, 1997 *Orson Welles*, i: *The road to Xanadu*. New York. Penguin.

Callow, Simon, 2006 *Orson Welles*, ii: *Hello Americans*. London. Jonathan Cape.

Carey, Mathew, 1942 *Autobiography*. Brooklyn, NY. E.L. Schwaab.

Carter II, Edward C., 1962 'The political activities of Mathew Carey, nationalist, 1760–1814'. Unpublished Ph.D. thesis. Bryn Mawr College, Pennsylvania.

Carter, Robert A., 2000 *Buffalo Bill Cody*. New York. J. Wiley.

Casella, Donna, 2013 'Mary Manning', in Jane Gaines *et al.* (eds), *Women film pioneers project*. New York. Columbia University Libraries, available at https://wfpp.columbia.edu/pioneer/mary-manning/ (accessed 31 May 2021).

Charles, M. ('A Trappist Monk'), 1991 *Father Peyton's rosary prayer book*. Dublin. Veritas Publishing.

Clarke, Gerald, 1988 *Truman Capote*. London. Hamilton.

Clarkin, William, 1984 *Mathew Carey: a bibliography of his publications, 1785–1824*. New York. Garland.

Clausius, Gerhard P., 1958 'The little soldier of the 95th: Albert D. J. Cashier', *Journal of the Illinois State Historical Society* (1908–1984), vol. 51, no. 4 (winter), 380–7.

Coakley, Davis, 1992 *Irish masters of medicine*. Dublin. TownHouse.

Cody, William F., 1994 *The life of Buffalo Bill*. London. Senate.

Collier, Robert, 1910 *In memoriam Peter Fenelon Collier*. New York. Privately printed.

Collins, David R. and Petie, Haris, 1971 *Great American nurses*. New York. J. Messner.

Comerford, R. V., 1998 *The Fenians in context* (2nd edn). Dublin. Wolfhound Press.

Conway, Katherine E., 1891 *Watchwords of John Boyle O'Reilly*. Boston. J. G. Cupples.

Conyngham, D. P., 1994 *The Irish Brigade and its campaigns* (reprint; first published 1869). New York. Fordham University Press.

Corner, George W. (ed.), 1948 *The autobiography of Benjamin Rush: his travels through life together with his commonplace book for 1789–1813*. Princeton, NJ. Princeton University.

Coughlan, Francis, 1977 'Pierce Butler, 1744–1822, first senator from South Carolina', *South Carolina Historical Magazine* 78 (April), 104–19.

Cox, Claude, 1995 'The Campbell–Stone movement in Ontario', *Studies in American Religion* 62.

Daly, Sean, 1984 *Ireland and the First International*. Cork. Tower Books.

Darby, Paul, 2009 *Gaelic games, nationalism and the Irish diaspora in the United States*. Dublin. University College Dublin Press.

Dawson, Lon, 2005 *Also known as Albert D. J. Cashier*. Chicago, IL. Compass Rose Cultural Crossroads Inc.

Dolan, P., 1974 'John McCormack, mastersinger: a short account of his American career', *The Sword of Light* (spring).

Doyle, D. J., 1947 'The Holland submarine', *An Cosantóir* vii (June), 297–302.

Doyle, David Noel, 1989 'The Irish in North America, 1776–1845', in W. E. Vaughan (ed.), *A new history of Ireland,* v: *Ireland under the Union, 1801–70*, 682–725. Oxford. Oxford University Press.

Doyle, Roddy, 2002 *Rory and Ita*. New York. Penguin.

Drew, Paul Redmond, 1996 'Sir William Johnson—Indian superintendent', *Early America Review* i, no. 2, available at www.varsitytutors.com/
earlyamerica/early-america-review/volume-1/sir-william-johnson-indi-
an-superintendent-colonial (accessed 31 May 2021).

Dryfhout, John H., 1982 *The work of Augustus Saint-Gaudens*. Hanover,
NH. University Press of New England.

Duggan, Keith, 2004 *The lifelong season: at the heart of Gaelic games*.
Dublin, TownHouse.

Dungan, Myles, 2006 *How the Irish won the West*. Dublin. New Island Books.

Dunne, Mick, 1997 *The star spangled final*. Dublin. Bank of Ireland/RTÉ.

Durand, John Francis, 1760 *Genuine and curious memoirs of the famous
Captain Thurot*. London. J. Burd.

Durey, Michael, 1997 *Transatlantic radicals and the early American republic*. Lawrence, KS. University Press of Kansas.

Eichacker, Joanne Mooney, 2003 *Irish republican women in America:
lecture tours 1916–1925*. Dublin. Irish Academic Press.

Elias, Stephen N., 1992 *Alexander T. Stewart: the forgotten merchant prince*.
Westport, CT. Praeger.

Elliott, C. A., 1979 *Biographical dictionary of American science*. Westport,
CT. Greenwood Press.

Ellis, Aytoun, 1960 *Heir of adventure: the story of Brown, Shipley & Co.,
merchant bankers, 1810–1960*. London. Brown, Shipley & Co.

Evans, A. G., 1999 *Fanatic heart: a life of John Boyle O'Reilly*. Boston.
Northeastern University Press.

Fanning, Samuel J., 1965 'Philip Embury, founder of Methodism in New
York', *Methodist History* iii, 16–25.

Feder, Chris Welles, 2010 *In my father's shadow: a daughter remembers
Orson Welles*. Edinburgh. Mainstream.

Ferguson, Kenneth (ed.), 2005 *King's Inns barristers 1868–2004*. Dublin.
King's Inns in association with the Irish Legal History Society.

Fetherling, D., 1974 *Mother Jones, the miners' angel* (1974). Carbondale,
IL. Southern Illinois University Press.

Feurer, Rosemary, 2013 'Mother Jones. A global history of struggle and
remembrance: from Cork, Ireland, to Illinois', *Illinois Heritage* (May),
28–33.

Fictum, David, 2016 'Anne Bonny and Mary Read: female pirates and
maritime women', *Colonies, ships and pirates: concerning history in the*

Atlantic world 1680–1740 (8 May), available at: https://csphistorical.com/2016/05/08/anne-bonny-and-mary-read-female-pirates-and-maritime-women-page-one/ (accessed 30 April 2021).

Fitzpatrick, Paul, 2013 *The fairytale in New York: the story of Cavan's finest hour*. Bray. Ballpoint Press.

Fitz-Simon, Christopher, 1996 *The boys*. Portsmouth, NH. Heinemann.

Flexner, James T., 1979 *Lord of the Mohawks: a biography of Sir William Johnson*. Boston. Little, Brown.

Fogarty, Weeshie, 2012 *My beautiful obsession: chasing the Kerry dream*. Cork. Collins Press.

Foxall, R., 1963 *John McCormack*. Staten Island, NY. Alba House.

French, Florence, 1917 'First authentic story of John McCormack's life and career', *Musical Leader* (June).

Goetzmann, William H. and Goetzmann, William N., 1986 *The west of the imagination*. New York. Norton.

Goff, Frederick R., 1976 *The John Dunlap broadside: the first printing of the declaration of independence*. Washington, DC. Library of Congress.

Gorn, Elliott J., 1986 *The manly art: bare-knuckle fighting in America*. Ithaca, NY. Cornell University Press.

Gorn, Elliott J., 1987 '"Good-bye boys, I die a true American": homicide, nativism, and working-class culture in antebellum New York City', *Journal of American History* lxxiv, 388–410.

Gorn, Elliott J., 2001 *The most dangerous woman in America*. New York. Hill and Wang.

Gosse, Phillip, 1954 *The history of piracy*. London. Cassell & Co.

Graham, Ian, 1993 'Rex Ingram: a seminal influence, unfairly obscured', *American Cinematographer* iv, 74–80.

Grant DePauw, Linda *et al.* (eds), 1972 *Documentary history of the first federal congress of the United States of America*. Baltimore, MD. John Hopkins University Press.

Green, James N., 1985 *Mathew Carey: publisher and patriot*. Philadelphia. Library Company of Philadelphia.

Gribble, Richard, 2003 'Anti-communism, Patrick Peyton, CSC, and the CIA', *Journal of Church and State* (summer), 535–58.

Gribble, Richard, 2005 *American apostle of the family rosary, the life of Patrick J. Peyton*. New York. Crossroad Publishing.

Griffith, Arthur (ed.), 1916 *Meagher of the Sword: speeches on Ireland 1846–1848*. Dublin. Gill.

Guiney, David, 1985 *Good days and old friends*. Dublin. PR Books.

Hafen, LeRoy R. and Hafen, Ann W., 1969 'Thomas Fitzpatrick', in LeRoy Hafen (ed.), *The mountain men and the fur trade of the far west* (10 vols; vol. 7), 87–105. Norman, OK. Arthur H. Clark Company.

Hafen, LeRoy R., 1973 *Broken Hand: the life of Thomas Fitzpatrick: mountain man, guide, and Indian agent.* Denver, CO. Old West Publishing Company.

Hagger, Bran, 2016 'Kay McNulty, ENIAC superhero' (22 August), available at: codelikeawoman.wordpress.com/2016/08/22/kay-mcnulty-eniac-superhero/ (accessed 30 April 2021).

Hamilton, Charles F. 1992 *Roycroft collectibles.* Tavares, FL. SPS Publications.

Hamilton, Milton W., 1976 *Sir William Johnson: colonial American, 1715–1763.* Albany, NY. University of the State of New York.

Hanley, Brian, 2004 'The politics of Noraid', *Irish Political Studies* xix, no. 1 (summer), 1–17.

Harding, William E., 1881 *John Morrissey: his life, battles and wrangles.* New York. Richard K. Fox.

Hearne, John M. and Corish, Rory T. (eds), 2005 *Thomas Francis Meagher. The making of an Irish American.* Dublin. Irish Academic Press.

Hitchcock, Mary E., 1899 *Two women in the Klondike.* Calgary, Alberta. University of Calgary Press.

Hogan, Robert, 1967 *After the Irish renaissance.* London. Macmillan.

House, Albert V., 1965 'The speakership contest of 1875', *Journal of American History* lii, 252–74.

Houseman, John, 1973 *Run-through: a memoir.* London. Penguin.

Houseman, John, 1986 *Unfinished business: a memoir.* London. Chatto & Windus.

Hughes, Robert, 1997 *American visions: the epic history of art in America.* New York. Alfred A. Knopf.

Humphrey, John T., 1994 *Pennsylvania births: Philadelphia county.* Washington, DC. Humphrey Publications.

Hutson, James H., 1980 'Pierce Butler's records of the federal constitutional convention', *Quarterly Journal of the Library of Congress* 37, 64–73.

Ingle, Sheila, 2014 'Elizabeth Hutchinson Jackson: the mother of President Andrew Jackson' (7 July), available at: https://sheilaingle.com/2014/07/07/elizabeth-hutchinson-jackson-the-mother-of-president-andrew-jackson/ (accessed 30 April 2021).

Ireland, J. de Courcy, 1967 'John Philip Holland: pioneer in submarine navigation', *North Munster Antiquarian Journal* x, no. 2, 206–12.

Isaacson, Walter, 2014 *The innovators*. London. Simon & Schuster.

Johnson, Captain Charles, 1724 *A general history of the robberies and murders of the most notorious pyrates*. London. Charles Rivington.

Johnson, Thomas H. (ed.), 1958 *Letters of Emily Dickinson*. Cambridge, MA. Belknap Press of Harvard University Press.

Kelly, Susan and Morton, Stephen, 2004 'Calling up Annie Moore', *Public Culture* xvi, 119–30.

Kenneally, Ian, 2011 *From the earth a cry: the story of John Boyle O'Reilly*. Cork. Collins Press.

Kenny, Kevin, 2018 'Irish emigration, *c.* 1845–1900', in James Kelly (ed.), *The Cambridge history of Ireland,* vol. iii, *1730–1880,* 666–87. Cambridge. Cambridge University Press.

Kent, Frank R., 1950 *The story of Alex. Brown & Sons* (first published 1925). Baltimore. Alex. Brown & Sons.

Key, Pierre V. R., 1918 *John McCormack: his own life story.* Boston. Small, Maynard & Company.

King, Seamus J., 1998 *The clash of the ash in foreign fields: hurling abroad*. Boherclough, Cashel, Co. Tipperary. S. J. King.

Kirwan, H. N. 1926 'An Irish-American sculptor—Mr Jerome Connor', *The Crystal* (May), 100–01.

Klein, Christopher, 2015 *Strong boy: the life and times of John L. Sullivan, America's first sports hero*. Guilford, CT. Lyons Press.

Konecky, Edith, 1989 *A place at the table*. New York. Ballantine Books.

Kouwenhoven, John A., 1983 *Partners in banking: an historical portrait of a great private bank, Brown Brothers Harriman & Co., 1818–1968*. Garden City, NY. Doubleday.

Labaree, Leonard Woods (ed.), 1969 *The papers of Benjamin Franklin,* xiii. New Haven, CT. Yale University Press.

Lacombe, Michele, 1984 'Frying pans and deadlier weapons: the immigrant novels of Mary Anne Sadlier', *English Canadian Writing* xxix, 96–116.

Lapp, Eula C., 1977 *To their heirs forever*. Wisconsin. Mika Publishing Company.

Ledbetter, G. T. (ed.), 2006 *The letters of John McCormack to J. C. Doyle*. Dublin. Zampano Productions.

Ledbetter, Gordon T., 1977 *The great Irish tenor.* London. Duckworth Press.

Leonard, Elizabeth D., 2001 *All the daring of the soldier.* New York. Penguin.

Leyda, Jay (ed.), 1970 *The years and hours of Emily Dickinson.* Hamden, CT. Archon Books.

Leyda, Jay, 1953 'Miss Emily's Maggie', *New World Writing* iii, 255–67.

Lindsay-Hogg, Michael, 2011 *Luck and circumstance: a coming of age in Hollywood, New York, and points beyond.* New York. Alfred A. Knopf.

Lipscomb, Terry W. (ed.), 2007 *The letters of Pierce Butler, 1790–1794: nation building and enterprise in the new American republic.* Columbia, SC. University of South Carolina Press.

Long, P., 1989 *Where the sun never shines: a history of America's bloody coal industry.* New York. Pargon House.

Longsworth, Polly, 1984 *Austin and Mabel.* New York. Farrar.

Luke, Peter, 1978 *Enter certain players.* Dublin. Dolmen Press.

Lunney, Linde, 2019 *Transatlantic lives: the Irish experience in colonial America.* Newtownards. Ulster Historical Foundation.

McAllister, Lester G., 2012 *Thomas Campbell: man of the book* (first published 1954). Eugene, OR. Wipf and Stock Publishers.

McCormack, Lily, 1950 *I hear you calling me.* London. W. H. Allen

McCracken, Harold, 1988 *Great painters and illustrators of the old west.* New York. Dover Publications.

McDonough, Jill, 2018 'The soldier: Albert D. J. Cashier (1843–1918)', in Mark Bailey (ed.), *Nine Irish lives: the thinkers, fighters and artists who helped build America*, 68–99. Chapel Hill, NC. Algonquin Books.

McElroy, Wendy, 1998 'The non-absurdity of Natural Law', Foundation for economic education website (1 February), available at: https://fee.org/articles/the-non-absurdity-of-natural-law/ (accessed 30 April 2021).

McElroy, Wendy, 2001 *Individualist feminism of the nineteenth century. Collected writings and biographical profiles.* Jefferson, NC. McFarland.

McEvoy, Dermot, 1978 'Roving eye', *Hibernia*, 23 November.

McGee, Eugene, 2014 *The GAA in my time.* Bray. Ballpoint Press.

Mac Liammóir, Micheál,1946 *All for Hecuba.* London. Methuen Publishing.

McManamin, Francis G., 1976 *The American years of John Boyle O'Reilly, 1870–1890.* New York, Amo Press.

McNickle, Chris, 1993 *To be mayor of New York: ethnic politics in the city.* New York. Columbia University Press.

McNulty Mauchly Antonelli, Kay, 2004 *The Kathleen McNulty Mauchly Antonelli Story* (published online 26 March), available at: https://sites.google.com/a/opgate.com/eniac/Home/kay-mcnulty-mauchly-antonelli (accessed 30 April 2021).

Magennis, P. E., 1934 'One of the faithful few passes', *Catholic Bulletin* (April), 339–43.

Malone, Aubrey, 2013 *Maureen O'Hara: the biography*. Lexington, KY. University Press of Kentucky.

Martinez, Raymond J., 1956 *The immortal Margaret Haughery*. New Orleans, LA. Hope Publications.

Mayer, Melanie J. and De Armond, Robert N., 2000 *Staking her claim: the life of Belinda Mulrooney, Klondike and Alaska entrepreneur*. Athens, OH. Ohio University Press.

Miller, Darlis A., 2012 *Captain Jack Crawford: buckskin poet, scout and showman*. Albuquerque, NM. University of New Mexico Press.

Mitchel, John, 1913 *Jail journal*. Dublin. M. H. Gill & Son.

Moore, Gerald, 1962 *Am I too loud?* London. Hamish Hamilton.

Morris, Richard K., 1964–5 'John P. Holland and the Fenians', *Journal of the Galway Archaeological and Historical Society* xxxi, nos 1–2, 25–38.

Morris, Richard K., 1966 *John P. Holland, inventor of the modern submarine: 1841–1914*. Annapolis, MD. United States Naval Institute.

Moss, Arthur Bruce, 1978 'Philip Embury's preaching mission at Chesterfield, New Hampshire', *Methodist History* xvi, 101–9.

Moss, Arthur Bruce, 1979 'Philip Embury's Bible', *Methodist History* xvii, 253–60.

Mott, Frank Luther, 1958 *A history of American magazines, 1741–1930*. Cambridge, MA. Harvard University Press.

Murphy, Edward F., 1958 *Angel of the Delta*. New York. Hanover House.

Murphy, James H., 1997 *Catholic fiction and social reality in Ireland, 1873–1922*. Westport, CT. Greenwood Press.

Murphy, Maureen, 1984 '*The Gael*, 1881–1904', *An Gael* ii, no. 2 (spring), 20, 22.

Murray, Aífe, 1999 'Miss Margaret's Emily Dickinson', *Signs*, vol. 24, no. 3 (spring), 697–732.

New York Architectural Book Publishing Company, 1985 *A monograph of the works of McKim, Mead and White 1879–1915*. New York. New York Architectural Book Publishing Company.

Ní Bhroiméil, Úna, 2003 *Building Irish identity in America, 1870–1915. The Gaelic revival*. Dublin. Four Courts Press.

Nicholson, James C., 2016 *The notorious John Morrissey: how a bareknuckle brawler became a congressman and founded Saratoga Race Course*. Lexington, KY. University Press of Kentucky.

Nilsen, Kenneth E., 1996 'The Irish language in New York, 1850–1900', in Ronald H. Baylor and Timothy J. Meagher (eds), *The Irish in New York*, 252–74. Baltimore. Johns Hopkins University Press.

O'Brien, Charlotte Grace, 1909 *Charlotte Grace O'Brien: selections from her writings and correspondence, with a memoir by Stephen Gwynn*. Dublin. Maunsel.

O'Brien, Gearóid, 1992 *John McCormack and Athlone*. Athlone. Old Athlone Society.

O'Brien, William and Ryan, Desmond (eds), 1948 and 1953 *Devoy's post bag* (2 vols). Dublin. Fallon.

Ó Buachalla, Breandán, 1979 '*An Gaodhal* i Meiriceá', in Stiofán Ó hAnnracháin (ed.), *Go Meiriceá Siar*, 38–56. Dublin. An Clóchomhar Tta, a d'fhoilsigh do Chumann Merriman.

O'Byrne, Robert, 2000 *After a fashion*. Dublin. Town House and Country House.

Ó Ceallacháin, Seán Óg, 1988 *Seán Óg: his own story*. Dublin. Brophy Books.

Ó Ceallacháin, Seán Óg, 1998 *Tall tales and banter*. Dublin. Costar Associates.

Ó Donnchadha, Tadhg ('Torna'), 1899 'Tuireadh Mhichíl Uí Lógáin', *An Gaodhal*, xviii, no. 5, 125.

O'Donnell, L. A., 1987 'Joseph Patrick McDonnell (1847–1906): a passion for justice', *Éire-Ireland* xxii, no. 4, 118–33.

O'Donovan, Donal, 1984 *Dreamers of dreams: portraits of the Irish in America*. Bray. Kilbride Books.

O'Dwyer, Paul, 1979 *Counsel for the defense*. New York. Simon & Schuster.

O'Dwyer, William, 1986 *Beyond the golden door*. New York. St John's University.

O'Grada, Cormac, 1975 'Fenianism and socialism: the career of J. P. McDonnell', *Saothar* i, no. 1, 31–41.

O'Hara, Maureen (with John Nicoletti), 2004 '*Tis herself*. New York. Simon & Schuster.

O'Hara, Pádraic, 2008 *The greatest Irish tenor: John McCormack a life in letters*. Ballina. Pádraic O'Hara.

O'Hehir, Michael, 1996 *My life and times*. Dublin. Blackwater Press.

O'Keefe, Timothy J., 1984 'The art and politics of the Parnell monument,' *Éire–Ireland* xix (spring), 6–25.

Ó Laighin, S., 1899 'Cailleadh Mhichil Uí Lócháin', *An Gaodhal*, xviii, no. 1, 4.

O'Leary, Liam, 1980 *Rex Ingram: master of the silent cinema*. Dublin. Academy Press.

O'Leary, Philip, 1994 *The prose literature of the Gaelic Revival 1881–1921. Ideology and innovation*. Philadelphia, PA. Pennsylvania University Press.

Ó Murchú, Giollamuire 1993 *Jerome Connor, Irish American sculptor 1874–1943*. Dublin. National Gallery of Ireland.

Ó Murchú, Giollamuire 1994 'The sculpture of Jerome Connor', *Kerry Magazine*, no. 5, 29–30.

Ó Murchú, Giollamuire 1998 'Connor, Jerome', in Günther Meißner (ed.), *Allgemeines Künstlerlexikon*, xx.

O'Sullivan, Michael, 2009 'Mary Ellen O'Connell—heroine of the American civil war', *Lough Gur District Historical Society Journal*, no. 15, 8–13.

O'Toole, Fintan, 2005 *White savage: William Johnson and the invention of America*. London. Faber and Faber.

Oliver, John Rathbone, 1930 'An unpublished autograph letter from Dr John Crawford (1746–1813) to General William Henry Winder (1775–1824)', *Bulletin of the Institute of the History of Medicine* iv, 145–51.

Parton, M. F. (ed.), 1974 *Autobiography of Mother Jones* (first published 1925). Chicago, IL. C. H. Kerr & Company.

Perkins, Edwin J., 1975 *Financing Anglo-American trade: the house of Brown, 1800–1880*. Cambridge, MA. Harvard University Press.

Peyton, Patrick, 1954 *The ear of God*. London. Burns, Oates & Washbourne.

Peyton, Patrick, 1967 *All for her; the autobiography of Father Patrick Peyton, CSC*. New York. Doubleday.

Phillips, Charles and Axelrod, Alan (eds), 1996 *Encyclopedia of the American west*. New York. Macmillan Reference.

Pleasants, Henry 1977 *The great singers from the dawn of opera to the present day*. London. Victor Gollanz.

Pound, Arthur with Day, Richard E., 1971 *Johnson of the Mohawks: a biography of Sir William Johnson, Irish immigrant, Mohawk war chief, American soldier, empire builder* (first published 1930). Freeport, NY. Books for Libraries Press.

Power, Arthur 1943 'Irish sculpture', *Irish art handbook*. Dublin. Cahill.

Prédal, René, 1970 *Rex Ingram, 1893–1950*. Paris. Anthologie du Cinéma.

Puirséal, Pádraig,1982 *The GAA in its time*. Dublin. Purcell family.

Quinlivan, P. and Rose, P., 1982 *The Fenians in England*. London. Calder.

Raistrick, Arthur, 1993 *Quakers in science and industry*. York. Sessions Book Trust.

Reel, Guy, 2006 *The National Police Gazette and the making of the modern American man, 1879–1906*. New York. Palgrave Macmillan.

Reynolds, Paige, 2016 'The avant-garde doyenne: Mary Manning, the Poet's Theatre and the staging of "Finnegans Wake"', *The Canadian Journal of Irish Studies* 39, no. 2, 108–33.

Riley, J. D. 1955 'Stephen MacKenna in New York', *Dublin Magazine* (October–December), 28–30.

Roche, James Jeffery, 1891 *The life of John Boyle O'Reilly, together with his complete poems and speeches, edited by Mrs John Boyle O'Reilly*. New York. Cassell.

Rockett, Kevin, 1996 *The Irish filmography*. Dublin. Red Mountain Media.

Rowlands, Penelope, 2005 *A dash of daring*. New York. Atria Books.

Scally, John, 1992 *The Earley years*. Dublin. Blackwater Press.

Scarry, J., 1973 'Finnegans wake: a portrait of John McCormack', *Irish University Review* iii, no. 2 (autumn), 153–63.

Schofield, William G., 1956 *Seek for a hero: the story of John Boyle O'Reilly*. New York. Kenedy.

Schwarz, Gregory C., Lauerhass, Ludwig and Sullivan, Brigid, 2002 *The Shaw memorial: a celebration of an American masterpiece*. Cornish, NH. Eastern National.

Scott, Alfred R., 1987 'Thomas Campbell's ministry at Ahorey', *Restoration Quarterly* iv, no. 29, 229–34.

Seaver, James E., 1856 *Life of Mary Jemison: Deh-he-wä-mis* (4th edn). New York. Miller, Orton & Mulligan.

Sewall, Richard B. 1974 *Life of Emily Dickinson*. London. Faber and Faber.

Seyfried, Vincent F., 1969 *The founding of Garden City, 1869–1893*. Uniondale, Long Island, NY. Salisbury Printers.

Sheafer, Frances B. 1903 'A sculptor of the people', *Appleton's Booklover's Magazine* (June), 623–8.

Shiels, Damian, 2013 *The Irish in the American civil war*. Dublin. Irish History Press.

Short, K. R. M., 1979 *The dynamite war*. Dublin. Gill & Macmillan.

Sikes, Lewright B., 1979 *The public life of Pierce Butler, South Carolina statesman*. Washington, DC. University Press of America.

Sioussat, St. George L., 1913 'Notes of Colonel W. G. Moore, private secretary to President Johnson, 1866–1868', *American Historical Review* xix, 98–132.

Sister Marie Emmanuel, 1962 'Angel of the battlefield', *Saint Anthony Messenger* (April), 8, 10–12.

Slattery, T. P., 1968 *The assassination of D'Arcy McGee*. Toronto. Doubleday.

Smith, M. H., 1980 *History of Garden City* (revised edn). Garden City, NY. Garden City Historical Society.

Smolenyak, Megan, 2017 '125th anniversary of Annie Moore and Ellis Island' (10 January), available at: www.megansmolenyak.com/125th-anniversary-of-annie-moore-and-ellis-island/ (accessed 30 April 2021).

Snow, Carmel and Aswell, Mary Louise, 1962 *The world of Carmel Snow*. New York. McGraw-Hill Book Company.

Spillane, Pat with McGoldrick, Eddie, 1998 *Shooting from the hip: the Pat Spillane story*. Dublin. Storm Books.

Steel, E. M. (ed.), 1988 *The speeches and writing of Mother Jones*. Pittsburgh, PA. University of Pittsburgh Press.

Stevens, Peter F., 2008 *Hidden history of the Boston Irish*. Charleston, SC. History Press.

Stewart, David, 1950 *The Seceders in Ireland*. Belfast. Presbyterian Historical Society.

Strong, L. A. G., 1941 *John McCormack*. London. Methuen & Co.

Szabo, Liz, 1995 'My heart bleeds to tell it: women domestics and the American ideal in Mary Anne Sadlier', University of Virginia, available at: https://www.xroads.virginia.edu/~Hyper/SADLIER2_OLD/Sadlier/Intro.html (accessed 30 April 2021).

Taft, Lorado 1903 *History of American sculpture*. New York. Macmillan.

Taft, Robert, 1948 'The pictorial record of the old west, iv: Custer's last stand—John Mulvany, Cassilly Adams, and Otto Becker', *Kansas Historical Quarterly* xiv, no. 4 (November), 361–90.

Taft, Robert, 1953 *Artists and illustrators of the old west 1850–1900*. New York. Scribner.

Tharp, Louise Hall, 1969 *Saint-Gaudens and the gilded era*. Boston. Little, Brown.

Thompson, David M., 1985 'The Irish background to Thomas Campbell's *Declaration and address*', *Journal of the United Reformed Church History Society* iii, no. 6, 215–24.

Tobin, Daniel (ed.), 2007 *The book of Irish American poetry: from the eighteenth century to the present*. Notre Dame, IN. University of Notre Dame.

Tolles, F. B., 1957 *James Logan and the culture of provincial America*. Boston. Little, Brown.

Tuite, Thomas P., 1909 'John Mulvany: great Irish painter...', *Gaelic American*, 6 March (photo); 3, 10 April.

Uglow, Jennifer, 1989 *The Macmillan dictionary of women's biography*. London. Macmillan.

Uí Fhlannagáin, Fionnuala, 1990 *Mícheál Ó Lócháin agus An Gaodhal*. Dublin. An Clóchomhar Tta.

Ulmer, S. Sidney, 1960 'The role of Pierce Butler in the constitutional convention', *Review of Politics* 22, 361–74.

Van Every, Edward, 1930 *Sins of New York as exposed by the Police Gazette*. New York. F. A. Stokes.

Via, Marie and Searl, Marjorie B. (eds) 1994 *Head, heart and hand: Elbert Hubbard and the Roycrofters*. Rochester, NY. University of Rochester Press.

Vreeland, Diana, 1985 *D. V.* New York. Vintage Books.

Wagner, Charles. L., 1940 *Seeing stars*. New York. G. P. Putnam's Sons.

Wakeley, J. B., 1858 *Lost chapters recovered from the early history of American Methodism*. New York. Carlton et Porter.

Walsh, Susan, 1992 '"With them was my home": Native American autobiography and *A narrative life of Mrs. Mary Jemison*', *American Literature* 64, no. 1, 49–70.

Ward, John, 1992 'McCormack on Brighton pier', *Record Collector* xxxvii.

West, Robert F., 1948 *Alexander Campbell and natural religion*. New Haven, CT. Oxford University Press.

Wharton, David, 1972 *The Alaska gold rush*. Bloomington, IN. Indiana University Press.

White, Robert H., 1935 'Elizabeth Hutchinson Jackson, the mother of President Andrew Jackson', *Tennessee Historical Magazine*, series 2, iii, no. 3 (April), 179–84.

White, Virgil D., 1990–92 *Genealogical abstracts of revolutionary war pension files*. Waynesboro, TN. National Historical Publishing Company.

Widmer, Mary Lou, 1996 *Margaret, friend of orphans*. New Orleans, LA. Pelican Publishing Company.

Wilkinson, Burke, 1992 *The life and works of Augustus Saint-Gaudens*. New York. Dover Publications.

Willcox, William B. (ed.), 1972 *The papers of Benjamin Franklin,* xvi. New Haven, CT. Yale University Press.

Williams, Hayley, 2015 'Invisible women: the six human computers behind the ENIAC' (10 November), available at: www.lifehacker.com. au/2015/11/invisible-women-the-six-human-computers-behind-the-eniac/ (accessed 30 April 2021).

Wilson, David A., 1998 *United Irishmen, United States: immigrant radicals in the early republic.* Ithaca, NY. Cornell University Press.

Wilson, Julia E., 1942 'An early Baltimore physician and his medical library', *Annals of Medical History,* 3rd series, iv, 63–80.

Wolf II, Edwin, 1974 *The library of James Logan of Philadelphia.* Philadelphia. Library Company of Philadelphia.

Worth, Paul W. and Cartwright, Jim, 1986 *John McCormack: a comprehensive discography.* New York. Greenwood Press.

Worth, Paul with McFarlane, Doreen (eds), 2018 'John McCormack Discography', available at: https://archive.org/details/MCCORMACK JOHNtenorARCHIVEDISCOGRAPHY (accessed 30 April 2021).

Worth, Paul with McFarlane, Doreen (eds), 2019 *John McCormack, a singer's life: memoirs and career of the beloved tenor.* Victoria, BC. Tellwell.

Wrather, Eva Jean, 2005 *Alexander Campbell; adventurer in freedom, a literary biography,* vol. 1. Fort Worth, TX. TCU Press.

Wright Jr, Robert K. and MacGregor, Morris J. (eds), 1987 *Soldier-statesmen of the constitution, Washington, D.C.* Washington DC. Center of Military History.

Wyss, Hilary E., 1999 'Captivity and conversion: William Apess, Mary Jemison, and narratives of racial identity', *American Indian Quarterly* 23, no. 3 and 4, 63–82.

Acknowledgements

We would like to offer heartfelt thanks to Ambassador Dan Mulhall for writing the foreword to this book, conveying his lived experience of Irish America: its rich history and its contemporary expressions.

Much gratitude also to Margaret Kelleher, chair of Anglo-Irish Literature and Drama at University College Dublin, for her enthusiasm, encouragement and time, and particularly for her assistance in choosing the entries for this book, as well in as reviewing draft material. Many thanks too to Maureen O. Murphy of Hofstra University for her helpful suggestions on figures for inclusion, also for revising her entries on Patrick Peyton and Michael J. Logan, and in particular for providing critical updates to her Annie Moore entry.

Many contributors kindly reviewed their entries prior to publication, and some submitted comprehensive revisions that greatly enhance the *Dictionary of Irish Biography* record. Particular thanks go to Angela Bourke for revising and expanding her entry on Maeve Brennan; Gordon T. Ledbetter for his enhancements to his biography of John McCormack; Owen McGee, for his updates to his entries for both Joseph Patrick McDonnell and John Philip Holland; and our always helpful former Dictionary of Irish Biography colleagues Linde Lunney and Lawrence William White, both for their revisions and their support.

Thanks also to contributors Johanna Archbold, Liam Barry-Hayes, Deirdre Bryan, Francis M. Carroll, Frances Clarke, Terry Clavin, Paddy Cunningham, Mildred Murphy DeRiggi, James E. Doan, Patrick M. Geoghegan,

Vivien Hick, Bridget Hourican, Sylvie Kleinman, David Murphy, James H. Murphy, Giollamuire Ó Murchú, Turlough O'Riordan, Adam Pole, Paul Rouse, Catherine B. Shannon and Alan Singer. When reaching out to contributors, we were sad to learn of the passing of Aidan Breen (d. 2013), late of Trinity, Queen's, Galway and Boston universities—may he rest in peace.

Huge appreciation goes to the RIA Publications Office team, in particular managing editor Ruth Hegarty, senior editor Helena King and designer Fidelma Slattery; to the Publication Committee; and to Sophie Evans of the RIA Library for helping with access to research materials during the Covid-19 closures.

We would like to thank Kate O'Malley, interim managing editor of the Dictionary of Irish Biography (2019–21), RIA executive secretary Tony Gaynor and the members of the DIB advisory board for their support; and to acknowledge the enormous work of DIB editors James McGuire and James Quinn.

Final thanks go to our families for their love and support: Kim Boland, and Fearghal, Abigail and Isobella Breathnach.

We would like to dedicate this book to the memories of two great gentlemen, both voracious readers: Peter Boland (1936–2020) and Anthony (Anto) Boland (1965–2021).

About the editors

LIZ EVERS is a writer and editor who has worked in the publishing industry in the UK and Ireland for many years and is the author of several popular reference books on diverse subjects, from Shakespeare to horology. She is a graduate of University College Dublin (BA English) and Dublin City University (MA Film). She joined the Dictionary of Irish Biography as researcher and project copy editor in 2018.

NIAV GALLAGHER is a medieval historian, specialising in the links between religion and politics in thirteenth- to fifteenth-century Ireland, Scotland and Wales. Among other roles, she has worked as a lecturer and as a researcher for genealogical and historical research company Eneclann, on several collaborative projects, including the National Archives Millennium Project and the Irish Battlefields Project. Niav is a graduate of University College Dublin (M.Litt.) and Trinity College Dublin (Ph.D.). She joined the Dictionary of Irish Biography as a researcher in 2018.

Index

Irish World 269
Israel 221
Iveagh Gardens, Dublin 115
Ivory, Thomas 231

Jackson, Andrew (d.1767) 9–10
Jackson, Andrew, Junior (1767–1845)
    3, 8, 10–11
Jackson, Elizabeth (*née* Hutchinson)
    (*c.*1740–81) 3, 8–11
Jackson, Hugh (d.1779) 10
Jackson, Robert 10
James, Henry (writer) 64
James, William (1771–1832) 64
James, William (psychologist) 64
Japan Times 115–16
Japanese Navy 160
Jay's Treaty (1794) 70–1
Jefferson, Thomas 43, 70, 231, 261
Jemison, Jacob 14
Jemison, Jane (*née* Erwin) 13
Jemison, Jesse (d.1812) 14
Jemison, John (d.1817) 14
Jemison, Mary (1743?–1833) (Deh-he-
    wä-mis) 3, 12–15
Jemison, Thomas 13
Jemison , Tommy (d.1811) 13, 14
Jerome Connor Trust 254
John P. Holland Torpedo Boat
    Company 160
John Wayne Birthplace Museum 143
Johnson, Andrew 50, 55
Johnson, Ann (Nancy) 35
Johnson, Anne (*née* Warren) 35
Johnson, Catherine (*née* Weisenberg)
    35, 37
Johnson, Captain Charles 5
Johnson, Christopher 35
Johnson Hall, New York State 37
Johnson, Sir John 35
Johnson, Mary 35
Johnson, Peter 37
Johnson, Sir William (1715–74) 32–7
Johnstown, New York 34, 37

Jones, George 201
Jones, Mary Harris (Mother Jones)
    (1837?–1930) 198, 200–2
Joyce, James 107, 109, 121, 124, 259
Junior Bazaar 290

Keane, John B. 132
Kearny, Stephen Watts (1794–1848)
    19
Kelley, Thomas 275
Kelly, Gertrude Brice (1862–1934)
    146–7, 162–4
Kelly, Jeremiah 163
Kelly, John Forrest (1859–1922) 146,
    163, 164
Kelly, Kate (*née* Forrest) 163
Kelly, Monsignor Paul 193
King George's War (1740–8) 35
Klondike 23, 65, 88, 90–2
Konecky, Edith (1922–2019) 293
Kyle, Henry 278

Labor Day 198, 212, 217
Labor Standard 216, 217
labour disputes 198, 201, 202, 216
labour movement 198, 216–17
    unions 198, 199, 201
Laetare Medal 248, 266
Lafayette, Marquis de 67, 68
Lancaster Volunteer Artillery 78
Larkin, James (Jim) 164
Laughton, Charles 137, 138, 140
Lawrie, Lee 118
Lea, Isaac 73
Lean, David 106, 121
Lee, General Robert E. 58–9
Légion d'honneur française 120, 242,
    286
Lemmon, Jack 124
Leo XIII, Pope 206, 266
Leslie, Captain James 9
Letchworth State Park, Castile, New
    York 15

NEXT IN THIS SERIES

Irish Lives in Sport